Must God Remain Greek? ⎯⎯⎯⎯⎯⎯⎯

Must God Remain Greek?

Afro Cultures and God-Talk

ROBERT E. HOOD

FORTRESS PRESS · Minneapolis

MUST GOD REMAIN GREEK?
Afro Cultures and God-Talk

Page 273 constitutes a continuation of the copyright page.

Interior design: ediType
Cover design: Patricia Boman
Cover art: "Possessed by the Spirit," sculpture in black serpentine by Nicholas Mukomberanwa. From the private collection of Louis Flessner. Photo by Frederick H. Gonnerman © 1990 Luther Northwestern Theological Seminary and used by permission. Spirit possession is a dominant motif in Shona traditional religion. In this work the artist captures the subject's trancelike pose. The strong vertical lines powerfully suggest the connection with the transcendent. Through the medium, the Spirit speaks.

Library of Congress Cataloging-in-Publication Data

Hood, Robert E. (Robert Earl), 1936–
    Must God remain Greek? : Afro cultures and God-talk / Robert E. Hood.
        p. cm.
    Includes bibliographical references and index.
    ISBN 0-8006-2449-1 (alk. paper)
    1. Black theology. 2. Africa, Sub-Saharan—Religion. 3. Blacks—Caribbean Area—Religion. 4. Liberation theology. 5. Christianity and culture. 6. Theology, Doctrinal. I. Title.
    BT82.7.H65 1990
    230'.089'96—dc20   90-44660
                                                        CIP

Manufactured in the U.S.A.   AF 1-2449

94   93   92   91   90   1   2   3   4   5   6   7   8   9   10

To Mark, Bruce, Kris, and Kitt
Outward and Visible Links to the Ancestors ————————

Contents

PART TWO
An Afro Grammar of Faith

Preface

When the third-century theologian Tertullian caustically asked, "What has Athens to do with Jerusalem?" he was protesting Christian use of the Greek philosophical legacy to elaborate the gospel revealed in Jesus Christ.

Tertullian's complaint has been taken up from time to time in history and theology. But Christian reliance on classical Greek and Roman patterns of thought has been pervasive and overwhelming, even by those who joined in protest against that legacy. In councils, controversies, condemnations, and crusades over 1500 years, the core notions of Christian life and thought — fundamental notions of God, Christ, the Spirit, redemption — were forcefully if not always gracefully hammered into the Greek mold. And when in the nineteenth century Christian missionaries sailed from Europe and the United States to impart the gospel to native peoples in the colonies of Africa, they carried, along with their message and a host of other cultural assumptions, their almost visceral faith in the Greek way of thinking.

Yet, must God remain Greek? Today it seems enormously important that Christianity be able to disentangle its religious self-understanding from its Greek patrimony. Despite its monumental contributions, the classical legacy now threatens the survival and integrity of Christian identity in this world of many and varied cultures, where even fellow Christians bear far different assumptions than their Euro-American counterparts about what is good, beautiful, and even real.

In part this is an issue of justice, of reverencing the autonomy and integrity of peoples whose non-Western values and thought patterns need not be jettisoned by their Christian commitment. In part it is a question of liberation, of Christianity's siding with marginalized Christians in their struggles against oppressive structures introduced by colonialism. Finally, on a very profound level, the issue marks a crossroad of Christian identity, an opportunity for Christian life and thought to be enriched and enhanced by appropriating the treasury of non-Western insights into the human situation and the divine life.

Such a theological trove, I believe, resides in the religious traditions of Africa and the African diaspora in the Americas. In this volume I seek to pose the dilemma and opportunity residing there for Christian theology. In Part 1, I introduce some of the more conspicuous Christian traditions. In Part 2, I unfold key theological motifs of traditional African-based religions and sketch how basic Christian concepts of God, Christ, the Spirit, and the saints might be leavened and renewed through use of those motifs. I invite readers to sample this wealth and to begin the process of renewing our religious reflection and identity on that basis.

Several people and institutions contributed much toward the research and completion of this work, and I am happy to acknowledge them. First, my two very able research assistants not only diligently went after many documents and other material but also posed imaginative critical questions to me. Mark Hansen is now a priest and doctoral candidate at Columbia University, and Thomas O'Dell, a former lawyer, is also now a priest.

Second, the Conant Fund of the Board for Theological Education of the Episcopal Church provided faculty fellowships for traveling to West Africa and the Caribbean, for which I am most grateful.

Third, Professors Richard Corney (Old Testament) and Deirdre Good (New Testament) — who are my colleagues at the General Theological Seminary and whose scholarship, judgment, and friendship I hold in high esteem — very kindly read some of the draft chapters and offered friendly criticism, for which I am also indeed grateful.

Fourth, a number of scholars and local people in Nigeria, Ghana, Haiti, Jamaica, and other Caribbean countries I visited assisted me with leads, introductions, collaborations, and hospitality. I am particularly indebted to the principal and staff at Immanuel Theological College in Ibadan, Nigeria, to the faculty of religious studies, University of Ibadan, Nigeria, to several Voodooists in the

Caribbean and the United States, and to the Rev. Daniel Darko (U.S.A.).

Fifth, I owe much appreciation and gratitude to my editor at Fortress Press, Michael West, who escorted the revisions of this work always in a supporting, felicitous, and enthusiastic manner.

Sixth, a special thanks is due Matthew Grande, reference librarian, and Alice Madden, faculty secretary at the General Theological Seminary, whose computer literacy and patience were valuable in producing the manuscript.

Robert E. Hood
The General Theological Seminary
New York

Introduction

Why is God so Greek to most Christians? This may sound like an odd question when many of us hardly consciously associate a nationality with God. And the term *Greek* is certainly not one most of us would connect with God — rather it conjures up a small, picturesque Mediterranean country in southern Europe, an exotic kind of cuisine, the setting for a delightfully sensuous and earthy film called *Never on Sunday*, or possibly, in some circles, it may evoke images of the Greek Orthodox Church. However, *Greek* is also descriptive of the way Christians think about God intellectually and talk about God theologically, for that thought and discourse have been shaped and defined by ancient Greek philosophical thought. To this extent, we can say that Christian theology has given God an "ethnic" or "ethnocentric" character that is Greek. Depending on how much they feel "at home" with this legacy, Christians can be divided into three groups: the "homies," the "adopted homies," and the "homeless."

Home, a word and concept with all sorts of associations, can be a place of nurture and formation, a source of good and bad experiences, and a metaphor for familiar surroundings, as in the expression "I feel at home." Home can also be a space for refuge and rest, a place to relax after the weariness of the heat of the day, or a shelter where we can complain, shout, laugh, and cry. It can be a place of protestation and a focus of conversation, a lodge of jubilation and self-affirmation.

Homey, a less familiar word to many, is a street expression in black culture. A "homey" is a person with whom you are at home and can relax, laugh, and cry because that person has been through the same stages of formation and rites of passage as you. You do

1

not feel threatened by a "homey" even when disagreements arise. Doctrines about God in the Christian tradition have reflected what scholars call a "Eurocentric" character. This means that in terms of theological concepts and doctrines, God has been transformed into a "homey" for large numbers of Christians in European cultures. The dominant intellectual concepts and thought patterns in these cultures reflect assumptions of what some conservative scholars call "Western civilization," which in turn is a descendant of ancient Graeco-Roman culture and of a Christendom that dominated Europe, North Africa, and Egypt until the Islamic invasion in the eighth century. Thus the term *homies* refers to those European Christians who are at home with concepts of God that have their roots in Graeco-Roman culture.

The second group, the "adopted homies," are New World offspring of the "homies." They should more appropriately be described as Euro-Americans because of their cultural and intellectual roots in Europe. "Adopted homies" are members of either the dominant white North American culture or the European-rooted South American cultures. Indeed the caste systems operating in much of Latin America are anchored historically and racially in European assumptions about indigenous cultures, traditional religion, and color. The assumptions were derived from European ideas about ancient Greek culture and its superiority, particularly in lands where aboriginal peoples and African descendants predominated. The religious worldview of those at the top of these American caste systems has been heavily influenced by the religion of their former European colonial rulers, hence the expression *adopted homies*.

But there is a third group, the "homeless": those whose cultures have not been shaped or greatly influenced by Graeco-Roman concepts and culture as found in European or Euro-American cultures and their attendant religion. They have their own ancient heritages and cultures, yet viewed from within the hegemony of Western culture and its domination of the Christian theological tradition, these cultures are homeless. This is especially the case for the cultures of the Caribbean and of Africa south of the Sahara, where the Christian church is currently mushrooming. The fundamental worldview in these cultures — a worldview rooted in African antiquity, in African survivals from slavery and the plantation era, and in the indigenous Indian cultures that European Christians tried to supplant — has not been primarily shaped by the Graeco-Roman legacy as it passed through European and American cultures. Thus the latter's hegemony in preserving and shaping Christian theology and doctrine has in effect rendered these African and African-based cultures intellectually homeless, even though they are well represented demographically in the church.

The European hegemony is furthered by classifying aboriginal, indigenous cultures and their traditions as "primitive." This allows the West (1) to internalize its own definition of what constitutes "advanced" thinking and civilization; (2) to construct an intellectual and historical hierarchy of thought and traditions with Graeco-Roman culture and its descendants at the top; (3) to distance itself from what it perceives as underdeveloped thought; and (4) to justify a morality of paternalism toward "primitive" cultures and worldviews. Less subtly, it provides cultures descended from the Graeco-Roman worldview with a foundation for claiming authority to determine what is worthy to preserve in the Christian tradition and who is worthy to interpret that tradition.

Some are prone to dismiss African traditionalist culture as limited in influence because many Africans have been educated in Europe and the United States and because former African and Caribbean colonies now have Western-style educational systems. The continued influence of these traditional cultures and customs, however, was attested to even as recently as 1987. The Kenyan Court of Appeal was called upon to rule in a dispute about whether a deceased husband, who was a member of the Luo tribe, should be buried according to the wishes of his wife, who was of a different tribe, or according to the traditions of the Luo. The wife claimed that her husband, a prominent lawyer, was Westernized and while living, paid little heed to tribal or ethnic traditions. Therefore, she contended, he ought not be bound to such traditions in death. Members of his tribe, however, contended that were he not given a proper tribal burial in the soil of his ancestors, his spirit would be restless and continue to torment the tribe and his survivors.

The court, consisting solely of Western-educated judges, decided *unanimously* against the wife and in favor of the husband's tribe. The court ruled that it is not possible for an African to dispossess himself or herself of the tribe and its culture and that this is particularly true of tribes, such as the Luo, that trace kinship patrilineally. Thus the tribe had prior claim on the husband's corpse and could bury him according to tradition.[1]

1. *New York Times*, May 16, 1987.

Such a judgment will seem alien to those who simply and spontaneously take for granted the Greek claims that have shaped Western civilization and Christian doctrine. These persons are Christians and others who no doubt laud as "civilized" (meaning sufficient and superior) the abiding ideas of such pre-Christian Greek classics as the writings of Aeschylus, Sophocles, Euripides, Plato, and Aristotle, works formerly read at university under the admonition that a well-educated, civilized person is expected to be conversant with these classical foundations of Western civilization. Implicitly, such a claim reinforces the idea of Greek civilization and literature as organizing tools for defining our own identity culturally and even our understanding of God and Jesus Christ theologically. When made explicit, it may strike some as too abstract, and others as foreign. But we all are products of a historical legacy and of educational systems whose cultural and intellectual values, ideals, and methods of thinking have been hugely influenced and shaped by ancient Greek intellectual thought. We take it for granted, like breathing, until challenged.

But in addition to the Greek influence, much of Western thought and values has been shaped by Roman patterns of thought. These have been handed down to us through the Latin writings of such people as Cicero, Julius Caesar, Lucretius, and Virgil, through the works of Seneca, Juvenal, and Pliny, through medieval Scholasticism and the Renaissance, and through the Protestant Reformation. Indeed the aim of the Renaissance was to revive classical antiquity and recapture the thought patterns and literature of the ancient Greeks and Romans as progenitors of European culture. Much of ancient Rome's influence lay with its being the capital of a Greek-speaking empire, even though it was a latinized city. The key bodies and officials dealing with law were located there: the senate, the ordinary magistrates, the consuls (chief judges who controlled the treasury), the praetors (urban magistrates who decided legal disputes between citizens), and the quaestors (judges with criminal and treasury jurisdiction). Its free citizens had a special status as a nationality unto themselves in the empire. Furthermore, when Emperor Constantine endowed the church in Rome with vast lands mainly in the West — for example in Gaul and Greece — he insured the Latin church's influence in the culture. Indeed when he became emperor, Rome was already a Latin city with a latinized populace, while the dominant Greek culture was dwindling. With the decline of the empire's central government in the third century A.D., the power of the provinces and of Rome began to wane.

Examples of the Graeco-Roman legacy that we in the West take for granted abound. We assume uncritically that there are fundamental, unchanging "principles" that anchor humanity and cultures. We speak of "truth" as a natural given in human affairs and discourse. It is customary to think of "action based on one's principles" and to speak of the "spiritual" being dissimilar to the "material," of "essences" in contrast to "becoming." Theologians and other intellectuals like to talk about "being" and "God as the ground or source of being," about "Jesus Christ as the Logos," about "God as the alpha and the omega," about "essences and accidents," and about "form and matter." All of these demonstrate the conquest of Greek metaphysics and philosophical patterns of thought in our ordinary and conceptual lives. They are commonplace and "natural," so much so that we have determined that such is the most appropriate way to preach and interpret God and Jesus Christ to other cultures.

Such a determination is characteristic not only of mainstream Christian denominations and churches. It also has shaped the character, message, and mission of pietists, fundamentalists, televangelists, Christian Scientists, and Mormons, among others. Adolf von Harnack noted that the person who played a major role as a conduit for funneling the church's hitherto variform Greek theology into the uniformed tidiness of Roman culture was the latinized African lawyer Tertullian (c. 160–225):

> He not only transferred the technical terms of the jurists into the ecclesiastical language of the West, but he also contemplated, from a legal standpoint, all relations of the individual and the Church to the Deity, and *vice versa*, all duties and rights, the moral imperative as well as the actions of God and Christ, nay, their mutual relationship.... God appears as the mighty partner who watches jealously over his rights.[2]

In three centuries the small primitive Christian church emerged in the vortex of the Graeco-Roman culture of the Roman Empire and established itself as an imperial, inclusive institution by appealing to the intellectual and educated classes of the empire. The overarching

2. Adolf von Harnack, *History of Dogma*, trans. Neil Buchanan, 7 vols. (New York: Dover Publications, 1961), 5:16-17.

environment of the empire in turn exercised a permanent influence on the Christian church's interpretation of the oriental Semitic God revealed in the Old Testament and the Aramaic-speaking Semitic figure of Jesus Christ in the New Testament. That this environment encouraged coherence, explanation, clarification, and inclusion as well as exclusion within the Christian church for these many centuries is to be applauded and commended.

The bequest of Graeco-Roman antiquity and of the Christian Latin Fathers, generously preserved and handed down by the Catholic Church in the West, particularly came into its own during the Reformation and Counter Reformation. The legacy of Greek antiquity and the Christian Greek Fathers and the Orthodox tradition was championed and handed down mainly in Byzantium, where it still governs thinking and spirituality in Eastern Orthodoxy today. So one may generalize and speak of Western culture and indeed mainstream Christian faith as descendants of Graeco-Roman thought, which also greatly shaped early and later Christian doctrines about God. At the same time, as we know from church history and the history of Christian doctrine, this also applies to theology about Jesus Christ, for only in Christ and through Christ do Christians know the true revelation of God.

This does not mean that there were not other competing cultural claims in the shaping of the Christian cultures of Western Europe, the New World, and the East. They are evidenced by the number of synods and councils convoked in the East to deal with other claims often cataloged by the Church Catholic as "heresy." Nor is it the case, as some claim, that Africa south of the Sahara was uncivilized in antiquity. Not only did some Greeks of antiquity, such as Herodotus (fifth century B.C.), who visited Egypt and Ilé-Ifè (in modern Nigeria), acknowledge the antiquity of African worldviews and traditions, but also, as I shall show later, the idea of Africa had some meaning even in the New Testament community, although biblical scholars gloss over it. What all of this means is simply that the power of the emperors, and later of the conquerors, "discoverers," colonizers, victors, and other ruling powers made them players in the history of Christian thought. They also helped to effect the claims of cultures shaped by Graeco-Roman and subsequent Renaissance and Enlightenment values. Their power stood behind declarations of the West's cultural supremacy to other cultures, including those of Africa south of the Sahara and the indigenous or aboriginal cultures already in place when Westerners descended upon their lands.

So Graeco-Roman and Renaissance/Enlightenment cultural dominance in Christian thought is also implicitly linked with conquest and power rather than just with natural selection and emergence of the fittest. As we shall learn, even the university contributed toward sanctioning this Graeco-Roman cultural and intellectual hegemony. Its disciplines of social anthropology and Egyptology were founded on eighteenth- and nineteenth-century European claims about the natural superiority of classical antiquity and the inferiority of most non-European cultures and ethnic groups, certainly those south of Egypt.

The Graeco-Roman packaging of Christian theology, dogmatics, languages, and traditions particularly raises acute issues of cultural and religious hegemony, called by less charitable people "cultural imperialism." Western Christians continue to exercise exclusive guardianship over the shape of Christian theology and over the debate about the meaning of Jesus Christ for a multicultural church and world; this is an especially crucial matter in Afro cultures, such as Africa and the Caribbean, where the church is growing rapidly. According to *The World Christian Encyclopedia*, as the Christian church began to institutionalize itself after A.D. 100 through its bishops, theologians, and, soon thereafter, its synods and councils, some 400,000 Christians lived in Africa, and many others were "evangelized": the "evangelized" being those who were aware of the gospel and the Christian faith but who did not yet confess to be members of the Christian faith. At the turn of this century, with missionary Christianity in full bloom in Africa, there were 10 million Christians and some 25 million evangelized people on that continent. It is projected that by A.D. 2000 there will be some 393.3 million Christians and some 695 million evangelized people in Africa.[3]

In 1900 there were only 369,430 Africans identified as Anglicans. By 1970 there were 7.8 million, and by the end of 1985 there were roughly 12.2 million — a growth rate of over 3000 percent since 1900. According to the most recent statistics, in 1988 there were over 14.9 million Anglicans in Africa, most of whom lived

3. David B. Barrett, ed., *The World Christian Encyclopedia* (Oxford: Oxford University Press, 1982), 778, 798.

south of the Sahara.[4] By contrast, in England, where the Anglican
Church was founded and is still the official established church of the
realm, in 1900 25 million were registered Anglicans; by 1970 that
number had expanded, but only to 29.3 million. By the end of 1985
that number was expected to have shrunk to 28 million. However,
according to the 1985 electoral rolls, out of some 25 million baptized Anglicans, only some 1.6 million are active. In North America,
a similar story can be told in comparison to Africa, even though sta-
tistically a majority of Americans claim belief in God and occasional
visits to church. Not only has the Episcopal Church shriveled to
2.5 million members, but mainstream Protestant denominations in
general are declining.[5]

The spread of the Christian faith in Africa is even more impressive when the rapidly growing African independent churches
are considered; these are estimated to number 5000–6000 different
bodies. These churches have radically changed a Christianity received
from the European colonizers, and their membership is said to be in
the millions. The independent churches are concentrated south of
the Sahara, instead of being in North Africa, Egypt, and Ethiopia,
where the faith was planted a long time ago.

And what about the Caribbean with its blend of the original
Indian cultures, the European cultures, and the African cultures,
all of which have formed and informed its religious traditions? The
membership of churches affiliated with the Caribbean Council of
Churches (CCC), which includes Roman Catholics, Anglicans, and
Protestants, in 1985 numbered more than 2 million or 38 percent of
the population. When other churches not affiliated with the CCC —
such as the various Evangelical, Seventh-Day Adventist, and indigenous churches — are added to this total, Christians make up at least
55 percent of the population in the English-speaking Caribbean.
And this figure does not include many of the Pentecostalists, whose
numbers are growing swiftly in the Caribbean.

Hence, the critical issue is whether Christianity within the traditions of these Third World cultures, where the Christian faith is
going from strength to strength in contrast to the West and the East
where it is in a state of "suspended animation," must be filtered
through Graeco-Roman religious thought and patterns in order to

    4. *Who Are the Anglicans? Profiles and Maps of the Anglican Communion*
(Cincinnati: Forward Movement Publications, 1988), 12–31.
    5. See "Mainline Churches," in *Emerging Trends* (Princeton, N.J.: Gallup Or-
ganization, May 1989), 1.

be considered legitimate and authentically Christian. In other words: Do Christians from Third World cultures have to become imitation Europeans or imitation North Americans before they can be considered fitting contributors to the formation and shaping of Christian thought? Must they steadily continue to contribute to their own *invisibility* within Christian thought by surrendering traditions and cultures long dismissed as "pagan," "animistic," "heathen," and "polytheistic"? We cannot neglect, overlook, or replace the major contributions of Graeco-Roman thought in formulating theologically the witness to and experience of the Christian God in the world, be those contributions from the apologetic, patristic, medieval, Scholastic, Reformation, Enlightenment, or colonial era. Still we also must remind ourselves that these contributions have in effect been universalized and sanctified by the church primarily based on the triumph of certain power factions that subsequently legitimized that victory and its accompanying ethnocentric claims by insisting that the Holy Spirit had led the assault. As Walter Bauer points out in his study of how orthodox doctrines came to be universalized, much had to do with the powerful position of Rome and of the church in Rome:

> At the beginning of the second century, Christianity as a whole is still called the "catholic church" by Ignatius, but by the end of that century it has become divided, as far as the Roman or Roman influenced outlook is concerned, into two distinct parts, the catholic or "great" church on the one hand and the *massa perditionis* ("condemned masses") of the heretics on the other.... This extremely powerful organism, although under great stress, knew how to rid itself even of the highly dangerous poison of Marcionism in the middle of the second century.[6]

Hence, a crucial question for the worldwide Christian church as it tries to take seriously Third World cultures, particularly those in Africa and in the African diaspora (e.g., in the Caribbean), is whether Greek metaphysics will continue to be used as a filter to authenticate its claims and understanding of God in Jesus Christ. For the Third World cultures in Africa and the Caribbean, must God remain Greek?

Or can there be a diversity of theological concepts about God's revelation that allows for alternatives to the Greek model, certainly

6. Walter Bauer, *Orthodoxy and Heresy in Earliest Christianity*, trans. and ed. Robert A. Kraft et al. (Philadelphia: Fortress Press, 1971), 229–30.

for Afro cultures? Can the theological treasure house of Christianity open up yet another account with African and Afro Caribbean cultures, an account in which those cultures are contributors rather than merely being recipients of the inheritances of Europe and North America? An answer to these questions may be provided by examining concepts in the cultural and religious milieu and in some of the indigenous churches in Africa and the Caribbean. These concepts in turn can be deployed in constructing theological alternatives and in thereby expanding the wealth of Christian doctrine. Such alternatives are intended to be a critical aid to Euro-Americans and Afro Americans and an assistance to African and Caribbean Christians. The issue is whether the thought patterns and worldviews of Afro cultures can be molds for reconfiguring the Christian vision of God, Jesus Christ, and the Spirit/spirits. Can these reconfigurations be as exportable as the Graeco-Roman models? Or must God remain in the Greek mode doctrinally for all of Christianity?

Consequently, Tertullian's question about what Athens had to do with Jerusalem is no longer the key question before us. Or at best his question may still be raised by Europeans and North Americans for their own doctrines. Rather, in light of the critical issue about inherited ethnocentric Christian doctrines, perhaps a more appropriate question is: What do Athens and Rome have to do with Egypt, Ethiopia, West Africa, East Africa, and South Africa? Likewise, what do Wittenberg, Geneva, Zürich, Canterbury, Edinburgh, Richmond (Virginia), and New York have to do with sub-Saharan Africa and the Afro Caribbean come of age?

PART ONE

Prophets, Healers,
and Liberators

1

African Indigenous Churches

The fastest growing Christian bodies in modern Africa are not the European- and American-founded missionary churches, but the African independent (indigenous) churches. These originated around 1862 and are now estimated to number at least some 5000 different denominations or churches in black Africa.[1] Their population is unknown but is thought to be in the millions. They have arisen in all parts of Africa, including Islamic North Africa.[2] The impetus for these churches varies, but it includes missionary, tribal, and political factors, the latter being particularly prominent.

The translation of scriptures into the tribal languages of African cultures by the missionaries had an effect on the literacy, self-esteem, and religious self-determination in modern Africa that was similar to the effect of the translation of the Latin Bible into the tribal languages of Europe during the Middle Ages. Many Protestant missionaries required that Africans be able to read one of the Gospels before baptism or confirmation. Africans discerned discrepancies between missionary Christianity and the Bible. Many, weary of missionary Christianity with its imported ethnocentric models, doctrines, rituals, liturgies, and music that rendered their traditional culture either invisible or subordinate to Western Christianity, desired a Christianity that affirmed the integrity of their own culture and worldview. Hence when they formed their own churches, they used the terms *independent* or *indigenous.*

The breaking point that led many Africans to express their discontent with missionary Christianity was the mistreatment of

1. Lamin Sanneh, *West African Christianity: The Religious Impact* (Maryknoll, N.Y.: Orbis Books, 1983), 206.
2. See a summary of which African nations have independent churches in David B. Barrett, *Schism and Renewal in Africa: An Analysis of 6000 Contemporary Religious Movements* (Nairobi: Oxford University Press, 1958), 18–36.

the first Yoruba Anglican bishop, Samuel Ajayi Crowther (c. 1809–1891). This mistreatment came at the hands of the Church Missionary Society (CMS) of the Church of England, which had founded congregations in Nigeria, Kenya, Uganda, and other parts of East and West Africa. Crowther had been taken from his village as a child by Moslem slave traders in the employ of the Caliphate of Sokoto in Nigeria. He was later rescued and taken to England by the Anglican missionary Samuel Crowther. He returned to his Yoruba homeland via the Niger area in 1857 as an educated Anglican priest. He organized congregations in Yorubaland and in 1864 was consecrated the first black Anglican bishop in Africa. The CMS restricted his authority to black clergy and catechists, even though white missionaries were in his diocese.

During a financial scandal, Bishop Crowther defended the African clergy accused of incompetence by British missionaries. After the white CMS secretary dismissed the African clergy in the Niger mission without consulting the bishop, Crowther protested. He consequently was chastised and reduced in authority even more by CMS. One observer writes: "Few scenes could have been more painful to watch than the grey-haired . . . Bishop of over 80 . . . , tormented and insulted by the young Europeans, trembling with rage . . . as he got up to announce his resignation from the committee."[3] Crowther's story of humiliation and degradation spread throughout Nigeria. A yearning for separation from white missionary Christianity increased as Nigerians recalled similar experiences of humiliation in other missionary churches. Most of these churches were of British and American origins. For example, in 1850 in Nigeria there were Anglican, Methodist, Church of Scotland Presbyterian, U.S. Southern Baptist, and Roman Catholic congregations, and all of them, even those few under indigenous clerical leadership, were ultimately under white control. The whites used the liturgies and doctrines of their respective home denominations to shape Africans' Christian life and beliefs in their congregations and schools.

Curiously, the link between Africa the motherland and Africa in diaspora also played a formative role in the rise of African independent churches in some places. Southern Baptist missions in Nigeria, for example, no longer received funds and personnel from the United States after the outbreak of the American Civil War; hence

3. J. F. A. Ajayi, *Christian Missions in Nigeria, 1841–1891: The Making of a Modern Elite* (Evanston, Ill.: Northwestern University Press, 1965), 253.

the white missionaries returned to the United States, where they remained until 1875. In the interim, Nigerian Baptists took charge of their churches, and they were assisted by American black missionaries who had remained in Nigeria when the whites left. These black missionaries worked with the Nigerians and others toward affirming an indigenous Christian identity among African Christians. For instance, J. C. Vaughan of South Carolina and J. M. and Sarah Harden carried on ministry in Abeokuta and Lagos, and Alexander Crummell and Edward Wilmot Blyden did mission work in Liberia.[4] In the early stages of the independent church movement, African indigenous clergy and lay leadership emerged from this ministry of black American missionaries.

Although Africans began leaving colonial Christianity as early as 1819 in Sierra Leone, the first surviving independent church was the United African Methodist Church in Nigeria, which split from the British-established Methodist Church in 1884. In 1888 the Nigerian Baptists in Lagos objected to white Southern Baptist missionaries who had returned and wanted to resume leadership in the congregations after an absence of many years. The Nigerian Baptists split off and called themselves Native Baptists, a name that Baptists in Jamaica also adopted in the nineteenth century. The Native Baptists did not initially understand themselves to be an African indigenous church, but rather an African-controlled branch of the Southern Baptist Church, with its headquarters in Richmond, Virginia. However, after an internal dispute in 1903, one group of the Native Baptists publicly identified with the growing African indigenous movement.[5] One observer described the historical and religious significance of this step:

> Without being aware of it, the Native Baptists in 1888 ushered in a new era of Christianity among the Yoruba. A spell had been broken, a door had been opened for Christians of every mission affiliation to find a dignified means of escape from the tyranny of the rule of the [missionary] societies. It was significant that the revolt first developed among the Baptists.... The glory of Baptist polity was the freedom

4. For the life and Pan-African ideas of Blyden in Africa, see Hollis R. Lynch, *Edward Wilmot Blyden: Pan Negro Patriot 1832–1912* (Oxford: Oxford University Press, 1970), 310–47.

5. James Bertin Webster, *The African Churches among the Yoruba, 1888–1922* (Oxford: Clarendon Press, 1964), 49; see also Sanneh, *West African Christianity*, 174–76.

which a local congregation exercised. The local congregation is *the* church in Baptist belief.[6]

Nineteenth-century European colonialism also motivated the movement toward African indigenous churches. In the 1870s the second phase of the Industrial Revolution, previously led by England, France, and the Netherlands, brought in additional players. By 1870 second-place France had been replaced by the United States. The United States pushed out first-place England by 1900, and Germany assumed second ranking. These, along with certain European countries such as Belgium and Italy, searched out new sources of raw materials to satisfy the increased consumer needs of their own new middle classes. But they also wanted the accoutrements of prestige and power, new lands and colonies. They needed status symbols of their industrial and military might within the club of superpowers. African colonies proffered one such symbol, hence the notorious scramble for land in Africa in the nineteenth century.

Whereas between 1800 and 1875 some 83,000 square miles of territories had been colonized by the Europeans, between 1875 and 1914 this figure jumped to 240,000 additional square miles. During this time England alone annexed some 66 million people to its empire. France added some 26 million people, Germany some 13 million, Russia some 6.5 million, mainly in Asia, and even the ministate of Belgium took over some 13 million Africans in the Congo to provide territorial *foie gras* for King Leopold.[7] In effect this club of imperialists dominated most of the world along with a few other players, as seen in the table on the following page.

The Berlin Conference on Africa in 1884–1885 was the arbiter that apportioned the spoils of the land scramble and established rules for further European acquisitions of African soil. By 1914 only ancient Ethiopia and modern Liberia, founded by repatriated American slaves in 1824, had not been appended by Europe.

Africans marshalled both political and religious resistance against colonialism, but most of the political nationalist movements of the period did not survive. One possible exception is the still-existing African National Congress (ANC) in South Africa, organized in 1912. Some of that nationalism took hold in the African congregations that began to secede from the mother churches in

---

6. Webster, *The African Churches*, 61.
7. L. S. Stavrianos, *Global Rift: The Third World Comes of Age* (New York: William Morrow, 1981), 264.

Overseas Colonial Empires in 1914[8]

Country with colonies	No. of colonies	Population Mother country	Colonies
Britain	55	46,052,741	391,582,528
France	29	39,602,258	62,350,000
Germany	10	64,925,993	13,074,950
Belgium	1	7,571,387	15,000,000
Portugal	8	5,960,056	9,680,000
Netherlands	8	6,102,399	37,410,000
Italy	1	35,238,997	1,396,176
TOTAL	112	205,453,831	530,493,654

quest of religious and political self-determination. Possibly the first ecumenical African indigenous church was the United Native African Church (UNA), a breakaway Methodist church established in 1891 in Nigeria. It sought to end nationalism and the divisiveness engendered by Euro-American denominationalism by incorporating African Anglicans, Methodists, and Baptists. At its inaugural meeting, it announced its purpose, " . . . that Africa is to be evangelized," and then went on to state "that the foreign agencies at work at the present moment taking into consideration climatic and other influences cannot grasp the situation." Finally it resolved "that a purely Native African church be founded for the evangelization and amelioration of our race, to be governed by Africans."[9]

However, not all scholars agree that political and social circumstances were paramount motivating forces in moving toward indigenous African Christianity. Kofi Appiah-Kubi of Ghana contends that a dominant factor was the colonial churches' unwillingness or inability to meet the spiritual needs of the African population within the context of its traditional culture, which included healing, prophesying, faith healing, visionary experiences, and the interpretation of dreams:

> For these Indigenous African Christian churches Jesus Christ remains the supreme object of devotion. He is the Savior, the Baptizer in the Spirit, the Soon-Coming-King, and the Healer. In contrast to a cold,

8. L. S. Stavrianos, *The World since 1500* (Englewood Cliffs, N.J.: Prentice-Hall, 1966), 236.
9. Minutes of the United Native African Church, August 14, 1891, 4 (cited in Webster, *The African Churches*, 68).

frigid, professionally-aired Christianity that is mainly interested in form, these churches are free, emotional, and to some extent fanatical in their Christian worship. Several of the churches are charismatic, lay, egalitarian, and voluntaristic in contrast to the established, professional, hierarchical, prescribed religion of the missionary churches.[10]

Thus African independent churches are not only legatees of European and American churches, but they also are evangelistic and apologetic missions for the integrity, antiquity, and truths of their traditional culture within the Christian faith. They deliberately dispute the traditional Graeco-Roman guardianship and Euro-American doctrinal control of that faith, as we shall see as we look at particular indigenous churches.

THE CHURCH OF THE LORD (ALADURA)

The most famous and widespread of the indigenous churches is the Church of the Lord, also called the Aladura (Yoruba: "the prayer people") Church of Nigeria. This African independent church has spread to Sierra Leone, Ghana, England, and the United States. Like many other indigenous churches, the Aladura Church was begun by an African prophet in one of the mainstream colonial churches. Joseph B. Shadare was an Anglican lay reader in the Church of the Saviour in Ijebu-Ode, some 40 miles south of Ibadan. During the influenza epidemic in 1918, Shadare assembled some people in his parish to form a prayer circle for combating the epidemic. One day a relative, Sophia Odunlami, testified about visions of the Holy Spirit and claimed that influenza victims relying on modern medicine were bound to die. Her visions told her they should use freshly fallen rainwater as a cure. She later joined Shadare's prayer group, which now practiced both prayer and faith healing and called itself the Precious Stone or the Diamond Society, possibly because Shadare was a goldsmith.[11]

The Precious Stoners were impressed with literature from an American Pentecostal church, Faith Temple in Philadelphia. Faith Temple taught adult baptism by the Holy Spirit, faith healing, and

10. Kofi Appiah-Kubi, "Indigenous African Christian Churches: Signs of Authenticity," in Kofi Appiah-Kubi and Sergio Torres, eds., *African Theology en Route* (Maryknoll, N.Y.: Orbis Books, 1979), 118.

11. Harold W. Turner, *History of an African Independent Church: The Church of the Lord (Aladura)*, 2 vols. (Oxford: Clarendon Press, 1967), 1:8.

personal holiness. The Precious Stoners broke with the Anglican Church in Ijebu-Ode in 1921 over the doctrine and practice of infant baptism. Then they affiliated with the Faith Tabernacle Church, which had a church in Lagos under D. O. Odubanjo and another in Ibadan, where the King of Ibadan (the *Olubadan*) was a member.[12]

One of the most outstanding figures in the early Aladura movement was Joseph Babalola. In October 1928 Babalola, a twenty-four-year-old Anglican truck driver, heard voices commanding him to leave his job and return to his home village of Odo-Owa Ilofa in the northern Nigerian province of Ilorin. He did, and after fasting and praying he had another vision that told him to preach God's judgment, call for repentance, demand the destruction of charms and idols connected with witchcraft, and teach the practice of healing through Christian prayer. He traveled to other Anglican churches with this message but had little success. In Ilesha he met the local leader of the Faith Tabernacle congregation, Babatope, an Anglican catechist. In December 1929 the two went to Lagos, where they met Shadare and Odubanjo and undertook preaching missions, drawing enormous crowds and preaching adult baptism by immersion, prophecy, and faith healing. Their missions led to a revival of the indigenous Christian movement in Nigeria and throughout West Africa.[13]

However, the person considered the real founder of the Aladura Church is Josiah Olunowo Oshitelu (1902–1962). In 1925 Oshitelu, a former Anglican teaching in a church school, had visions and a strong call to begin a ministry apart from the established Anglican Church. After praying and fasting for a year, he spent an additional two years undergoing what he called "spiritual training" in a small village in the bush. Oshitelu's biography is helpful in understanding the propensity of this overachiever.

Oshitelu was a first-generation Christian of traditionalist, illiterate parents. His mother became pregnant when infant mortality in Nigeria (attributed to witches) was high. She and her husband went to a traditionalist priest who knew Ifa divination. After consulting Ifa, the priest promised them a male child who would survive and have a splendid future of distinction and great influence. In thanksgiving, as is still the custom in Africa, they celebrated this news by

12. Ibid., 10.
13. Ibid., 16–17.

naming the child Ifakoya, meaning "Ifa has avenged my cause."[14]
When he was baptized Anglican on August 28, 1914, in Ipenu, they
gave him the Christian name of Josiah, and at the Yoruba naming
ceremony they gave him his grandfather's name, Olunowo ("God
has honor").

His first vision came when he was enrolled in a theological
course in preparation for the Anglican ministry. The vision told him
to pray daily and destroy all charms and medicines at home. In August 1926 he had another vision, this one directing him to preach
the gospel and to call people to repentance. After this vision he described himself as "Holy Oshitelu, for whom the Lord opens the
way."[15] This increased his fame, and Babalola, now known throughout Nigeria for his prophecy and healing, came to visit him. Given
the Yoruba tradition of hierarchy and respect for the authority of
elders, this was an unusual gesture on the part of Babalola, who
was the older and more prestigious of the two. Oshitelu noted in
his journal that this encounter meant that God had given him even
greater authority than Babalola. Oshitelu lectured Babalola, telling
him of his visions in which they were working together and a holy
man wrote Oshitelu's name first, that of his assistant, Daniel Ajayi,
second, and Babalola's name third. Babalola was obviously irritated
and disappointed, but Oshitelu told him that the vis.on revealed that
Babalola was third among the *prophets* and not merely a leader of the
Faith Tabernacle Church, the role of prophet being the equivalent
of the rank of "apostle" in the New Testament church.[16]

Eventually Shadare, the other great personality in the early African indigenous Christian movement in Nigeria, could no longer
ignore Oshitelu and invited him to conduct a revival at his Precious
Stone Church in Ijebu-Ode. He disagreed with Oshitelu's practice
of extracting public confessions from supposed witches during services: "Knowledge that somebody is a witch can bring no benefit
to anybody."[17] They also disagreed on Oshitelu's claim of special
knowledge of certain "holy names" or "seal words" — especially
the secret name of Jesus Christ — with innate divine power to effect miracles. As tensions between the two leaders heightened, their
respective followers parted ways.

14. Ibid., 36.
15. Ibid., 43.
16. Ibid., 18.
17. Ibid., 22.

Oshitelu died in 1962, but his mark in African church history has been established through the Church of the Lord (Aladura) churches and similar indigenous African churches that use the African experience and African traditions to come to grips with the message of Jesus Christ. This struggle of these churches is unrestricted by the traditions, concepts, and doctrines of European and North American images of a Greek God.

The Aladura Church grew rapidly in Yoruba-speaking as well as non-Yoruba areas in Nigeria, including predominantly Muslim northern Nigeria. It also spread to other parts of West Africa and to England and the United States; it has attracted Nigerians, non-Nigerians, and non-Africans alike. Oshitelu took elements of the traditional African culture that had been strictly forbidden by the missionaries and incorporated those elements into the Aladura Church. Some of those elements were polygamy (he himself had eight wives at one time), removing one's shoes before entering the church, interpreting dreams and visions as a direct communication with Jesus Christ and the Holy Spirit, and veneration of ancestors. The actual beliefs and God-talk of the Church of the Lord (Aladura) as well as other African independent churches will be examined later. Here it is important simply to emphasize that the Aladura Church, the largest of the indigenous churches in Nigeria, was one of the first to give credibility to using African traditional culture as a vehicle for interpreting the Christian faith.

THE CHERUBIM AND SERAPHIM CHURCH

The Cherubim and Seraphim Church is another large independent church. Like the Aladura Church, it began as a prayer and faith-healing movement among the Yoruba and then spread beyond West Africa. It began around 1925 under Moses Orimolade Tunolashe. Tunolashe's fame spread after he revived an Anglican teenage girl from a long trance. Soon he and the girl, Christiana Abiodun Akinsowon, teamed up and conducted prayer and healing missions, attracting large numbers of inquirers and followers. After several days of prayer and fasting, in September 1925 they were told to name their circle of followers *Seraphim* after the angels that had appeared in their visions. Two years later they added *Cherubim* to the name. Soon Tunolashe was known as Baba Aladura, "Praying Father," and his society was popularly called Egbe Aladura.[18]

As both his title and the band's name reflect, prayer was crucial to their mission and identity. It was, on the one hand, the way the people received benefits and fulfillment of wishes and hopes; and, on the other hand, prayer was the vehicle through which divine instruction and guidance for daily life were revealed. The Cherubim and Seraphim group adopted the Yoruba concept of *orisha*, the divinities in traditional religion, a concept also taken to the New World and found in such Yoruba-descended traditional religions as Santeria (Cuba) and Candomblé (Brazil, where the *orisha* are called *orixa*). The Cherubim and Seraphim group also incorporated dreams and visions as important sources of communication between God and the earthly. Likewise, they "Christianized" Ifa divination found in traditional Yoruba religion.

Eventually there was disagreement and a separation between Orimolade and Abiodun over the influence of a young female convert in the life of Baba Aladura and the church. But the movement continued to grow. Abiodun and her people went to Abeokuta, the historic city where the Anglican Church in Nigeria was first established, and won over the paramount chief, the Alake, along with others. Another equally significant symbol for Abiodun and her group was the establishment of the movement in the city of Ilé-Ifè, the most sacred spot in Yoruba tradition. The movement received extraordinary credibility when the city's king, the chief guardian of Yoruba tradition and religion, asked the prayer group to pray for his unwell son. In Ondo, also in Yorubaland, some 1500 people joined the church, led by the daughter of a paramount chief, who burned charms and idols in a public ceremony in a churchyard. After the death of Orimolade in 1933, the movement took a decided interest in Nigerian revivalism of the 1930s, which was largely fueled by the Aladura movement. Under the influence of revivalism, the ever-growing prayer band or sect became a church.[19] It is now one of the largest churches in Nigeria, with branches in England and in New York, Chicago, Florida, and Houston. A number of divisions have occurred in the Cherubim and Seraphim Church, particularly as it established branches outside Nigeria. Those branches emphasize the

18. Sanneh, *West African Christianity*, 190–91.
19. Ibid., 192–93.

primary role of the prophet/leader in faith healing and prophesying through dreams and visions.[20]

THE CHURCH OF JESUS CHRIST ON EARTH (ZAIRE)

In addition to the large Aladura and Cherubim and Seraphim churches in Nigeria, a significant indigenous church was established among the Kongo in Zaire under the prophet Simon Kimbangu (1889–1951). Formerly the Belgian Congo Free State, as distinguished from the other French-speaking former colony also called the Congo (now called the People's Republic of the Congo), the area now called Zaire was unified by King Leopold II of Belgium in 1885. Until 1908, Leopold ruled it with unprecedented repression and brutality, treating it as his private playground, even though he never once set foot on its soil. Leopold acquired it largely through treaties with various tribes. Henry Stanley, who was troubled by the horrors of the slave trade he saw there, negotiated these treaties on behalf of the king from 1879 to 1885. The infamous Berlin Conference On Africa in 1884–1885 established the present borders and awarded this territory to Belgium.

This ancient land, once the Kongo kingdom, has a rich history preceding colonial civilization. Its people are known to have produced iron tools some 2000 years ago, and they were particularly powerful during the Middle Ages before the arrival of Diogo Cão and the Portuguese and their slave trade in 1482. In 1908 the king gave the land to Belgium as a colony, and the Catholic Church was established as the dominant Christian church, although some Protestant churches also were permitted to settle there. When the Congolese sued for independence in 1960, Kimbangu's church had become such a populist nationalist movement to be reckoned with that both the colonial and the postcolonial authorities had to negotiate with it for support and public stability.

The Eglise du Jésus Christ sur la terre par le prophète Simon Kimbangu (The Church of Jesus Christ [on Earth] through the Prophet Simon Kimbangu), popularly called the Kimbanguist Church, is located in six countries and has been a member of the World Council of Churches since 1969. The founder was educated

---

20. Interview with V. A. Iyamu, supervising apostle, Eternal Sacred Order of Cherubim and Seraphim of Nigeria, October 10, 1989, New York; see also Sanneh, *West African Christianity*, 190–94.

at a Baptist mission near his village of Nkamba, and like Shadare in
Nigeria, he was called as a prophet during the 1918 influenza epidemic. He described his call as first hearing a voice saying, "I am
Christ, my servants are unfaithful. I have chosen you to witness to
your brethren and to convert them."[21] Afraid and thinking himself
unworthy, Kimbangu left the mission and moved to Kinshasa (formerly Leopoldville), where he took up work as a laborer, but soon
returned to his village.

His ministry as a prophet first became known when he healed a
sick woman in 1921; a bit later he raised a child said to have already
died. Rumors raced back and forth about this healer, and people
began to flock to his village to see him. There Kimbangu held services in front of his compound. He also quoted scripture constantly,
which was unusual at the time, causing people to clamor for Bibles
and hymnals. The colonial authorities heard about him, and fear-
ing civil unrest from such a political and uncontrolled following,
they arrested him in September 1921, claiming he was inciting disrespect of the colonial authority and racial hatred against whites. He
was imprisoned, tried, and remained in prison — mostly in solitary
confinement — for thirty years until a natural death in 1951. Even
before the trial, the authorities, taking no chances, ordered that he
be soaked in cold water and beaten with a whip to prevent any kind
of seizure by the Spirit.[22] After his death in prison, his body was
returned to his village of Nkamba in what the Kimbanguists call an
"ark." The ark is now located in the center of what is now called
Nkamba-Jerusalem.

In spite of his imprisonment, the movement, led by his wife,
became and continues to be one of the most powerful African independent churches in Zaire and indeed in all of Africa. His followers
call him Ngunza, "Prophet-Messiah," which took on added meaning after his death. He was lauded as a martyr, and his martyrdom
has been compared to Christ's passion: "He whom God sent as a
Saviour to the blacks was *betrayed* to the Authorities.... Finally the
authorities decided to put him to death by force of arms. But no
sooner did they make him stand up and fire at him, than he appeared
in our country. He came to Kinzwana and to Kituenge, where he

21. Marie-Louise Martin, *Prophetic Christianity in the Congo* (Johannesburg:
Christian Institute of Southern Africa, n.d.), 4 (cited in Benjamin C. Ray, *African Religions: Symbol, Ritual, and Community* [Englewood Cliffs, N.J.: Prentice-Hall, 1976],
195).
22. Ray, *African Religions*, 197.

made himself known. . . . It was then that he himself appointed the *apostles* and ordered them to create places of prayer."[23]

Healing is the primary ministry of this church, although like other indigenous churches, there is also a very stringent code of morality in which drinking, charms, idols, consumption of palm-wine, smoking, and polygamy are forbidden. Healing is always done in the name of Jesus Christ. "Hold fast to Jesus Christ," Kimbangu said to his followers. To non-Christians he would say, "Change your mind, believe in Jesus Christ, and He will save you," which apparently had an amazing effect on the population, for hundreds left their jobs to go on pilgrimages to his village, called the "New Jerusalem," and hospitals suddenly had an excessive number of unoccupied beds due to patients and future patients flocking there.

As his popularity grew, some of his more radical followers began to politicize the church as a protest movement, urging the black population to cease paying taxes and to boycott work on the government railway, which was of major importance for transportation and commerce. Kimbangu was called by some nationalists the "ruler of Africa" and by others the "Messiah," and hymns about him sprang up. These hymns combined religious and nationalist moods, much like some of the Psalms in the Old Testament and slave songs in the United States:

> The Whites revile Thy name,
> Show them Thy love, Lord.
> O Jesus, hear us,
> We cannot weary,
> For at the last Trump we shall be gathered together.[24]

In addition to Christianizing the African tradition of healing by spirits and being a beacon for liberation, Kimbangu also "Christianized" another important element in African culture, the ancestors. He referred to them as sources of spiritual renewal and political awakening, particularly in the matter of nationalism. But this was not antiwhite chauvinism, as the Belgians charged. As one of his prayers puts it:

23. Georges Balandier, *Sociologie Actuelle de l'Afrique Noire* (Paris: Presses Universitaires de France, 1955), 432–33 (cited in Ray, *African Religions*, 198).

24. Efraim Andersson, *Messianic Popular Movements in the Lower Congo* (Uppsala: Almqvist & Wiksells Boktryckeri, 1958), 282.

I thank Thee, Almighty God, Maker of heaven and earth. . . . Heaven
is Thy throne and earth . . . Thy footstool. Thy will be done on earth
as it is in heaven. Bless all peoples of the earth, great and small, men
and women, whites and blacks. May the blessing of heaven fall on
the whole world so that we all may enter heaven. We pray to Thee
trusting that Thou dost receive us, in the name of Jesus Christ, our
Saviour. Amen.[25]

The community life of the Kimbanguists centers around three
major liturgical events: April 6, commemorating Kimbangu's ministry of healing and preaching; October 12, the date of his death;
and December 25, which, being Christmas, is associated with divine
incarnation and care for children. Worship is largely conducted by
laity with the clergy acting as coordinators or masters of ceremonies.
It is a very Bible-centered church and singing is an essential part of
the worship, although dancing is not included as a sign of joyousness
as in some other indigenous churches.[26]

ZIONIST CHURCHES IN SOUTH AFRICA

Harold Turner divides the African independent churches into two
groups: (1) the Ethiopian churches: those that seceded from the
established Euro-American denominations and strongly emphasize
African traditions, such as polygamy and dancing, hence the ancient word "Ethiopian" as a synonym for Africa, and (2) the Zionist
or Apostolic churches: indigenous churches emphasizing prophecy,
healing, and possession by the Spirit.

The Ethiopian churches usually support the traditional doctrines and polity of the church from which they departed.[27] The
term *Ethiopian* as a classification was actually coined by a European,
Bengt G. M. Sundkler, in his study *Bantu Prophets in South Africa.*
Focusing on Ps. 68:31 ("Let bronze be brought from Egypt; let
Ethiopia hasten to stretch out her hands to God") and Acts 8:26-39
(the story of the Ethiopian eunuch and Philip), Sundkler traced the
term to black Christians in South Africa.[28] Interestingly enough,

25. Marie-Louise Martin, *Kimbangu: An African Prophet and His Church* (Oxford: Basil Blackwell, 1975), 49 (cited in Sanneh, *West African Christianity*, 208).
26. Sanneh, *West African Christianity*, 208-9.
27. Harold W. Turner, *Religious Innovation in Africa: Collected Essays on New
Religious Movements* (Boston: G. K. Hall, 1979), 57.
28. See ibid., 96.

both of these passages were also favored by black American slave preachers in the antebellum period, since for them — as for African Christians — Ethiopia was an ancient symbol of an independent, liberated, and self-governing African Christianity theologically and liturgically separate from European and American Christianity.

The Zionist and Zion Christian churches — which fall in the second category of indigenous churches — stress possession by the Holy Spirit, speaking in tongues, parallels between Christian saints and African ancestors, the forbiddance of sorcery and witchcraft, baptism by total immersion, and a number of taboos, such as those on medicine, tobacco, and alcohol. They also highlight faith healing, dancing, drumming, and establishing their own future "Zion" one day.[29] In 1913 there were an estimated 30 separate indigenous Zionist bodies in South Africa; in 1955 there were about 1200; today they are estimated to number about 3000.

Zion is a popular term for several indigenous churches in South Africa and refers to Zionist churches in general as well as to the large Zion Christian Church. Furthermore, *Zionist* may also refer to Zion City, Illinois, which had a great influence on some of the Zionist churches through the missionaries of the Catholic Apostolic Church in Zion, founded by the Rev. John Alexander Dowie (1847–1907). The missionaries came to the Zulu in 1908. They preached faith healing instead of medicine and physicians, and urged the Zulu to prohibit tobacco, alcohol, and pork.[30]

The beginnings of black Zionist churches in South Africa can be traced to a combination of factors: (1) the teachings of a disaffected Afrikaner minister in the Dutch Reformed Church, Petrius Louis Le Roux, who was sent by that church as a missionary to the Zulu in Wakkerstroom ("Rapid Stream") in the Transvaal; (2) black nationalism stirred up by the battles between the Zulu and the Boers; and (3) the black Pentecostal movement in the United States.

After he arrived in 1893 in the Transvaal, Le Roux from the very beginning ministered to whites, coloreds, and Zulu who lived on the Snake River, the site of the decisive battle between the Zulu and the Boers, a battle which continues to be a vital part of Afrikaner ideology. Le Roux and other white clergy interested in divine healing and the Zulu language began to call themselves "Zion" because

29. Ibid., 97.
30. Bengt Sundkler, *Zulu Zion and Some Swazi Zionists* (Oxford: Oxford University Press, 1976), 30.

of the inspiration and comfort they found in the Dutch Reformed Church hymnal called *Zions Liedere*.

After a crisis caused by the severe illness of his fifteen-month-old daughter in 1900, Le Roux was expressly attracted to the teachings of Dowie. Refusing to give their daughter medicine, Le Roux and his wife had been using only prayer to try to cure her, but both had become resigned to her dying. A Zulu who believed in Dowie's teachings told them to pray day and night. They did so and the girl got well. Soon thereafter Le Roux resigned the Dutch Reformed Church to be a missionary solely among the Zulu. He organized a Zulu Zion community in Wakkerstroom and held the first Zionist baptism among the Zulu in May 1904. The baptism was conducted by an American, Overseer Daniel Bryant, from Zion City, Illinois.[31]

The black Pentecostal movement in the United States also had a telling influence on the Zionist movement in South Africa. This influence came largely through the Azusa Street Mission revival in Los Angeles in 1906. Literature and pamphlets from this Pentecostal revival circulated widely in South Africa. A white American Zionist leader, John Lake, who was greatly influenced by the Azusa Street Mission and a "spiritual vision of Africa," came to South Africa in May 1908 along with two friends. There he preached his first sermon at a Zionist chapel in Johannesburg and had a great impact on many Africans. Some of the white South African Zionists looked askance at these activities, but Le Roux himself was persuaded that they were genuine works of God.

One African who was also persuaded was Job Chiliza (1886–1963), founder of the African Gospel Church and one of the most charismatic leaders in the Zionist movement. A shoemaker by trade, Chiliza at the time had been a minister at the American Mission Board for six years, but increasingly felt that the mission did not "teach the Spirit." After later visiting a Zionist church, where he said he heard six teenage girls possessed by the Holy Spirit preach, he decided to be rebaptized by the Holy Spirit in 1922 in the Zion Church of Le Roux, but this too failed to satisfy his hunger. He drifted to Archibald Cooper, a South African Pentecostalist from Cape Town who also had been greatly influenced by the Azusa Street Mission. Chiliza joined Cooper's Full Gospel Church and was baptized yet again, this time in the Umhlatuze River, along with four other Africans.

31. Ibid., 22.

Soon the Africans teamed up and established their own African Full Gospel Church, which sought its independence from Cooper's congregation in 1942, but was refused. So as Richard Allen and Absalom Jones in the early nineteenth century left the Methodist Church to found the African Methodist Episcopal Church and St. Thomas African Episcopal Church in Philadelphia, Chiliza and his team seceded along with some 7000 members and went over to another white-led American church, the Pentecost Holiness Church, naming their indigenous Zionist church the African Gospel Church. They located in Durban, adopted the taboos of the other Zionist churches, and added their own taboo against the sacrifice of goats as offerings, claiming that such offerings eroded the biblical avowal that Jesus Christ has been offered as a sacrificial *lamb* for our sins.[32]

Perhaps the most prominent and best-known Zionist churches are the Nazaretha Church in Durban, founded by Isaiah Shembe, and the Zion Christian Church, founded by Ignatius Lekganyane. The Nazarites' annual festival in July at Ekuphakameni, Natal, a festival that attracts thousands, has become a media event even in South Africa's white media. Shembe, paralleling the experience of other leaders in African indigenous churches, was once an unskilled farm laborer and had no formal education. When he was a young man, he had a vision directing him to climb a mountain and to move into a cave at the top of the mountain, which he did. While sleeping in the cave, he had a dream. In the dream he saw his own decaying corpse with a warning, "If you do not leave *ukuhlobonga* [sexual sins], you will never see me again. It is this which hinders your spirit from unity with our Spirit. Because you dwell in a filthy carcass, you may not unite with us."

He awoke startled, decided that this was a warning from God, and set himself apart for a ministry. One of the first things he did was to get rid of his four wives, whom he had married according to the African tradition of polygamy. Afterwards the vision came again and told him he would be healed only by Jehovah God, not human medicines, and also that he must exorcise demons and heal the sick. Immediately thereafter he traveled as an itinerant preacher throughout the Orange Free State preaching this message. Never having been baptized, in 1906 Shembe was baptized by a Baptist minister, William M. Leshaga, in a river.[33]

32. Ibid., 85–89.
33. Ibid., 162–64.

Shembe started the Nazaretha Church in 1911 outside Durban on a spot he named Ekuphakameni, "the Elated Place." At that site in 1912 he had yet another vision. This vision commanded him to go to a mountain called Inhlangakazi to pray. At first he resisted, but when he was told that he would die immediately if he went elsewhere, he hurried to Inhlangakazi. This experience for him paralleled Moses' journey into the wilderness of Sinai. In January 1913 he returned to the mountain with his congregation. There he had yet another vision, this one of skeletons, one of whom promised that he would not die but would receive power from God. They remained there in retreat for two weeks, and the pilgrimage has since become the church's "Feast of the Tabernacles," which each year attracts tens of thousands of Nazarites for preaching, praying, teaching, and dancing.[34]

Soon after the pilgrimage, rumors of Shembe's powers of demon exorcism and healing spread rapidly, attracting even more people. In the beginning, a number of Zulu chiefs were suspicious of his church, but several eventually joined, thereby signaling official approval and persuading still others to join, although hundreds had already joined the church before the chiefs. A link between Zulu royalty and the Nazarites was forged when Shembe's daughter married a Zulu king some years later.

As with most of the African independent churches, Nazarites' beliefs are to be found in their worship, particularly the hymns, preaching, and ceremonies. Their hymnal, *Izihlabelelo zama Nazaretha* (Hymns of the Nazarites), contains over 180 hymns, all written by Shembe, plus a liturgical supplement. According to Shembe's son, Johannes Galilee Shembe, his father wrote down each of these hymns after he heard a woman's or a girl's voice singing it. He could never see the woman, but could clearly hear her singing the unfamiliar words. As he came out of a vision or walked down a road, he would hear the voice and would write down the words, while humming or singing the tune that was born with the words.[35]

The hymnody strongly praises God and views humanity as suffering and confused, searching for wholeness and healing rather than looking for forgiveness of sins. Christ is understood primarily as one who empowers:

34. Ibid., 167–68.
35. Ibid., 186.

Shembe always said, God and Jesus Christ are the same, they are not to be separated. When he said Jesus Christ, he meant God — and vice versa. What Shembe did, he did in the name of God. Shembe believed in Jesus Christ. If you believe — do the works of Christ and the "greater things" which he has promised! When we are told that this is not "Christian," we are simply not interested. But I know that as a Christian I shall one day stand in the presence of God. I shall have to give account for all my acts and all my sermons. If I have told lies, I shall be judged.[36]

The hymns focus primarily on two themes: Ekuphakameni and the human situation. Ekuphakameni, as already mentioned, is the Zion for the Nazarites, but in distinction to the conceptions of other Zionists and Millennialists, this Zion lies not in the future but in the here and now, where the people assemble to sing and dance in praise of God:

> I remember Ekuphakameni,
> where is assembled
> the saintly congregation
> of the Nazarites.
>
> I remember Ekuphakameni,
> where the springs are
> Springs of living water
> lasting for ever.[37]

Ekuphakameni is also a place of rest, where the wicked will cease from troubling and the weary will find refuge. It is compared to the heavenly Zion in some hymns:

> Let me hurry, let me hasten
> to enter Ekuphakameni
> before the Gates are shut.
> [Chorus]
> Come, come into Ekuphakameni
> and listen to its word.[38]

But the hymns also portray the primal human situation of suffering, which is seen as being the result of humanity's rupture with the wholeness of creation given to Adam and Eve in Eden:

36. Ibid., 196.
37. Ibid., 198.
38. Ibid., 200.

A voice sounded
at sunset
in the garden of Eden
at sunset
[Chorus] Adam, what have you done,
the earth was injured.
The voice of the beasts
that had dwelt in Eden cries,
Alas, where are we going
[Chorus ...]
We parted from our fathers,
the earth is injured.
Help us, Jehovah, bring out Adam;
Adam was chased from the garden of Eden.[39]

Like the Zionist churches, the Zion Christian Church has a political function. The latter is largely a Zulu-dominated church in northern Transvaal, and in general it has supported the South African government's policy of apartheid. Its annual Easter festival at Zion City Moria, attended by hundreds of thousands, is not only a media event but also attracts political leaders. The church was founded in Lesotho by Ignatius Lekganyane in 1925, and Zion City Moria was established at the same time. Its support of the government has been based on the conviction that as most of its leaders are Christians (members of the South African Dutch Reformed Church), they deserve the loyalty of other Christians. It was at Zion City Moria that some 5 million followers witnessed Bishop Lekganyane bestowing a very controversial honorary membership on former State President Pieter W. Botha on Easter Sunday in 1985.

CHURCH OF CHRIST IN AFRICA (KENYA)

While most of the indigenous churches in West, central, and southern Africa separated from European and American missionary churches liturgically, culturally, and theologically, a very different kind of independent church arose in parts of East Africa. One of these, the Church of Christ in Africa (CCA), started among the Luo in Kenya and in many ways resembles other indigenous churches. Historically, however, it has understood itself as a nationalist reform movement within the Anglican Church, thus viewing its relation

39. Ibid., 202.

to the Anglican Church as being similar to that of the Church of England to the Roman Catholic Church in the sixteenth century.

The result of the consolidation of several indigenous movements within the colonial Anglican Church in Kenya, the Church of Christ in Africa was started in 1948. However its origins lie in the revival movement that swept East Africa from 1926 onward, and the roots of its expansion lie in the mass Luo withdrawals from both the Anglican and Catholic churches in the 1950s. In order better to understand the CCA, as well as other revival-based indigenous churches, it is helpful to see them in relation to the indigenous Spirit-based churches, the latter being those that sharply separated from the European and American missionary churches. The revival movement emphasizes a personal experience of Christ as necessary for conversion and an internalizing of values and taboos of the particular church and its leader, whereas the Spirit movements emphasize the Spirit possessing the person. Revival thrives among evangelical Anglicans in East Africa, say some scholars, because of its "background of ordered church government, of liturgical worship and of a theology which, however much it may ignore them, is at least aware of its historical roots.... Revival tends to regard the revival of the church as its primary object."[40] The Spirit movements, on the other hand, tend to be wholly African with little or no contact with European missionaries.

John V. Taylor observes that the revival movement came about because Africans lost confidence in the spiritual leadership of the British and Europeans, especially given their assumptions about spiritual and cultural superiority and natural dominance over the Africans.[41] The written and orderly prayers of Anglican liturgy sounded empty to the Africans, and they insisted on extempore praying as well as visible manifestations of the Spirit. The movement began mostly with lay leadership that recognized only Jesus Christ as the leader of the church. The lay persons thus did not recognize the leadership of the bishops and proclaimed that Jesus Christ alone commissions people to preach, not the bishop. Because of this early emphasis on the laity, there were men and women preachers and leaders in the movement from its beginning. Furthermore, "walking

40. F. B. Welbourn and B. A. Ogot, *A Place To Feel at Home: A Study of Two Independent Churches in Western Kenya* (London: Oxford University Press, 1966), 18.

41. John V. Taylor, *The Growth of the Church in Buganda* (London: SCM Press, 1958), 102.

in the light" (meaning that one is able to document one's conversion in the light of Christ) is necessary for membership and leadership in the church. Thus, church members refused to be teachers in colonial Anglican church schools because it meant teaching sinners, collecting money, and working with other teachers who were not "walking in the light." This emphasis on seeing the light and walking in the light led to other taboos, such as not being godparents and marriage witnesses for non-*Jeromol* (from the Luo word *remo*, "blood," meaning salvation and healing through the blood of Jesus; hence non-*Jeromol* means "not people of the blood"), not attending their funerals, even if immediate family, and not wearing wedding rings and Anglican liturgical vestments.[42]

In 1957 the leaders of the CCA were expelled from the Anglican Church by the bishop of Mombasa. This seriously divided the Anglicans, who eventually regrouped in 1960 under a new name, the "Province of the Church of East Africa." Nevertheless, the CCA still considered itself a renewal movement within the Anglican Church and in March 1958 appealed to the archbishop of Canterbury as head of the Church of England and titular head of the Anglican Church to consecrate a bishop and ordain some of its laity to the priesthood to minister to them. They argued that this was urgent because the 16,000 members and 130 churches that had left the Anglican Church had only seven clergy among them. In July they wrote a second letter, noting that the membership had now grown to 20,000 but had only two more clergy than in March. The archbishop refused the requests, whereupon the CCA ordained one of its own, A. M. Ajuoga, calling him a "supervisor" rather than bishop to emphasize theologically that he was "first among equals," but not superior to or above other clergy.[43]

The CCA is a legally recognized church in Kenya today with an estimated membership of some 170,000. Most come from the Luo and Luyia ethnic groups, but other tribes are represented as well, since the church has spread to Uganda and Tanzania. The church upholds the Trinity, the two sacraments of holy baptism and Holy Eucharist, believers' baptism, and monogamy. Polygamists may be baptized on the basis of Acts 17:30: "God overlooked the times of ignorance"; however, they may not hold church office, a stricture based on Titus 1:6 and 1 Tim. 3:2. They may also take the Eucharist,

42. Ibid., 34–35.
43. Ibid., 56–60, passim.

since Jesus allowed even Judas to celebrate the Last Supper with him
and the other apostles. All people regardless of social standing or
marital condition can be members if they believe in the love com-
mandment of Christ and are prepared to be baptized by water by a
licensed priest in the name of the Spirit.[44]

INDIGENOUS ELEMENTS OF WORSHIP

In a survey of some West African independent churches, Kofi
Appiah-Kubi, a Ghanaian scholar, discovered the following common
features, particularly in worship: (1) the Bible, (2) the naming ceremony, (3) the marriage ceremony, (4) the rite of baptism signifying
purification, (5) healing, and (6) hymnody.[45] In what follows, I shall
discuss a number of these elements that have particular relevance for
the goals of the present study.

The naming ceremony, important in all African cultures, includes all of the extended family, the village elders, and the ancestors, although the naming of the baby is decided variously. For
example, in the Yoruba tradition an elderly woman visits the parents
seven to nine days after the child's birth and then shows the child to
the public for the first time. The officiant at the ceremony, who may
be a parent, grandparent, or a senior member of the family, actually
names the child, having consulted with the parents earlier, and then
touches its mouth with several "naming materials," such as palm oil
(which signifies "ripe old age and affluence"), kola nut (= "warding
off evil"), fish (= "a safe journey through life"), or honey or sugar
cane (= "enjoying the sweetness of life"). Thereafter, each naming
material is passed around, first to the mother, then to the father, and
afterwards to others present, and each person consumes part of it
and passes it on.[46]

Among the Igbo, the naming ceremony, which happens 25
days after the birth of the child, begins with the elders of the village
blessing the mother (her first appearance in public after the birth)
and asking the ancestors for blessings and hospitality in welcoming
the baby into the family. The eldest man from a selected party of
four family members — usually the eldest man and woman in the

44. Ibid., 70–71.
45. Appiah-Kubi, "Indigenous African Christian Churches," 121–25.
46. J. Omosade Awolalu and P. Adelumo Dopamu, *West African Traditional Religion* (Ibadan: Onibonoje Press and Book Industries, 1979), 175–77.

family, a married daughter, and a son of a married daughter — lifts the child up, prays for it, and pours water upon it to symbolize the blessings to flow upon it like the flowing waters of a river. The father then names the child, and the party of four in unison repeats the name to the others present.[47]

For the Akan of Ghana, the naming takes place after the seventh or eighth day, the assumption being that if the child still lives on that day the ancestors and the supreme deity must have blessed the child. Some indigenous churches incorporate this ceremony into their own liturgy by having the baby brought to church on the eighth day, at which time the father gives three names to the pastor. The pastor meditates and chooses one of them for the child as the right name. Then, using water, salt, and honey, the pastor charges the newly named baby "to take up the cross of Christ and follow him in the wilderness, in the bush and in the villages."[48]

The naming ceremony is crucial in itself but is also crucial because it legitimizes the birthright. Illegitimacy in African society is understood not primarily as a blight upon a child born outside wedlock. The key issue is not the marital status of the parents; rather the key matter is whether the child can lay claim to a name from the father:

> What makes one illegitimate [in Yoruba society]? It is culture-bound.
> . . . A child may be a product of adultery, but if he/she is not disowned by the man who had sexual relations with his/her mother, there is no case of illegitimacy. The naming ceremony is therefore first and foremost the means of initiation of a newly born child to a cultural family. By it a child has full right to all the family obligations and privileges.[49]

Another common element of the indigenous churches is their practice of the African marriage ritual. Because children and fertility are highly prized in Africa, marriage is a very important social goal, and unmarried people are a puzzlement. For these reasons the Catholic Church — with its vow of priestly celibacy — has many problems recruiting priests in Africa. Further, unlike many marriages in the West, marriage in Africa is not simply a contract between

---

47. Ibid., 185.
48. Appiah-Kubi, "Indigenous African Christian Churches," 123.
49. T. M. Ilesanmi, "Naming Ceremony among the Yoruba," *Orita: Ibadan Journal of Religious Studies* 14, no. 2 (December 1982): 113.

two private persons or a sacrament of the church; it is an arrangement involving families and communities. Parents and elders are involved in the complicated negotiations and counsel that precede a marriage. Among the Akan in Ghana, once the parents of the future bride have agreed to the marriage arrangements, including the dowry, the ancestors are asked to "seal" the marriage and a wine libation is offered to them to show the completion of the formalities.[50]

Many of the African independent churches intentionally avoid Western marriage symbols, such as rings, wedding cakes, wedding gowns, and so on. The Aladura churches use the following instead: (1) the Bible to symbolize fidelity; (2) bananas to symbolize hope that the couple will have many children (bananas are used because the banana tree is constant and very plenteous in Africa); (3) a coconut to symbolize maturity in the marriage (coconuts are used because they take so long to ripen); (4) an orange to symbolize sound body and mind; (5) bitter kola nuts to symbolize long life and wisdom; (6) salt to symbolize that the couple is chosen by Christ to be the salt of the earth, which must not lose its savor; (7) honey to indicate a sweet marriage with no bitterness; and (8) a seven-branch candelabra to represent the eyes of the Almighty God, who is asked to be forever with the couple.[51]

A fourth common element has to do with the significance of baptism. In the Zionist churches, baptism is important as a rite of purification. Sprinkling or pouring water rather than total immersion in flowing waters in a river or stream is considered the "Mark of the Beast" (Rev. 13) and a sign of colonialist churches. The new identity of the believer is made public by this ceremony of baptism through total immersion and a pilgrimage to the mountain: "A sacred place, a Zion, as in the Old Testament." For the Zionists, Zion provides an identity in a land dominated by whites, a land where blacks have no legal rights to possess land.[52]

Another factor that is common among the independent churches is the fact that their theological beliefs can best be discovered from their prayers and hymns. As Harold Turner observes, traditional concepts like "marks" or "signs" of the church go askew with these churches.[53] Because of that, Westerners must use other

50. Awolalu and Dopamu, *West African Traditional Religion*, 191.
51. Appiah-Kubi, "Indigenous African Christian Churches," 123–24.
52. Sundkler, *Zulu Zion*, 315.
53. Harold Turner, "Independent Churches of African Origin and Form," in

criteria — for instance, the hymns — to understand the theology of the churches. Their hymns as sources of theology parallel the use of hymnody in the early church, which employed hymns for theological and spiritual purposes. This is a practice that was echoed in the slave songs and gospel songs of American blacks, a legacy continued to this day in the black churches in the United States.

The New Testament abounds with remnants of Christian hymns in support of claims about Jesus Christ (see, e.g., Eph. 5:14; Phil. 2:5-11; 1 Tim. 6:15-16; Rev. 15:3-4). Gregory of Nazianzus (fourth century) used hymnody to exalt certain Christian mysteries and to dispute heresies. Likewise, the famous "Trisagion" (Gk., "thrice holy"; 451 at the Council of Chalcedon), "Monogenes" (Gk., "only begotten"; c. fifth century), and "Te Deum" (c. fourth century[?]) illustrate the use of hymns for devotion and doctrine. The critical issue is this: If hymns are so significant in defining the Christian tradition doctrinally within an ancient theology shaped by Graeco-Roman traditions, then why can't hymns be used in the same way within an African context?

One noticeable characteristic in many of the hymns is the triumphant christology. In the hymnbook of the Cherubim and Seraphim Church, Jesus is called "the Big Boat which cannot be sunk" — in other words, he is the one who calms the seas and dispels the chaos that is always threatening human life. In the hymns Jesus is also called *Okuruakwahan*, meaning the one who has overcome the strong man; *Ogyampanturudu*, the great wind that precedes the first rain after the dry season; and *Odokotobonnuare*, the farmer who is able to cultivate stony land that formerly was fit only for thorn bushes. One hymn describes total surrender to Christ in this way: "Jesus is the day of the month when I get my pay. The Chief of Christians whose shade-tree grows money, whose knife cuts great chunks of meat. The big house which takes in travelers. The unused farm where grows the wild yam. The Sea, which gives us fat fish."[54]

Likewise, the victory of Jesus' resurrection is acclaimed in such accolades as the "first-born child who knows Death's antidote. Jesus

Claude Geffré and Bertrand Luneau, eds., *The Churches of Africa: Future Prospects* (New York: Seabury Press, 1977), 109.

54. *Holy Hymn Book of the Universal Cherubim and Seraphim Organization* (Lagos: Boladele Bros., n.d.), Hymn 30. All of the titles and attributes cited above are found in this hymnal.

is the wall which bars Death from entry and makes many hearts leap for joy."[55] He is "the resurrected body who raised himself from three days in the grave. Storehouse of wisdom! Jesus is the one who shouted at Death and Death ran from his face."[56] A constant theme of urgency in the hymnody is that Jesus Christ is the redeemer who acts in dramatic ways in the here and now.

At the same time, the Holy Spirit and the gifts of the Spirit promised in the New Testament are also emphasized, particularly possession by the Spirit and the experience of the Spirit in ecstasy and dancing at worship. These are seen as having pastoral benefits: "The practice of comforting the despairing and the uncomforted (through drumming, clapping, dancing, and spirit possession) is one of the hallmarks of the churches' attraction."[57] The leader of the Zionists in Zimbabwe speaks of the place of ecstasy in the liturgy as follows:

> In Psalm 149, verses 3 and 4, we read: "Let them praise his name with dancing, making melody to him with timbrel [translated as drums] and lyre [translated as the African piano]. For the Lord takes pleasure in his people. . . ." The Bible is our witness that we please God with our drumming. But many do not understand what we are doing and they think that we are playing. Look also at Psalm 150. There we read: "Praise him with trumpet sound; praise him with timbrel and dance."[58]

Indigenous worship practices are an important reason for growth among these churches because those practices embrace the fringe, the underprivileged, and the disadvantaged in African society, although a number of middle-class and professional people also have joined. The missionary churches during colonialism appealed largely to the educated and the professional Africans, such as civil servants, lawyers, physicians, and teachers, most of whom viewed these emerging churches with some contempt and probable embarrassment. They looked upon these churches with disdain because they saw them as emphasizing "heathen" or "superstitious" practices in the traditional culture. However, these indigenous churches provide refuge for people wanting solutions to spiritual problems and dilemmas, such as how to deal with diseases or

55. Ibid., Hymn 31.
56. Ibid., Hymn 29.
57. Appiah-Kubi, "Indigenous African Christian Churches," 120.
58. Ibid., 125.

illnesses, how to protect oneself from enemies, and how to interpret dreams. As one Western critic acknowledges: "These [churches]
present themselves as a 'place to feel at home,' a personalized community of love within African societies, an accepting community
ready to include polygamists and to find a place for ancestors, and
to maintain the authentic values of social life in traditional African
cultures."[59]

African politicians are known to consult the leaders of indigenous churches for their prophecies and advice on social problems,
health problems, barren women, job promotions, and so on. Consequently, in many African countries, such as South Africa and Nigeria,
to mention only two, the political orientation of the African independent churches is of some concern to the state:

> The concept of church and state held by Aladura churches is one of
> harmony, with the Church having the spiritual oversight while the
> State exercises the temporal authority. But the Church must reserve
> the right to direct the State with revelations received in visions, in
> matters of public interest, and to criticize or even to condemn the
> government whenever it enacts policies of oppression and injustice.
> The Aladura believe society must be freed from all the besetting prob-
> lems of sickness, fear, insecurity, etc., so that the spirit of God could
> freely in-dwell it and ultimately manifest the Kingdom of God. In
> this way the Aladura churches have remained more dynamic and virile
> than the "older" churches.[60]

Even the repressive South African government tries to entice
indigenous churches, such as the largely Zulu Zionist Christian
Church, to support its policy of apartheid, not because of a belief
in African prophecy, but because an alliance with that church's large
following gives the government additional credibility in the larger
black community and international circles.

A. A. Abiola, of the Cherubim and Seraphim Church, summa-
rizes the role of these indigenous churches in postcolonial Africa:

> We Aladuras in Nigeria are a peculiar church. We want to remain
> peculiar. We want to remain indigenous. We represent God's own
> way of revealing Himself to Africa: this is why we are peculiar. Many
> people who do not understand us ridicule us. They say we are not

59. Ibid., 109.
60. Akin Omoyajowo, "The Aladura Churches in Nigeria since Independence," in Edward Fashole-Luke et al., eds., *Christianity in Independent Africa* (London: Rex Collins, 1978), 108.

sophisticated, that we are not educated. We know these things, but we are happy that we are an indigenous church, practicing Christianity in the indigenous way and worshipping God by this means. God does hear us in this indigenous way and has been doing marvelous work through our hands. Hallelujah![61]

61. Cited in ibid., 110.

2

Caribbean Indigenous Religions and Churches

Afro traditional religion in the Caribbean began when Christopher Columbus brought colonialism and African slaves to Hispaniola (Spanish: *Isla Española*, "Spanish island") in the fifteenth century.[1] In order to sustain the commercial ventures of the Spanish, Portuguese, British, Dutch, and French, a slave labor force was needed for the plantation economy that developed. After the decimation of the Indians, the slave labor was supplied through importation of African slaves. Fortified by conventional Christian piety and attitudes about Africa and infidels, European Christians viewed slavery as a means of bringing mercy to "heathen" African slaves and saw slavery and their economic ventures as "blessed" vehicles for fueling an emerging global market economy. Most of the slaves were imported from West African tribes, although some were cargoed from central and East Africa and Mozambique in southern Africa and stacked in slave "castles" built along the coast of West Africa; the slaves were held in these "castles" until slave ships transported them to the Caribbean and other parts of the New World.

While defining a Caribbean identity or consciousness or culture with any precision is difficult, for our purposes the term *Caribbean* refers to peoples and cultures with two fundamental characteristics: they are located within the Caribbean Sea or lands that touch that sea; and they are linked intimately with former African slaves, with native-born Indians, or with East Indians freighted over to sustain the island economies of the European planters. This definition would include not only the Caribbean islands but also Belize in Central America, and Guyana, Surinam, and French Guiana in South

---

1. Robert Debs Heinl and Nancy Gordon Heinl, *Written in Blood: The Story of the Haitian People, 1492–1971* (Boston: Houghton Mifflin, 1978), 13.

America. The Caribbean historian Franklin Knight insists that the political fragmentation of the Caribbean does not erase the cultural similarities:

> [The] forces that have resulted in the balkanization of the region have varied more in degree than in kind. This assertion, however, does not imply any underestimation of the accumulative impact of historical traditions, linguistic forms, administrative differences, and general ignorance. To deny these differences would be to deny the political realities of the Caribbean. . . . All the societies of the Caribbean share an identifiable *Weltanschauung*, despite the superficial divisions that are apparent. . . . Moreover, the Caribbean peoples, with their distinctive artificial societies, common history, and common problems, seem to have more in common than the Texan and the New Yorker, or the Mayan Indian and the cosmopolite of Mexico do.[2]

We are thus speaking of an area that contains many nations and lands and some 30 million people who are popularly called West Indians but who are actually a mixture of original Indian populations, African slaves, Asians, and Europeans. There is thus great diversity in the Caribbean, yet as someone has pointed out, all of the territories together could fit into the large King Ranch of Texas.[3]

Some of the better-known Caribbean religions, often called cults by Europeans and North Americans, are Voodoo in Haiti and the Dominican Republic, Santeria in Cuba and Puerto Rico, Shango in Trinidad, Grenada, and St. Lucia, and Kumina and Pocomania in Jamaica. On the South American continent there are such Afro traditional religions as Candomblé, Xango, and Macumba, which are found in Brazil, and Winti, which is found in Surinam. These religions, which are blends of African traditional religion and Christianity, mostly Catholicism, took various forms depending on a host of factors on each island or land mass. They became the traditional non-Christian religions of Caribbean Afro cultures, retaining the essential traits, beliefs, and worldviews of the religion of their African forebears. In the Caribbean, Christianity itself has not proved immune to the traits and worldviews of these Caribbean religions.

---

2. Franklin W. Knight, *The Caribbean: The Genesis of a Fragmented Nationalism* (New York: Oxford University Press, 1978), x–xi.
3. Abraham F. Lowenthal, "The Caribbean," *The Wilson Quarterly* 6 (Spring 1982): 117.

HAITIAN VOODOO

It has been said that Haiti is 95 percent Catholic and 150 percent Voodoo. In the late eighteenth century, slaves in Haiti called upon Voodoo as a source of empowerment to help them battle the French, and the Haitian Revolution (1791–1804) began and triumphed to the chanting and drumming of Voodoo. Neglected by most European and North American historians for obvious reasons, the Haitian Revolution against the French, as well as other Europeans, is as significant in the history of ideas as the French and Russian revolutions. The adaptation of African traditional religion to the New World not only showed that the spirits travel well, but also established a fortification for the slaves resisting wholesale conversion to the European Christian God. Boukman — a *houngan* (Voodoo priest), maroon, and leader of the initial rebellion against the French colonists — made the following distinctions between the God of the Europeans and the liberating God of the Africans:

> The god who created the sun which gives us light, who rouses the waves and rules the storm, though hidden in the clouds, he watches us. He sees all that the white man does. The god of the white man inspires him with crime, but our god calls upon us to do good works. Our god who is good to us orders us to revenge our wrongs. He will direct our arms and aid us. Throw away the symbol of the god of the whites who has so often caused us to weep, and listen to the voice of liberty, which speaks in the hearts of us all.[4]

The pervasiveness of Voodoo in Haitian culture is further documented in the paintings of such Haitian artists as Hector Hyppolite (1894–1948), Philome Obin (b. 1892), Jasmin Joseph (b. 1923), Wilson Bigaud (b. 1931), Ernst Prophete (b. 1950), and Celestin Faustin (b. 1977), and in the metal sculptures of Georges Liautaud (b. 1899) and Serge Jolimean (b. 1952).

Although Voodoo is deeply rooted in Haiti, there have been many attempts to rid the nation of this religion. These attempts have been made mostly by some intellectuals, the elite, and especially the Roman Catholic Church, which is predominant in Haiti. Recognized as the state church in an 1860 concordat between the Vatican and the government, one of its first objectives was to destroy Voodoo in alliance with the president at the time, Fabre Nicolas Geffrard

---

4. Cited in C. L. R. James, *The Black Jacobins: Toussaint l'Ouverture and the San Domingo Revolution* (New York: Vintage Books, 1963), 87.

(1859–1867), a member of the elite classified as a *griffe* ("24–39 parts white," according to the classification of the famous Moreau de Saint Méry); Geffrard called Voodoo "these last vestiges of barbarism and slavery, superstition and its scandalous practices."[5] In 1896 the bishop of Cape Haïtian, in the north of Haiti, scorned Voodoo as "this ignoble African paganism."

In the 1920s and early 1940s the church, again with state support and finances, organized a *campagne anti-superstitieuse* against Voodoo, during which the church published special catechisms attacking Voodoo; these catechisms declared that a *houngan* was "the principal slave of Satan" and stated that the *loa* (spirits) were envoys of the evil one. This campaign was essentially a cultural and political war between the predominantly black (*noire*) population, with its roots in Africa, and the small, francophile, mulatto (*mulâtre*) elite. In Prophete's painting depicting such a campaign in the 1920s (*Campagne anti-superstitieuse en 1927*), as the military and the priests force people to surrender their Voodoo implements, in the bottom corner of the painting, a woman is seen slipping away to hide hers, knowing that Voodoo will again emerge after this action fails.

Eventually even the Catholic Church began to understand how much Voodoo had permeated the whole of Haitian culture. In a letter to the Vatican in 1951, Bishop Paul Robert of Gonaïves, who began the anti-Voodoo campaign, relented in his hatred of this "African paganism," and urged that to understand the culture and mentality of Haiti, the church must find "points of contact" between Voodoo and the Christian faith. "There exist in Voodoo practices which are able to assist us wonderfully in understanding the sense of the Christian calling and even of the priestly and religious vocation," he wrote, although he continued to insist that Voodoo is pagan and that the church must insist that Catholics totally abandon its practice.[6] Robert was eventually expelled in 1962 by President François Duvalier (1957–1971), who himself supported and engaged in Voodoo both as a part of Haiti's cultural heritage and for political reasons. Robert was attacked in the following tones: "Under the cover of the anti-superstition drive, Bishop Robert organized or

    5. Cited in David Nicholls, *From Dessalines to Duvalier: Race, Colour and National Independence in Haiti* (Cambridge: Cambridge University Press, 1979), 84.
    6. Ibid., 198.

tolerated the pillaging of archaeological and folklore riches of the diocese."[7]

Historically, Voodoo is a descendant of the traditional African belief in spirits (*loa*) providing for, protecting, and rebuking the human community; these spirits are seen as the basis of sound communal living and individual survival. Like the role of the black church among its members in the United States, Voodoo has been a bond of solidarity and a vessel of identity and selfhood for the *noires* of Haiti, the black descendants of the African tribes thrown together as slaves in an alien Christian environment. Voodoo, therefore, is a living religion that has influenced and formed much of Haitian culture; it deals with good, not evil (black magic), spirits in the cosmos with which persons must ally themselves and not offend, for such offense leads to disorder. "Voodoo songs and prayers which are orally transmitted from one generation to another are for the Haitian masses what the Bible is for Christians and the Jews and the Koran for Muslims: a source of religious inspiration for their everyday life."[8]

Many Western etymologists have supported the idea that the term *Voodoo* is a corruption of the French *Vaudois*, while others have created new terms altogether: *Vodou, Vaudou,* or *Vodoun.* However, as Métraux points out, just as the French tried erroneously to claim that Creole is merely a *patois*, merely a corrupted form of Old French, so too it is erroneous to try to find a French root for *Voodoo.* It is from the Fon (Dahomey: today the Republic of Benin), where most of the slaves in Haiti came from, and means simply "spirit" or "sacred object."[9]

Having forged a labor force from the Fon, Guinean, Yoruba (now Nigeria), Ashanti (Ghana), Mandingo (Senegal), and Congo (both the Peoples' Republic of the Congo and Zaire) cultures, neither the Spanish nor the French slave masters had reckoned that the slaves' traditional religion would adapt to repressive conditions and empower them to begin and succeed in the first triumphant black revolution in the New World. Jean Price-Mars, the noted systematician of Haitian Voodoo, suggests that the "unification" of

7. *New York Times*, November 17, 1962.

8. Michel S. Laguerre, *Voodoo Heritage*, Sage Library of Social Research (Beverly Hills, Calif.: Sage Publications, 1980), 17–18.

9. Alfred Métraux, *Voodoo in Haiti*, trans. Hugh Charteris (New York: Schocken Books, 1972), 27.

what came to be Voodoo most likely happened when the slaves were preparing for their revolution against the French.[10]

As in African traditional religion, the cosmos in Voodoo belief is under the influence of spiritual beings: (1) God, the supreme deity; (2) divinities or lesser spirits; (3) ancestral spirits; (4) evil spirits. Lacking in this scheme is the conflict between the material and spiritual worlds that predominates in Western religious thought, that conflict being a legacy of Greek philosophy; rather in Voodoo the two orders are joined, and while the spirits move freely between them, they control the forces in the material order. As one African scholar notes:

> Man has need of the spirit-world, while the minor spirits have need of man to gladden their hearts, to feed with fat things. It must be pointed out, however, that between the world of men directed by the spirits and the spirit-world, there reigns order, not chaos. The spirits can topple the order of the world as a punishment for man's offenses, but man has ways and means of pressing this or restoring the order when upset.[11]

The legacy of the various African cultures of the slaves in Voodoo is that the cosmos is believed governed by a supreme being with his divinities (*loa*) or spirits; these *loa* keep things in balance, act as intermediaries between God and humankind, function as protectors of the community, the family, and individuals, and are like governors each with his or her own assigned jurisdiction. Divided generally into two liturgies or rites — the Rada liturgy and the Petro liturgy — Haitian Voodoo also includes divinities and spirits (*mystères*) from the Nago rite (Nigeria), the Congo rite (Zaire and Angola), the Igbo rite (Nigeria), and common spirits shared by all these rites. Again, many like to speak of Voodoo as a synthesis of African and Christian religion. But I agree with Métraux in his observation:

10. Jean Price-Mars, *Une Etape de l'Evolution Haïtienne* (Port-au-Prince: Imprimerie La Prense, 1929), 127. He also says that the word *houngan* (Voodoo priest) is derived from central Nigeria, where it means "fire" or "the warmth of fire" (p. 144). One of the earliest to identify Voodoo and to analyze its beliefs was M. L. E. Moreau de Saint-Méry, *Déscription Topographique, Physique, Civile, Politique et Historique de la Partie Française de l'Isle de Saint Domingue*, 3 vols. (Philadelphia, 1797) (Abr. Eng. ed.: *A Civilization That Perished*, ed. and trans. Ivor Spencer [Lanham, Md.: University Press of America, 1985]).

11. See Stephen N. Ezeanya, "God, Spirits, and the Spirit World," in Kwesi Dickson and Paul Ellingworth, eds., *Biblical Revelation and African Beliefs* (London: Lutterworth Press, 1969), 36.

All who have concerned themselves with Voodoo have been pleased to list the many things it has borrowed from Catholicism. . . . No one has raised the question whether the Voodooist ranks the beliefs which he holds from his African ancestors on the same level as those he derived from the whites. An example usually cited of the fusion of the two cults is the identification of African gods and spirits with Catholic saints. . . . This was a mistake, for in most cases there has been no real assimilation or common identity. The equivalence of gods and saints only exists insofar as the Voodooist has used pictures of saints to represent his own Gods.[12]

The name of God in Fon is Nana-Buluka, who is both male and female, but in Voodoo he is Le Bon Dieu, who created the *loa* for service to humanity. Métraux insists that Haitians think of him as a kind of nice old father, easygoing and not given to anger. They often confuse God with natural phenomena or fate, so that even common illnesses are often referred to as "illnesses of God," as are poor weather and disasters. God is associated with events unsuitable to evil spirits and trickster spirits, which sometimes appear unasked at a Voodoo ceremony to liven it up.[13]

Deren, in opposition to the above interpretation, says that the name of God among Haitians is Le Gran' Maître; this God is the source of the entire universe but is too distant to be worshiped directly. Possibly for this reason, few Voodoo chants are directed toward God. However, as in Dahomey, this God did create the twins Mawu and Lisa, from whom all the other divinities and spirits came. The divinities govern creation, but they themselves cannot create. This is the gift of the supreme deity alone. "They can help a garden grow and can bring rain, but they did not create either the seed or the water."[14] Even the Christian God does not pose a problem for Voodoo, since the libation for *les mystères, les morts,* and *les marassa* (these being the *loa* who communicate with human beings through first mounting them and then possessing them) and the libation for the ancestors and the divine Twins who symbolize the dual or "twinned" nature of humanity (e.g., the material and spiritual, the mortal and immortal, the human and divine) can also be offered to the Father, Son, and Holy Spirit. As a Haitian prayer goes: "I am asking the Saints, the Dead, the Marassa, you who are my only

12. Métraux, *Voodoo in Haiti,* 324.
13. Ibid., 83–84.
14. Maya Deren, *Divine Horsemen: The Living Gods of Haiti* (New York: Documentext, McPherson & Company, 1953), 55.

defense before God, you who are placed for my defense against the infernal enemy, do not stop helping me during my life."[15]

But in Haitian Voodoo, a distant God does not mean always an uninvolved or unconcerned God. Even with the absence of songs addressed to the supreme deity, Voodoo is aware of the power and the unique authority of God, as is African traditional religion, which also lacks temples, chants, and direct worship of the supreme deity. This is seen in a Voodoo chant of thanksgiving addressed to Ezuli, the *loa* of love and fertility, protectress of the weak, the needy, and (since she lives in the sea) the seafarers:

> Zili o Zili o Zili o Zili o
> In the sea — my boat turned upside down.
> Without God's help we would have drowned.
> God, we called you and you assisted us.[16]

Likewise, in a Voodoo song that is of probable Congo origin and that is sung before the spirit or *loa* appears, God's power and authority are acknowledged: "Greeting to you, Congo. / After God, I welcome you."[17]

God is the source of everything in the universe, even evil, although he does not will evil forces upon humankind. Melville Herskovits discovered in his field studies in Haiti that even the *bocor* (priests of black magic) ask permission from God, as well as from the devil, before they engage in black magic rites: "Good and evil are two brothers; life and death are two brothers. All four come from God. They do not come from the *loa*."[18]

Haitians' entire environment, even their Catholicism, is shaped by the *loa* of Voodoo, especially in rural areas, where most Haitians live:

> The supernatural world of the common people of Haiti is a vast, rich, and unexplored world. It is peopled with thousands of gods who may at any time come down a rocky mountain trail, or up from the bottom of the sea, or out of the springs where people drink, to enter the hounfor [the ceremonial area] of the Vodoun priest or the humblest of thatched huts. . . . Yet whenever they come they are recognized for what

15. Cited in ibid., 57.
16. Cited in Laguerre, *Voodoo Heritage*, 73.
17. Ibid., 111.
18. Melville J. Herskovits, *Life in a Haitian Valley* (New York: Octagon Books, 1975), 247.

they are. The things they say and do bear the mark of their character and their special powers, and usually there is little disagreement over their identity.[19]

It is interesting to note that during Carnival in Haiti, while the elite dance to European music and cassettes, the poor usually dance in their areas to Voodoo tunes, accompanied by Voodoo drums and rattles. When the United States invaded Haiti in 1915 — the occupation stretched until 1934 — one of its first campaigns was to strike against Voodoo by burning the drums. Herskovits notes that even the drums witness to the use of Christianity by Voodoo because they must be baptized with holy water and prayers before being used. "Since the world is ruled by God, it is necessary to invoke God with the ritual of His Church before the rites to placate the loa may begin."[20]

Dancing, a vital part of the culture, is also influenced by the traditional religion of Voodoo:

> Dancing touches on virtually every aspect of life in Haiti. It plays a part in the supplication of loa, the placation of the dead, and the making of magic; in the consecration of a hounfor, the installation of a houngan, and the initiation of cult members; in planting, harvesting, and house-building. Catholic Church holidays, Nine Night, baptisms, the election of a new president, and ordinary social gatherings — all are celebrated in part, at least, by dancing.[21]

Thus, the culture in which Haitian Christianity has been formed is heavily impregnated by Voodoo, a cultural legacy of the slaves and their traditional religions. The Haitian church and government have from time to time undertaken purges of Voodoo, but they have been singularly unsuccessful. Of course, François ("Papa Doc") Duvalier understood Haitian culture in this regard fully and completely, thereby being able to exploit it for his own use, including, in spite of his brutalities, ridding the Haitian Catholic Church of its dependence on French bishops and insisting on Haitian bishops instead. Voodoo shapes the worldview of most Haitians, even some of the elite, and provides its own God-talk in one of the most Africanized cultures in the New World. The issue is how to use it to interpret Jesus Christ and the Spirit in Caribbean Afro cultures.

19. Harold Courlander, *The Drum and the Hoe: Life and Lore of the Haitian People* (Berkeley: University of California Press, 1960), 19.
20. Herskovits, *Life in a Haitian Valley*, 273.
21. Courlander, *The Drum and the Hoe*, 130.

CUBAN SANTERIA

Another very widely practiced traditional religion in the Caribbean is Santeria. Associated usually with Cuba, Santeria has spread into other Spanish Caribbean cultures, such as Puerto Rico, just as Voodoo has spread from Haiti into the Dominican Republic. Indeed emigrants to the United States from Puerto Rico and Cuba have brought their traditional religion with them, so that *botanicas* (shops selling herbs, etc.) have sprung up in Spanish-speaking urban areas to provide all the necessary implements for Santeria ceremonies. These ceremonies are usually held in secret, unlike ceremonies in Haitian Voodoo or Trinidadian Shango, which can be attended by outsiders.[22]

The first African slaves were imported to Cuba in 1511 under Spanish colonialists, mostly cattle ranchers and tobacco farmers. With the capture of Havana by the British in 1762, the island's economic system was changed into a sugar-based monoculture, thereby necessitating a larger labor force for the plantations. Compared with the black population on other Caribbean islands, that of Cuba was relatively small up to 1788 — about 100,000 freed and enslaved. In February 1789 King Carlos IV assented to foreigners and Spaniards selling unlimited numbers of slaves to Spanish American colonies, including Cuba. Hence, from 1792 until well into the nineteenth century, Cuban plantation owners and merchants imported blacks directly from Africa with demographic results shown in the table that follows:

CUBAN POPULATION GROWTH, 1774–1841[23]

Class	1774	%	1827	%	1841	%
White	96,440	56.9	311,051	44.1	418,291	41.6
Freed	36,301	20.3	106,494	15.1	152,838	15.1
Slave	38,879	22.8	286,942	40.8	436,495	43.3

Derived almost intact from Yoruba, Santeria stresses communing with God and the spirits (*orisha*) for counsel, help, and guidance; the ancestors; sacrifice as a means of empowerment and encouragement; and divination, which interprets the present and the future

22. For a report on Santeria in the United States, see Joseph M. Murphy, *Santeria: An African Religion in America* (Boston: Beacon Press, 1988).
23. Franklin W. Knight, *Slave Society in Cuba during the Nineteenth Century* (Madison: University of Wisconsin Press, 1970), 22.

with the aid of cowry shells, seashells, and coconut rinds, which are known as *dilogun* (probably derived from the Yoruba word for "sixteen," *erindilogun*, since sixteen cowry shells are used in divination). Like other Caribbean traditional religions, Santeria is a syncretism of the Catholic faith and African traditional religion. In eastern Cuba, for example, the Virgin of Cobre is identified with Oshun, the *orisha* of water, brass, gold, love, marriage, children, and money. St. Francis is identified with Orunmila, the *orisha* for divination and wisdom. St. Peter is associated with Oggún, the *orisha* for metal, iron, and war. And St. Anthony is identified with Elegguá, the *orisha* for crossroads and corners, the communicator for the other *orisha*, and also the guardian of the family and home. Likewise drumming, songs, prayers, libations, and possession by the *orisha* are important. Santeria has retained all of the Yoruba names for *orisha*, foods, rituals, powers, and priests, although there are some Spanish names as well.

Rooted in the Spanish word *santo*, Santeria means "worship of the saints," the "saints" being the *orisha*. A *santero* is a devotee who has qualified after a long apprenticeship with a mentor and after witnessing many ceremonies prior to his or her "birthday." The "birthday" happens at an initiation ceremony, the *asiento*, meaning "seat."[24] During the ceremony, the head of the initiate becomes the "seat" of the saint, since, as in Voodoo, the saint, like the *loa*, "mounts" the initiate, who then becomes the "horse" of the particular saint.[25]

This and other ceremonies usually take place in the *cabildo*, the special house or meeting place where the traditions are handed down to new initiates and current devotees. Each person upon birth into Santeria is assigned an *orisha* who functions as guardian angel, and a particular birthstone, a plant, and a beneficent animal such as the goat, turtle, elephant, or the pigeon. Animals that are spiritually harmful, like reptiles, poisonous insects, some breeds of frogs, birds of prey, rodents, crocodiles, and lizards, are not used.[26]

The creation stories of Nigerian Yoruba have been readily adapted by its Cuban descendant, Santeria, with some refinements. Olodumare (God) is understood to be a godhead consisting of three

---

24. Ironically, during slavery in Spanish colonies, *asiento* also was the contract granted to a company or individual by the crown for the privilege of importing slaves to Spain's American colonies.

25. Migene González-Wippler, *Santeria* (New York: The Julian Press, 1973), 13.

26. Ibid., 19.

separate but equal spirits: (1) Olodumare Nzame, the creative principle who created the heavens, galaxies, and all plant and animal life, including the first human; (2) Olofi, overseer of human affairs and taboos; and (3) Baba Nkwa. Olodumare Nzame created the first human being from mud in his *imago dei* and endowed him with intelligence, eternal life, and beauty. But the first man, appropriately named Omo Oba (*Oba* is Yoruba for "king"), soon was so filled with pride in his own beauty and intelligence that he angered Olodumare, who in turn ordered Nzalam, the lightning bolt, to destroy him. However, since Omo Oba had been created with eternal life, the lightning bolt failed to destroy him and he ran away, hiding himself in the bowels of the earth. There, as in some medieval Christian legends about Lucifer, Omo Oba still lives among fire and brimstone created by Nzalam's lightning, and, calling himself Olosi, has become the great tempter of humanity.[27] As the result of Nzalam's failed attempt, the earth became dry and barren; however, filled with compassion, the three spirits of the godhead came down to earth and filled it with new life and agriculture. They also created a new man to dominate the earth, but without eternal life; he is called Obatalá, who is also a major divinity in Yoruba.

According to this myth, Olofi was assigned supervision of earth's affairs, while the other two spirits in the godhead, Olodumare Nzame and Baba Nkwa, continued their work elsewhere in the universe and galaxy. Olofi, therefore, effectively became humanity's link to Olodumare, and in that capacity he immediately established a table of commandments to remind believers of their covenant relationship with Olodumare and of the taboos. The commandments are: (1) do not steal; (2) do not kill except in self-defense or for nourishment; (3) do not eat human flesh; (4) do not covet someone else's property and possessions; (5) do not curse with God's name; (6) honor your parents; (7) accept what God provides and be content with your fate; (8) do not commit suicide or fear death; (9) teach your children the commandments; and (10) obey and respect God's laws and taboos.

Obatalá, depicted as a warrior dressed in white (his favorite color is white), was given a wife, Oddudúa, always portrayed as a black woman breastfeeding a baby; she is thus the *orisha* for fertility. They had two children, a son, Aganyú, *orisha* of the volcano and father of Changó, and a daughter, Yemayá (Yoruba, *Yeye omo*

27. Ibid., 24.

eja, "the mother whose children are the fish"), *orisha* of the waters and motherhood.[28] They in turn married each other and had a son, Orungán, who was so good-looking and talented that his father became unwell from envy and died. After Aganyú died, Yemayá climbed to a mountaintop and died while pregnant, whereupon her stomach split open and fourteen offspring were born. These became a part of the Yoruba pantheon of divinities and include Changó, the god of thunder and lightning and one of the most feared but also one of the most sought after divinities in Santeria; Oba, wife of Changó and divinity of the Oba River as well as patroness of justice and teacher of the memory; Dada, divinity of unborn children and gardens; and Orisha-Oko, divinity of the fields and harvests who makes land and women fertile. Each of them also has an equivalent in the iconography of the Catholic Church: Olorún-Olofi is understood as the Crucified Christ; Obatalá, father of the divinities, as Our Lady of Mercy (Las Mercedes); Oddudúa, mother of the divinities, as St. Claire; their son Aganyú as St. Joseph; Yemayá, his sister and wife, as Our Lady of Regia; Orungán as the baby Jesus; Changó as St. Barbara; and Dada as Our Lady of Mount Carmel.[29]

From the point of view of Western morality, the interesting thing in these stories is that neither incest nor the exchange of sexual roles — that is, representing male Santeria *orisha* as female Christian saints — seems to bother the devotees. This is again possibly a carryover from the African tradition where people are able to live among contradictions unbothered by Greek or Western rules of consistency and logic. It is also an example, such as we found in Haitian Voodoo, of the traditional religion sometimes assimilating the Christian God and saints.

Some *orisha* are more powerful than others, and there is a group of seven that are particularly powerful. Known as the *Las Siete Potencias Africanas* (The Seven African Powers), these superpower *orisha* include Obatalá, Elegguá, Changó, Oggún, Orúnla, Yemayá, and Oshún, and are called upon especially during great crises. They control every physical and emotional aspect of earthly life. For example, Obatalá, second in command to Olofi, represents space and the heavens and is the divinity of purity. In some legends he is a woman and, as already noted, within the Christian iconog-

---

28. Migene González-Wippler, *Rituals and Spells of Santeria* (New York: Original Publications, 1984), 33.
29. Ibid., 26–29.

raphy of saints, he is portrayed as Our Lady of Mercy. When someone wants to get rid of troubling evil pressures or forces, Obatalá is petitioned. Often at ceremonies, a small white bag filled with pieces of cocoa butter, coconut, and powered eggshell is passed all over the body as a prayer is offered to Obatalá for peace and purity.[30]

Elegguá, another of the powerful Seven, is considered the most powerful *orisha* after Obatalá; his good will must be sought at all times. *Orisha* of change, he makes things happen and has many attributes — for instance, he is the guardian of cemeteries; he protects Ifa; and he protects those associated with Eshu, often represented as the Christian devil. Each year on August 24 Eshu roams the streets and villages creating havoc and trouble. Elegguá also controls life and death. In Christian statuary he is represented as the Guardian Angel, although some *santeros* identify him with St. Anthony.[31]

The next most powerful and most popular *orisha* is Changó, usually represented as St. Barbara. *Orisha* of fertility and virility, he is primarily in charge of lightning and thunder, as in Yoruba. His color is red, symbolizing the fire of lightning and passion. One way of pacifying him during a dreadful thunder and lightning storm is to burn some of the palm branches distributed by the Catholic Church on Palm Sunday.[32]

Other divinities in this powerful club are Oggún, in charge of war and metals, provider of employment, and patron of metal works — his assistance is sought in overcoming an enemy; Orúnla, overseer of divination and the master of the past, present, and the future; Yemayá, who was discussed above; and Oshún, female *orisha* of love, marriage, and boldness. Flamboyant and liking a good life, she is also represented as the patroness of Cuba, La Caridad del Cobre.[33]

Something ought to be said about the *babalawo*, who combines the sacrificial role of the Christian priesthood with those of herbalist, confessor, and diviner. His most important duty is the divination of the Table of Ifa. The Yoruba scholar J. Omosade Awolalu, a Nigerian, points out that in Yoruba as in other ancient religions and cults, people come to the *babalawo* when they want to know the will of the deity and the plight of their own situation, both present and

30. González-Wippler, *Santeria*, 104–5.
31. Ibid., 105–9.
32. Ibid., 109–13.
33. Ibid., 113–23.

future, if possible. There are various kinds of divination, but the best known is that of Ifa, which Santeria has adapted. During the Yoruba ceremony — which is conducted with cowry shells, pieces of broken pottery, animal teeth, and sesame seeds — the *babalawo* pulls together many of the elements of traditional religion: homage to the ancestors, invocation of the oracular spirit, interpreting conditions through elaborate and complicated patterns of palm nuts that only he is able to interpret. Divination tells persons what the divinities desire and what the future holds for them. It also usually ends in some kind of sacrifice, be it for the better or for the status quo.[34]

The *babalawo*'s other most important task is knowing the correct sacrifice at major rituals and ceremonies of Santeria. Sacrifice both in African traditional religion and in the Caribbean religions such as Santeria and Voodoo has frequently been misunderstood by Western Christians, whose liturgies have either trivialized or spiritualized this important offering to the divine. In the traditional religions of Africa and the Caribbean, including Santeria, sacrifice is a religious act in which something is offered to the deity or divinity in thanksgiving, for penance, or as a petition for a change in one's fortunes and situation. Awolalu makes the point that sacrifice is usually made to gain the intercession or favor of the divinities and spirits under the supreme deity.

> It is believed that life should be preserved, and its preservation and continuation depend upon the favor of the beings which have the power to sustain or destroy it....[Yoruba] know that they depend upon these spiritual powers for material prosperity, for good health, increase in crops, in cattle and in the family; they consider it expedient to show their gratitude to the givers of good things. That is why thanks, which is due the benefactors, are given in the form of thanksgiving sacrifice.[35]

But sacrifice also has an aspect that is bound up with evil and suffering. The forces of destruction in the cosmos, which cause mishaps and evil, can be counteracted through offering sacrifice to gainsay the anger and vengeance of the divinities and the spirits. In addition, sacrifice is often a petition for the purification of a person or a community that has broken a taboo or committed a sin. In many parts of Africa, before the practice was abolished by the

34. J. Omosade Awolalu, *Yoruba Beliefs and Sacrificial Rites* (Harlow, England: Longman, 1979), 120–32, passim.
35. Ibid., 137.

colonial powers, the highest sacrifice for taking away the offense or sins of a community or a people as well as epidemics and diseases was to offer a human being as a scapegoat.

Santeria, like other Caribbean traditional religions, also has its special feast days. Common both to Santeria and Haitian Voodoo is the Feast of John the Baptist on June 24; John the Baptist is also the patron saint of Puerto Rico and a favorite saint in Hispanic cultures. It is thought that divine forces are particularly powerful on this day, so *babalawo* are in much demand for divination. Unmarried women sometimes ask for divination on June 24 in order to discover whether they will marry a rich man or a poor man in the future. Another custom attached to this day is bathing in seawater, a "rebaptism" under the patronage of St. John the Baptist. Some claim that Santeria's celebration of this feast is the reason beaches in Puerto Rico are always so crowded on June 24.[36]

Good Friday and Holy Saturday are also significant feast days for Santeria. Since Good Friday is believed in Santeria to be the day when God absented himself from the earth, people and the cosmos are thought to be most vulnerable to malevolent powers on that day. Because of God's absence, evil forces cannot be stopped on this day, but on Holy Saturday God renews nature and the good forces prevail over the evil powers. Called "Saturday of Glory" in Cuba, on that day the *santeros* pick herbs believed to have the *aché* or "strength" or "grace" of the soon-to-be resurrected Christ. Later when the first rains of May come, the herbs, having been stored in the homes of the *santeros*, are boiled in some of the rainwater and the resulting liquid is used to cure diseases.[37]

TRINIDADIAN SHANGO

In Trinidad the legacy of African traditional culture and religion is known as Shango. Because slaves were not imported to Trinidad in great numbers until late in the eighteenth century, that legacy came to Trinidad after it had come to the other islands in the Antilles and long after Columbus discovered the island in June 1498. Named by Columbus to honor the Holy Trinity, its original inhabitants were Arawak Indians. Trinidad was largely ignored by the Spaniards until 1592, when Domingo de Vera established a permanent settlement

36. Ibid., 141.
37. Ibid., 143.

at San Josef de Oruna (now St. Joseph). Trinidad's slave population did not increase until 1777, when French planters from Grenada came to the island with their slaves after being promised land and tax abatement by Spain, which hoped to develop and defend the island against an increasingly aggressive Britain. Prior to this, the Arawak Indians made up the labor force on the Spanish plantations, where tobacco, cotton, sugar, coffee, and mostly cocoa were grown.

By 1779 there were over 500 settlers, mostly French, and nearly 1000 slaves residing and working on Trinidad. In 1783 both white settlers and freed coloreds were officially recognized as residents as a part of Spain's colonial foreign policy under the Cedula [Decree] of Population. Each immigrant settler was promised thirty acres of land and half as much for each slave brought with him. After five years both whites and coloreds could become citizens. As a result, a substantial colored propertied class was created in Trinidad under the Spanish because freed coloreds soon outnumbered white settlers.[38] The regulations regarding who could settle in Trinidad were not without restrictions, however. It was stipulated that each settler had to be Roman Catholic and a subject of a state friendly toward Spain. Trinidad very quickly became a predominantly French and Roman Catholic colony with a slave labor force and a plantation economy, the French and black slaves largely replacing the Spanish-Indian population. According to the 1784 census, 2550 freemen, 2462 slaves, and 1491 Indians lived on Trinidad. By 1797, some 6627 freemen (now including both whites [2151] and coloreds [4476]), 10,009 slaves, and 1082 Indians made up the population.[39] Most of the French slaves had been cargoed from Angola, the Blight of Benin (Yorubaland), the Gold Coast (Ghana), the Windward Coast (modern Ivory Coast and Liberia), and Senegambia.[40]

In October 1796, under French pressure, Spain declared war on Britain, which then speeded up its attacks on the ports of Trinidad. In February of the following year, Trinidad was surrendered to the British, who held it until independence in 1962. Its population and culture are a mixture of African, Spanish, French, British, Indian, and Chinese elements. (The Indians and Chinese were brought over by the British to augment the labor force on the plantations

38. Bridget Brereton, *A History of Modern Trinidad 1783–1962* (Kingston, Jamaica: Heinemann, 1981), 13–14.

39. Ibid., 16.

40. Philip D. Curtin, *The Atlantic Slave Trade: A Census* (Madison: University of Wisconsin Press, 1969), 170.

and to build construction projects.) The slave community practiced African traditional religion, Obeah, Islam, and some Christianity via Roman Catholicism, Anglicanism, and the Baptist faith, which was brought to Trinidad by a group of American ex-slaves who had fought on the side of the British in the War of 1812 and had settled there after Britain's defeat.

Later, after the 1833 emancipation, some 8000 Africans came to Trinidad between 1841 and 1861, and they brought with them their traditional religion. One group that has retained its traditional religion even to the present day are the Radas, who came from Dahomey; their religion, like all traditional African and slave religions in Trinidad, was called *Obeah* by the colonists. However, the traditional religion that came to be adapted overall in the Afro culture of Trinidad was the Yoruba-derived Shango (Changó in Cuba; Shango in Haiti; Xangó in Brazil), which emerged as a full-fledged religion in the nineteenth century. To identify this as the Afro traditional religion in Trinidad is not to slight Hinduism, which the East Indians brought with them after the British imported them as indentured servants after the abolition of slavery in 1833. The respective religions and faith in Trinidad also reflected the color stratification found in other Caribbean cultures: the whites and Creole elites were Anglicans and Catholics; the colored middle class represented a spectrum of denominations; the black lower class were Protestants and Catholics but also Shangoists and Spiritual Baptists.

George E. Simpson calls Trinidadian Shango a "neo-African" religion in that it is named after Shango, the Yoruba *orisha* of lightning and thunder, and was brought by the Yoruba migrating to Trinidad in the nineteenth century.[41] Shango includes a number of deities; its pantheon is more decentralized than that of Haitian Voodoo; and it includes a number of "powers," in addition to Shango himself. Shango is only one among equals, albeit an important one. Most of the names of the gods are Yoruba in origin, and some of the gods are also Santeria *orisha* and Voodoo *loa*: Alufon (Olufon), Elephon, Emanjah, Eshu (Esu), Obalufon, Ogun, Obatalá, Oshún, Oya, and Yao. But its pantheon also includes non-Yoruba deities. Its legends and myths about a supreme deity are not as sophisticated or developed as in Yoruba or its legatee, Cuban Santeria. The

41. George Eaton Simpson, *Black Religions in the New World* (New York: Columbia University Press, 1978), 73. See also his "Shango Cult in Trinidad," *African Notes* 3 (1965): 11–21.

deity Elephon, also called Daluphon and Shakbear, is identified as the "Eternal Father," and Obalufon, sometimes called Abalophon, is identified with Jesus Christ.[42]

The syncretism between Catholicism and African spirits evident in other Afro Caribbean traditional religions also occurs in Shango. Alufon, for example, is identified with the Holy Spirit, although it is not the supreme or chief spirit as might be expected from the Christian understanding of the Holy Spirit. Emanjah, the female spirit of rivers, is identified with St. Anne and St. Catherine; Eshu with Satan; Ogun, the Yoruba *orisha* of iron, metal, and taxi drivers, with St. Michael; Oshún, the goddess of the ocean, with St. Philomena and St. Anne; Oya, the mistress of the winds and rains, with St. Catherine and St. Philomena.[43] All have their cults and communicate with each other through the messenger known as Elegba or Elegbara, also known as Legba in Haitian and New Orleans Voodoo. A great many Catholic prayers — such as the Hail Mary — hymns, and devotional materials — such as crucifixes, candles, rosaries, and incense — are very much a part of the rituals.

Divination, healing, possession, and sacrifice of animals are also important parts of Shango. This is not too dissimilar from the litany of saints, spirits, and ancestors (*Priè Ginin*) in Haitian Voodoo, that litany being a blend of Catholic prayers and invocations to the saints and Voodoo rituals. It begins with Catholic hymns ("An angel of the Lord said to Mary / That she will give birth to Jesus / She has been chosen since the beginning of the world / She will give birth by the operation of the Holy Spirit"),[44] followed by the *houngan* naming male and then female Catholic saints, followed by the naming of Voodoo saints and ancestors.

An interesting relationship between Shango — with its mixture of Catholic ritual and implements — and Protestantism exists in Trinidad through the Spiritual Baptists. Thought to have come from St. Vincent, the Spiritual Baptists (also called "Shouters") of Trinidad constitute a twentieth-century religion among the descendants of the slaves. Forbidden by the British from 1917 to 1951, as they were in St. Vincent from 1912 to 1965, the Spiritual Baptists have a liturgy that centers on possession by the Holy Spirit.

42. George Eaton Simpson, *Religious Cults of the Caribbean: Trinidad, Jamaica, and Haiti* (Rio Piedras, P.R.: Institute of Caribbean Studies, 1970), 18.
43. Ibid., 18–20.
44. Cited in Laguerre, *Voodoo Heritage*, 156f.

Both Shango and the Spiritual Baptists use baptism as entry to the cult, but in Shango baptism can be performed only by a known "Shouter" leader. Called "mourning," the candidate for baptism stays in a "sacred chamber" or tomb, often a separate structure located near a church, for three days, known as a "temporary death." The people "lying in the tomb" are called pilgrims. On the third day the pilgrim is "lifted" and "released." At the end of the ceremony, food is offered to the spirits as well as sacrifices of pigeons or other fowl. Herskovits describes the Spiritual Baptists as the "point of transition between African religion, represented in Trinidad by the Shango cult, and undiluted European forms of worship."[45] Apparently Shangoists also hold "prayer meetings" at Spiritual Baptist churches and even conduct services in their churches in the course of the year.[46]

As already noted, Shango lacks a hierarchy, although great respect is given Shango himself. The powers are invoked at different centers or *palais*; each center has its own leader, and people move between the various centers for different ceremonies and festivals. However, in recent years Pa Neezer, the most knowledgeable leader of rituals, became known as the "king" or chief resource master of ceremonies. Since Neezer's death, several leaders have claimed to be his heir. Today, Shango is on the move, *palais* are growing, and it has become more and more of an acceptable African enrichment of Trinidadian culture. Shango is accepted by the educated as well as the poor, and is particularly attractive to young people wanting a distinct Trinidadian identity. Some scholars attribute this attraction to the black power movement of the 1960s and 1970s with its emphasis on blacks' African heritage. That movement, which began in the United States, spread throughout the Caribbean.

JAMAICAN CHURCHES AND TRADITIONAL RELIGIONS

Jamaica, whose early history is dotted with maroon wars of liberation from and slave rebellions against slavery, is justifiably proud of its Afro Caribbean heritage. As in Haiti and the United States, black religion played an important empowering role during such resistance. Interestingly enough, it was American black clergy who served as

---

45. Melville J. Herskovits and Francis S. Herskovits, *Trinidad Village* (New York: Alfred A. Knopf, 1947), 305.
46. Simpson, *Black Religions in the New World*, 79.

the impetus for the emergence of Jamaican churches that incorporate African traditional religions. Although it took some time before these churches began fully to incorporate the elements of traditional African religions, evidence shows that even prior to this time, traditional African beliefs, such as the veneration of ancestors, were practiced by many slaves at burials on the plantations, especially during the "Nine Night" services, a mourning period for the dead lasting nine days and nights. Also many of the vessels used in ceremonies reveal the legacy of the African traditions being mixed with Christian elements.

The Spanish were the first Europeans to set foot on Jamaica, arriving in 1509, but the British took the island from Spain in 1655. The first shipment of Africans arrived around 1517. The Africans were mostly from the Ashanti in present-day Ghana, the Mamprussi, Dagomba, and Nankansi in Guinea, the Yoruba and Igbo in present-day Nigeria, and the Kilkongo of modern Zaire. At the time of the English settlement there were about 1500 slaves and a similar number of Spaniards who grew cocoa, indigo, various kinds of citrus plants, and, of course, sugar. In his *History of Jamaica* Edward Long records that in 1655, 76 percent of the island's population was white (British and Spanish) and 24 percent was African. By 1673 the white population had decreased to 47 percent (8500) and the slave population had increased to 53 percent (9500). Toward the end of the century, in 1690, the number of whites remained about the same as in 1673, but the slave population had grown to over 40,000.

The slaves looked after crops originally developed by the native Arawak Indians: tobacco, corn, potatoes, and cotton. Later in their own plots they added a foodstuff from West Africa that is still the national dish in Jamaica, ackee. The British were late in permitting missionaries to work among the slaves, the first being Moravian missionaries (Church of the United Brethren) from Saxony in Germany, who had first arrived at St. Thomas, Virgin Islands, then a part of the Danish West Indies, in 1732. These missionaries arrived in Jamaica in 1774. Then came the black American Baptists, who arrived in 1783. Among them were men such as George Liele and Moses Baker. Some of those American Baptists were very influential in starting the indigenous Native Baptist Church. The American Baptists were followed by the Wesleyan Methodists in 1789. Thomas Coke, a close friend of John Wesley, did missionary work mostly among freed mulattoes in the towns, while others worked with the slaves on the sugar plantations and in the towns. The Anglican Church

did little work among the slaves, calling them the "home heathen."
One exception to this was an annual mass baptism, which Anglican
clerics conducted at the request of the plantation owners.

It is estimated that when emancipation abolishing slavery took
effect on August 1, 1834, there were about 311,000 slaves in Jamaica (almost 90 percent of the island's population). Their owners
received £6,149,955 in compensation.[47] Many slaves were members
of one of the American or European churches; many were members
of the indigenous movements; some took part in both. By 1841,
not counting the blacks in the established Anglican Church and the
indigenous Native Baptist Church, about one-third of the black population — approximately 100,000 — belonged either to a European
or an American church; most of them were either Baptist or Wesleyan Methodist.[48] During this period there were black revolts —
the most renowned occurred in 1831 (it was led by Sam Sharpe,
a Native Baptist lay preacher) and in 1865. Unlike the plantation
owners in the United States, who beat, restricted, and jailed missionaries as "outside agitators," the plantocracy in Jamaica allowed
them to work reasonably unrestricted among the blacks. And although there was general anxiety about Jamaica's economic future
after the emancipation decree, so much so that open discussions
were held about secession from Britain and union with the southern states of the United States, such alignment with the U.S. slave
states did not materialize.

Native Baptists

African religious survivals in Jamaica were first developed by the
Native Baptists, an indigenous church started by black American
ex-slaves and slaves who came with their owners when the lat-
ter migrated to the island as British loyalists after the American
War of Independence. Among the ex-slaves was George Liele from
Georgia, the first ordained black Baptist minister, who arrived in
Kingston in 1783. Liele had been given his freedom by his owner,
who died in the Revolutionary War. But his owner's survivors dis-
agreed about the actual status of Liele, so, for his own security,
Liele went to Kingston, where he attracted a large following and

---

47. Cyril Hamshere, *The British in the Caribbean* (London: Weidenfeld and
Nicolson, 1972), 148.

48. James M. Phillippo, *Jamaica: Its Past and Present State* (1843; reprint,
London: Dawsons, 1969), 290–91.

built a chapel. However, soon some of his flock split and established the "Native Baptists." Among early Native Baptist leaders were some other black Americans: Moses Baker, George Gibb, and George Lewis.

These Native Baptists practiced baptism by immersion in the name of the Father, Son, and Holy Spirit, a practice similar to rites long known among traditionalists in Africa, who baptized in lakes and streams. The Native Baptists also connected the interpretation of dreams with the Holy Spirit. In fact, for them dreams and visions quickly became prerequisites for baptism rather than "right" doctrine. John the Baptist became more important than Jesus Christ since they reasoned that as John baptized Jesus, he must have had more authority originally. In this respect the emphasis on John the Baptist reminds us faintly of the theology of some of the early patristic Fathers, such as Origen, Ambrose, and Leo the Great, who esteemed John's role so highly that they said he was given "pre-natal grace" by God during the Visitation to Mary (Luke 1:41).

But there are also parallels to the Mandeans, an ancient Middle East cult sometimes called the "Christians of St. John." Dating from the first or second century and existing today along the Tigris and Euphrates in Iraq, in Iran, and in cities like Baghdad, Mandeans revered John the Baptist and also accentuated the rite of baptism. Baptism for them was the ritual preparation for a person's entry into salvation as well as the protection from sins and transgressions. In fact, Mandeans called all baptismal waters "Jordan" after the river in which John baptized Jesus. But baptism was also preparation for ascension after death. Lacking baptism, no Mandean could pass into the next world of light after death, and priests who were backsliders had to undergo several baptisms in their lifetimes. However, it must be quickly added that there is no evidence that Mandeanism reached into Africa. Nevertheless, the tenor of their belief in John the Baptist matched the sentiment in an early Native Baptist prebaptismal hymn still sung in Jamaica:

> John a Baptist — Do my Lord
> Me pray for sin — Do my Lord
> Me pray for my soul — Do my Lord
> Remember you duty — Do my Lord
> Sinner dead he must — Do my Lord

Me pray for keep me out of de fire —
Do my Lord.[49]

The Holy Spirit and possession by the Spirit also play major
roles in Native Baptist ritual, since it is the Spirit that gives life,
knowledge, and healing. Indeed, fired up by the Spirit with their
eyes set on freedom, many of the early black rebels leading insur-
rections against the colonial system and plantocracy were leaders in
the Native Baptist movement; among these leaders were Sam Sharpe,
George Taylor, and Robert Gardner in the 1831 rebellion, and Paul
Bogle of the Morant Bay rebellion in 1865. In fact, by 1830 Native
Baptists had become so strong that they were viewed as an African
Christian alternative competing with the Christianity of the Europeans in Jamaica.[50]

Myalism

Another surviving remnant of African traditional religion appeared
among the Native Baptists after emancipation, namely Myalism.
However, one plantation owner, Monk Lewis, claimed to have witnessed Myal dancing among the slaves as early as 1818, and some
scholars maintain that Myalism appeared in Jamaica as early as 1760.
Certainly by the nineteenth century it had Christian syncretisms. On
the other hand, some devotees of another Afro Caribbean religion,
Kumina, maintain that Myal is a spirit rather than a belief; they say
this spirit possesses people in a violent way: "Myal is de ting dey
call a spirit where you' head 'pin roun' an' you drop an' you' 'kin
pupalich ('somersault') 'pon your neck, you see."[51]

Its etymology is thought to begin in Central Africa, since the
stronghold of Myal is St. Thomas's Parish, many of whose residents
are descendants of Central African tribes and who commonly speak
about possession by certain ancestral spirits as "catching Myal."
Others think Myal is of West African origin, having been brought
by Akan slaves (from Ghana); still others think the name may have

49. Cited in Barry Chevannes, "Revival and Black Struggle," *Savacou* 5 (June
1971): 29.

50. Philip D. Curtin, *Two Jamaicas: The Role of Ideas in a Tropical Colony,
1830–1865* (Cambridge: Harvard University Press, 1955), 32–34.

51. From an interview with a Kumina queen in Jamaica by Maureen Warner
Lewis, *The Nkuyu: Spirit Messengers of the Kumina* (Kingston, Jamaica: Savacou Publications, Mona, 1977), 59.

come from the plant in Jamaica called the "myal weed."[52] Manifested mainly in dancing, Myal was believed by the slaves to protect them from being killed by Europeans as well as from Obeah magic.[53] They would drink a concoction of water and West Indian spinach (*calalu*), which when uncooked and left soaking in cold water for a period of time becomes a strong narcotic. Then they danced until they reached ecstasy and complete disorientation, after which they were revived by another remedy.

Because Myal also stresses dreams and visions as necessary credentials preceding baptism as well as drumming and possession by the Holy Spirit, many confuse it with the religion of the Native Baptists. Some scholars claim that even the Great Revival that took Jamaica by storm in 1861–1862 and again in 1866 was basically Myalist. But this is more likely testimony to the common African religious legacy of both beliefs. It is not to be denied, however, that the Great Revival had political overtones for black Jamaicans that were linked to Africa in the rebels' minds: "Tell the Sons and Daughters of Africa, that a great deliverance will take place for them from the hand of Oppression," read a sign on the wharf in Hanover, "for, said the Voice, they are oppressed by Government, by Magistrates, by Proprietors, and by Merchants."[54]

Such cries for freedom and liberation clothed under the worldview of traditional African religious belief among the slaves were early on understood by slave owners as a threat to the peace and stability of the Jamaican social structure, so much so that in December 1781 the legislature enacted a law proscribing death or other punishment for "any negroe or other slave who shall pretend to any supernatural power."[55] Such priests, including the Obeah-men, provided the slaves with the "courage to be" (to use Paul Tillich's phrase) — the daring to survive based on a belief in the supreme god

52. Orlando Patterson, *The Sociology of Slavery: An Analysis of the Origins, Development and Structure of Negro Slave Society in Jamaica* (Rutherford, N.J.: Fairleigh Dickinson University Press, 1967), 186.

53. According to F. G. Cassidy, it may have come from the Ewe (Ghana) *maye* (evil) and *le* (to grasp, to take hold of), hence the understanding "to take hold of the evil" of Obeah. In Ivor Morrish, *Obeah, Christ and Rastaman: Jamaica and Its Religion* (Cambridge, England: James Clarke, 1982), 46.

54. Monica Schuler, "Myalism and the African Religious Tradition," in Margaret E. Crahan and Franklin W. Knight, eds., *Africa and the Caribbean: The Legacies of a Link* (Baltimore: Johns Hopkins University Press, 1979), 75.

55. Cited in Noel Leo Erskine, *Decolonizing Theology: A Caribbean Perspective* (Maryknoll, N.Y.: Orbis Books, 1981), 31.

and the divinities of African traditional religion. One eighteenth-century writer describes the empowerment Jamaican slaves believed they received from Myalism through the "Myal dance": "The lure hung out was, that every negro, initiated into the myal society, would be invulnerable by the whitemen, and although they might in appearance be slain, the obeah man could at his pleasure restore life."[56]

Myalism also claims to interpret the will of the spirits to the community and worshipers and to counteract injury conjured or invoked by Obeah, the negative side of Jamaican traditional religions, although historically the "Obeah-man" was also an important link between the customs and beliefs of the homeland of Africa and the conditions in the New World.[57] Professor Noel Erskine, himself a Jamaican, suggests that the Obeah-man through his charms and amulets provided protection and assurance for the slaves in their struggle to survive the brutalities and cruelties of the slavery system. The Obeah-man also acted as a broker for a male slave trying to court a female slave as a means of revenge on a fellow male slave.[58] In general, then, we can say that in contrast to Myal, Obeah is considered sorcery that is bent on doing injury to a person's enemy by way of charms, poisons, and catching the enemy's shadow. Obeah deals with evil spirits, whereas Myal deals with good spirits and counters the evil magic of Obeah, particularly in freeing shadows of the living from the magic of Obeah.[59] Many Jamaicans believe that unless a person's shadow is released from the power of Obeah, that person will wear away and soon die.[60] One Jamaican slave explained Obeah's evil power in the following terms: "When him set obeah for somebody him catch dem shadow, and dem go dead."[61] Indeed an important role of the Bible was to act as a charm or symbol of "white Obeah" — it was believed to protect slaves from slave owners and thus was to be carried at all times. (I cannot be certain if there is a direct link, but it is impressive to see Jamaican Christians of

56. Cited in Erskine, *Decolonizing Theology*, 47.

57. This term is thought to have come from the Ashanti (Akan) word *obayifo*, meaning "wizard" or "witch." An Obeah-man is thought to have the ability to leave his body in order to travel at night and bring harm to the enemies of others.

58. Erskine, *Decolonizing Theology*, 29.

59. Patterson, *Sociology of Slavery*, 187–95.

60. Martha Warren Beckwith, *Black Roadways: A Study of Jamaican Folk Life* (New York: Negro University Press, 1929), 144.

61. Cited in Patterson, *Sociology of Slavery*, 187.

all varieties carrying their Bibles with them to church on Sundays, even today.)

The relationship between Myalism and Obeah may also have something to do with the fact that the former is the ancient tribal religion of the Ashanti (Akan). Many of the Myal priests from Akan ethnic groups became Obeah-men in Jamaica because they were forbidden to practice openly in slave religious assemblies except under Christian auspices. In this dual role as an Obeah-man or Obeah-woman the Myal priest also gained authority in the black community.[62] But the Myal priest, though aware of the skills and powers of the Obeah-man, was considered a doer of good rather than evil.

In common with African tradition, Myal deals with healing as well as with interpreting the Spirit and the spirits. A man or a woman wanting to be a Myal priest or priestess begins a long apprenticeship, first learning the healing powers of plants, herbs, and trees, after which he or she is made to dance until possessed by a Myal spirit. The initiate falls to the ground ("rooted") in a trance, where she or he remains for several days. It is believed that during this trance, the person is in fact in the spirit world communing with the spirits about healing powers. Upon being revived, he or she is given a "bush-bath" — a bath with special herbs. After this person has qualified to use good medicine, called "bush medicine," for countermanding the evil medicine of Obeah, people, particularly in rural areas, go to the Myal priest or priestess for herbal and spiritual medicine. Some suggest that, little by little, much of Myalism has been incorporated by the Native Baptists.

Kumina

The most Africanized of the cults in Jamaica is the Kumina cult (sometimes spelled Cumina). The cult is a legacy from the Congo, and its name is thought to come from *kumona*, "to see" or "possession," or from *kumunu*, "rhythm, the spirit of rhythm," or even "lion."[63] It too came into prominence during the emancipation period when many of the newly emancipated slaves, now apprentices and indentured servants according to British law, continued to be

---

62. Joseph J. Williams, *Voodoos and Obeahs: Phases of West India Witchcraft* (New York: Dial Press, 1932), 145.

63. Zora Neale Hurston claims that "koo-min-ah" means "the power," which she witnessed in a "house" built for a duppy (*Voodoo Gods* [London: J. M. Dent, 1939], 56–60).

oppressed. But at the same time, its roots in Jamaica can be traced at least to 1730. This suggests that its reappearance at the time of the emancipation and later in the 1930s meant either that it went underground during those respective intervening periods or that it decayed and was restored.[64]

Membership in a Kumina group, called a "bands," is inherited at birth rather than being taken on through conversion or voluntary membership, although this rule is not strictly enforced, especially when a new person appearing at a ceremony is acceptable to the ancestors at that same ceremony. A "bands" is not a commune, but members sometimes do reside together at the "seal or mission ground," the place of assembly for the "bands." The "seal," focused around a tall pole in the yard, is the most sacred part of the "ground," for here the ancestral spirits ascend and communicate. Members in "bands" may or may not have experienced the spirit.

According to Simpson, unlike devotees of Voodoo, Santeria, and Shango, Kumina devotees do not venerate the old African deities, but rather the ancestral spirits. The remembrance of the ancestral spirits, what Christian liturgy calls the anamnesis, happens in Kumina under what they call zombies, although these are not to be confused with the zombies in Haiti.[65] These ancestral zombies are (1) sky divinities, the highest ranking spirits — 37 of these have been identified and they have names like Obo, Jubee, Belgium, Flash, Sango, Beeal, and Goomba; (2) earth-bound divinities — 62 of these have been identified and they have names like Macoo, Biko, Kachee, Ezekiel, Mabell, Augustus, King Makoo, and Chickee; and (3) ancestral zombies, spirits of the deceased members of families living in an area — these return to dance at Myal dances and bear the names of persons, e.g., Jimmy Snate, Sophie Bartly, Archie Pierce, and Grace Baily, among others. Thought to be spirits who are actually the equivalents of holy men and women who lived on earth, they act as guardians for the earthly family, as in African cultures. Some of them have become such powerful spirits that they excel the earth divinities in power.[66]

---

64. The earliest written note about Kumina dates from 1730. For the note, see Charles Leslie, *A New History of Jamaica* (Dublin: Oli Nelson, 1741). The note is cited in Patterson, *Sociology of Slavery*, 201.

65. Simpson, *Black Religions in the New World*, 99. For an intriguing investigation of zombiism in Haiti, see Wade Davis, *The Serpent & the Rainbow* (New York: Simon and Schuster, 1985).

66. Simpson, *Religious Cults of the Caribbean*, 162–63.

There are several reasons for invoking the spirits in Kumina, but most invocations pay respect to the ancestors of the worshipers. "Memorial dances [sometimes called 'black and white dances'], given in honor of a deceased member of the family, entombment dances (a service added to a memorial dance), and 'crop-over dances' marking the end of 'nine night' after a death (crop-over dances are also given to celebrate the end of a cane cutting season) are among the major Cumina ceremonies."[67] The memorial dance is intended to assure rest to the spirit of the departed zombie and to ensure that he or she and all the other ancestors are happy. Should the dead not be properly honored and proper rituals executed, their spirits will wander about forever and menace the living members of the family.

The cottonwood tree, hailed in Kumina as a dwelling place for both good and evil spirits ("duppies"), is an important part of the liturgical life. It is also the place for "catching shadows," also an important aspect of the Kumina leader's work.[68] One Jamaican Kumina queen described her going inside the cottonwood tree during her apprenticeship as a return to the womb for new life and at the same time a journey into the tomb toward death. For Kumina, the opposite of death is not life but birth. While in the cottonwood tree the apprentice learns the secret knowledge for invoking the ancestral spirits of the dead (*nkuyu*) and for healing.[69] At the cottonwood tree's base the good medicine of Kumina counters the bad medicine of Obeah when the latter tries to "catch the shadow" of an individual.

Kumina devotees believe that a person's spirit has a personal aspect that is always within the person as long as he or she lives, and an aspect that "walks beside" the person, called the person's "shadow" or "duppy." When the person dies, the personal spirit ascends to the King Zombie, Oto, unless the person has been possessed by a zombie while on earth, in which case the "duppy" at death joins other ancestral zombie spirits and returns to earth for various duties. The "shadow" or "duppy" spirit remains buried with the corpse unless

67. Ibid., 99.

68. Beckwith, basing her assertions on studies of rural Jamaica, says that the cottonwood tree is both feared and venerated because it is thought to be inhabited by evil or trickster spirits. Only cottonwood trees planted over a grave are "dealt with" by Myal men to counter Obeah. A cottonwood tree will not be cut down unless there is first a propitiatory offering (*Black Roadways*, 145).

69. See this important interview in Lewis, *The Nkuyu*, with additional commentary in Edward R. Brathwaite, "Kumina: The Spirit of African Survival in Jamaica," *Jamaica Journal* 42 (September 1978): 45–63.

it chooses to come out from time to time. "Catching a person's shadow" is a chief purpose of Obeah-priests and priestesses when they want to inflict harm on one's enemy. The fact that some of Kumina's ritual involves the cottonwood tree suggests that at some point there may have been an intermingling of Myalism and Kumina. The use of Myal rituals can checkmate the power of Obeah in this area, with the aid of the cottonwood tree. Some scholars say that a duppy is primarily a mischievous spirit of Obeah living in cottonwood trees and bamboo forests, but not controlling them.[70]

As in African traditional religion and other Caribbean traditional religions, drumming, invocations, and chanting are vital to Kumina. The chanting includes both English and inherited untranslatable African words, just as Haitian Voodoo ceremonies include both French and Latin as well as no longer understandable African expressions. Interestingly enough, the chants and songs are first "lined" by a leader, something still found in some U.S. black churches; this is a process whereby a leader sings or recites the first line or verse of a hymn and the congregation repeats it afterwards. In the United States this is frequently done in small black congregations lacking a pianist or organist, particularly in the South and inner-city churches in the North.

Another interesting feature in Kumina is the ring dance, which resembles a part of slave worship in the antebellum American South called the "ring shout." In Kumina the devotees form a ring and step to the rhythm of the drums. But the people not only dance with their feet, but also with their hips, shoulders, and indeed their entire bodies, a movement characteristic in the Caribbean, Africa, and black America. They dance counterclockwise in a ring in order to evoke the spirits, each of which has his or her own distinctive dance style.[71] In the "ring shout" U.S. slaves formed a ring, clapped their hands, stamped their feet, and step-danced counterclockwise in a circle. Daniel Payne (1811–1893), a bishop in the African Methodist Episcopal Church, utterly disliked this African legacy and labeled it "heathenish" and the "Voodoo Dance," complaining that many of his pastors not only tolerated it, but openly encouraged it.[72] The father-son team of John and Alan Lomax, collectors of eth-

---

70. Lewis, *The Nkuyu*, 70. However, Martha Beckwith records a rural Jamaican in the 1920s saying that neither the soul nor the body "makes" the duppy, but the person's shadow (*Black Roadways*, 98).
71. Simpson, *Religious Cults of the Caribbean*, 100.
72. Daniel Alexander Payne, *Recollections of Seventy Years* (1886; reprint, New

nic folklore, witnessed a ring shout in Louisiana in 1934 and found similarities between it and rituals in other black communities in the United States and in the Caribbean: the song is danced with the whole body, including the belly and the hips; dancing moves counterclockwise in a circle; the entire worship is mostly dancing and singing; a call-response takes place between the leader and the chorus, with much repetition of rhythm rather than melody; the dancing and singing intensify and accelerate "until a sort of mass hypnosis ensues. . . . This shout pattern is demonstrably West African in origin."[73] The "mass hypnosis" was no doubt spirit possession induced by the ring shout.

Jamaican Revivalism

Although not direct descendants of African traditional religion, indigenous Jamaican "revival" churches should not be overlooked. In some parts of Jamaica revivalism is also called Revival Zion and Pocomania (or Poku-kumina).[74] Some have asserted that revivalism in Jamaica dates from the 1860s, while others have argued that it began much earlier. One Jamaican planter observed that after the American Revolutionary War, blacks came to Jamaica "blending important [Christian] truths and extravagant puerilities," such as a reliance on visions and the interpretation of dreams, so that they might qualify "for full admission to the community." They too fought the power of Obeah with their own gifts of being able to communicate with the spirits.[75]

The differences between revivalism and Pocomania are sometimes more apparent to Jamaicans than to outsiders, but generally Pocomania has a more negative reputation among Native Baptists and revivalists. One of Jamaica's leading sculptors, Kapo (Mallica Reynolds, 1911–1989), who was also a minister in the revivalist

York: Arno Press and the New York Times, 1969), 254–56 (cited in Albert J. Raboteau, *Slave Religion* [New York: Oxford University Press, 1978], 69).

73. John A. Lomax and Alan Lomax, *Folk Song U.S.A.* (New York: Duell, Sloan & Pearce, 1947), 335.

74. Since "Pocomania" is the more familiar term, for the sake of consistency, I shall use it to refer to what Edward Seaga, the former prime minister of Jamaica and student of Jamaican African survivals in religion, claims should properly be "Pokumina." The misspelling came about through Spanish phonetics and vocabulary. Hence "poco-mania" ("little madness") described the frenzy and spirit possession that had their roots in the African legacy and confirmed Catholic ideas about African religion being primarily superstitious. See Edward Seaga, "Revival Cults in Jamaica: Notes Towards a Sociology of Religion," *Jamaica Journal* 3 (June 1969): 4.

75. Phillippo, *Jamaica: Its Past and Present State*, 267–79.

movement in Jamaica and bishop of St. Michael's Revival Tabernacle, which he founded in Brooklyn, New York City, pointed out that
the revivalists emphasize the Bible, prayer, sick-visits, and healing,
whereas Pocomania emphasizes experiencing and communicating
with the spirits, particularly ancestral spirits.[76] Simpson, however,
identifies Pocomania as a branch of revivalism that (1) includes
more singing and spiritual dancing in its ceremonies as a means
of communion with the divinities than the revivalists or Revival
Zionists, who use more preaching and biblical references in their
services; (2) makes more frequent use of witchcraft and magic; and
(3) tolerates the use of rum and ganja (marijuana) in its services,
although Simpson admits that some Revival Zionists also make use
of magic.[77]

The revivalists and devotees of Pocomania share some common features in their worship and liturgy. The place of worship
for revivalists usually has a tall pole, the most important part of
which is the "seal," also called the "center." The pole sometimes
carries the name of the church or meeting place. It may be sur-
rounded by various other kinds of symbols or by a box (called
an ark) in which the Bible is placed. The ark is also understood
to be the office or abode of the spirit, although the spirit is not
confined to this ark. This bears some structural similarity to the
poteau-mitan in a Haitian Voodoo *hounfor* or temple, where rituals
and ceremonies to the *loa* take place. The *poteau-mitan* is a center
post along which the *loa* or spirits descend and enter the *peristyle*,
the ceremonial space in and around which dancing, ritual movements, libations, *vévé* (designs of wheat flour or powdered maize
drawn on the ground by the *houngan* or *mambo* to evoke the *loa*),
and offerings take place.[78] Whether spirits in revivalism use the
pole for the same purpose is not clear. However, the Holy Spirit
does possess worshipers as do other spirits, including (1) heavenly
spirits; (2) earth-bound spirits; and (3) ground spirits. Heavenly
spirits embrace the triune Christian God, the archangels Michael,
Raphael, and Gabriel, and some saints. The earth-bound spirits consist of Old Testament biblical prophets, such as Samuel, Jeremiah,

76. *Intercom* 3, no. 1 (Spring 1977): 42.
77. Simpson, *Black Religions in the New World*, 111; see also his *Religious Cults
of the Caribbean*, 190.
78. For a good explanation of *veve* in Haitian Voodoo, see Milo Riguad, *Ve-
ve: Diagrammes Rituels du Voudou* (New York: French and European Publications,
1974); see also Deren, *Divine Horsemen*, 86–150.

Ezekiel, Isaiah, David, Solomon, Daniel, and Joshua; New Testament figures such as Matthew, Mark, Luke, John, the Blessed Virgin Mary, Peter, and James; but also Satan and his helpers, especially Rutibel, but these are not desired spirits. The ground spirits include the spirits of dead relatives and of revivalist leaders of the past. These spirits are called shepherds or shepherdesses, and they inspire, commune, assist, and protect the devotees from evil and danger.

However, revivalists, devotees of Pocomania, and Zionists all differ about how highly the ground spirits ought to be regarded. Pocomania works primarily with ground spirits and "fallen angels," who are not evil but are good and more attentive to human requests. Why they are called "fallen" is not clear.[79] Simpson points out that revivalists like to speak of themselves as "traveling under" a spirit, which means to be a follower of a particular spirit or category.[80]

Major liturgical objects used by revivalists include wooden crosses, vessels of consecrated water, white candles, red flags, Bibles, flowers, machetes, and drums. All of these are used to evoke and invite the spirits or divinities, which are very numerous in revivalism's pantheon. God as supreme being does not enter the ceremony, although God is considered the creator and lord of the universe. Some believe Jesus Christ descends to the ceremonies, but unlike the spirits, never possesses a worshiper. This simply documents his superior presence at the ceremony.[81]

A partial list of the spirits and their attributes is as follows:

Christ is merciful.
Gabriel is the head angel around the throne of Almighty God, Minister of the Midnight wind; cross and war-like.
Jeremiah is the chief prophet because "him suffer deep." He cuts and clears away "destruction." . . .
God sends death and judgment messages.
Michael is the minister of the Lord's Day (the Angel of Peace).
Samuel is the minister of Blood.
Rutibel concentrates on evil deeds.
Raphael is chief minister of the Archangel group; minister of the General Wind.
Matthew, Mark, Luke and John can be helpful to everyone.

79. Seaga, "Revival Cults in Jamaica," 10.
80. Simpson, *Black Religions in the New World*, 113.
81. Ibid., 112.

Satan may be used if an important case is in court.
Solomon was black....
God and the saints are for everybody.[82]

Not only do the spirits and the Holy Spirit possess the devotees at ceremonies, they also commune with them in dreams and visions — a form of communion inherited directly from African culture, although this is not unique to Africa, as is apparent from the Old Testament and documents from other ancient cultures. Through such possession the person is informed of coming events and receives warnings about enemies. Revivalist services themselves include Bible readings, "spiritual" dancing, the use of drums, tambourines, and rattles, preaching, possession by the spirit, hymn singing, and some public healing.

Unlike Haitian Voodoo, Cuban Santeria, and Trinidadian Shango, Jamaican revivalism does not try to syncretize African divinities with Christian saints. Revivalists believe that the cosmos is fundamentally spiritual, occupied by many spirits with their own jurisdictions. Spirits are also intermediaries to the supreme being. But spirits within Jamaican revivalism can be bifurcated in exercising their powers, and thus are capable of doing both good and evil to humankind.

Although revivalists have been more influenced by Baptists than by Catholicism, nevertheless they include symbols in their liturgy borrowed from both churches: crucifixes, candles, Bible verses, texts from Protestant hymns, emotional preaching, and much hymn singing. Baptism by immersion is also an important rite borrowed from the Baptists, but, as one scholar cautions, "revivalists do not run into the water under possession by a god, as novitiates often do in Africa, but as a baptismal candidate is immersed the spirit may descend on him and produce a possession hysteria that — at least in its outward appearance — is almost indistinguishable from that brought on by the African water deities."[83]

82. Beckwith, *Black Roadways*, 345.
83. Simpson, *Religious Cults of the Caribbean*, 116.

3

Liberation Theologies in Afro Cultures

God-talk about the Christian God from the perspective of Afro cultures also has to be rooted in the social and economic realities of those cultures, particularly the cultures of southern Africa and the Caribbean. The racial politics of a white minority in southern Africa since the Second World War, beginning with white Rhodesia (now Zimbabwe) and continuing with the aberration called apartheid in South Africa, have shaped the context for the formation of South African liberation theology. South African liberation theology initially was closely akin to the black consciousness movement headed by Steve Biko, just as North American black liberation theology arose from the black power movement in the United States.[1] In Jamaica the social and political context has been conditioned by a combination of a former colonial plantocracy, an internal caste system, and class distinctions, all of which have given rise to the Rastafarians and their reggae music as expressions of cultural and religious liberation. The Rastas and reggae music have spread not only throughout the

---

1. This chapter will focus on liberation theologies in the Caribbean and South Africa. Liberation theology in black U.S. culture has been widely discussed in works such as: Klauspeter Blaser, *Wenn Gott schwarz wäre...* (Zürich: Theologischer Verlag, 1972); James H. Cone, *A Black Theology of Liberation* (Maryknoll, N.Y.: Orbis Books, 1970); idem, *Speaking the Truth: Ecumenism, Liberation, and Black Theology* (Grand Rapids, Mich.: William Eerdmans, 1986); Jacqueline Grant, *White Women's Christ and Black Women's Jesus: Feminist Christology and Womanist Response* (Atlanta, Ga.: Scholars Press, 1989); J. Deotis Roberts, *Liberation and Reconciliation: A Black Theology* (Philadelphia: Westminster, 1974); idem, *A Black Political Theology* (Philadelphia: Westminster, 1974); Cornel West, *Prophesy Deliverance: An Afro-American Revolutionary Christianity* (Philadelphia: Westminster, 1982); Gayraud S. Wilmore and James H. Cone, eds., *Black Theology: A Documentary History, 1966–1979* (Maryknoll, N.Y.: Orbis Books, 1979); Theo Witvliet, *The Way of the Black Messiah* (Oak Park, Ill.: Meyer-Stone, 1987).

Caribbean, but also to the United States, Europe, Africa south of the Sahara, and beyond.

SOUTH AFRICA'S APARTHEID CULTURE

The story of apartheid in South Africa has become a familiar one in all parts of the world, although all of the details may not be so well known. When the Dutch, who also took along a trading company (the East India Company), invaded the territory of the Khoikhoi (called the "Hottentots" in English) in 1652, the historical aggression of a European people in search of land and markets against an indigenous people — an aggression already at play in the Americas — was extended to the tip of Africa. Although the Portuguese discovered the Cape (which they called Cape Bogador) in the fifteenth century, they chose not to settle there. Instead they moved on to the more lucrative territories (for their purposes) of western Africa, where they founded the export industry of slave trading from Africa to Europe and the New World. Both the English and the Dutch also understood their mission to be "saving" heathen infidels by offering them a taste of Christian culture and civilization. Indeed the first prayer offered to the Christian God by the leader of the Dutch trading company petitioned God "for the propagation and extension (if that be possible) of Thy true Reformed Christian religion among these wild and brutal men."[2]

The British invaded and occupied the Dutch territory in 1795, thereby leading to ongoing rebellions by the descendants of the original Dutch and French, the Boers (Afrikaners). The Afrikaners finally went farther east on their "Great Trek" (*Vortrekkers*) in covered wagons into traditional Zulu territory, now Natal and Transvaal. While these Afrikaners wanted more opportunities for land than were possible under the British, they also ventured elsewhere because they disagreed with the British policy of "equality" among the "coloreds" and the whites. The Afrikaners held all nonwhites to be inferior and viewed policies fostering equality as threats both to their own social status and to the colonial system of contract labor, a system that had granted them control and power over blacks and other nonwhites.

At the same time they believed that their trek into the far country was a God-willed and inspired mission; this belief was not

---

2. Cited in George M. Fredrickson, *White Supremacy: A Comparative Study in American and South African History* (New York: Oxford University Press, 1981), 12.

dissimilar to the religious ideology that gripped the early New England Calvinist settlers in the United States. This conviction, still a source of tenacious patriotism in white South Africa, is not to be underestimated in examining apartheid. For example, certain of their own divine Manifest Destiny, the Afrikaners have determined that, though a minority, they should hold on to 85 percent of the land in modern South Africa, most of that being arable land, while restricting the black majority to the remaining 15 percent, most of which is not arable.

> For the Vortrekkers religion was the only available source of intellectual authority. But it sufficed for their purposes because it deemphasized the evangelical implications of the New Testament and stressed Old Testament or Hebraic precedents for the exclusiveness and isolation of a "chosen people." ... They have persuaded themselves by some wonderful mental process that they are God's chosen people, and that the blacks are wicked and condemned Canaanites over whose head the divine anger lowers continually.[3]

After these Boer Vortrekkers defeated the Zulu at the Battle of Blood River on December 16, 1838, they established the Republic of Natal, which in turn was annexed by the British in 1843 in an imperial fashion. Eventually the British recognized Boer independence in the Transvaal and the Orange Free State, thereby planting the seeds for the present-day Republic of South Africa. Two wars between the British and the Boers, one in 1880 and one in 1899, resulted in the defeat of the latter both times. At the end of the second war, in 1902, the British signed a peace with the Boers and set up the South African Native Affairs Commission to sort out the first "homelands" policy — a policy that separated Africans and whites instead of laying foundations for a multiracial society. In 1910 London recognized an entity called the Union of South Africa under a minority English-speaking government, even though the majority of the white minority was Afrikaner and the overwhelming majority of the total population was black (coloreds being included under the designation *black*). In 1912 the African National Congress (ANC) was founded to organize nonviolent protests against the increasing number of racial segregation laws and to argue for a multiracial society in South Africa.

3. Ibid., 173.

Originally called the S. A. Native National Congress, the ANC represented from its very beginning a cross-section of British black southern Africa. Assembled at Bloemfontein, chiefs of different ethnic groups, intellectuals, heads of political associations, clergy, teachers, and journalists came together from South Africa, Bechuanaland (now Botswana), Basutoland (now Lesotho), and Swaziland. The ANC was modeled after the U.S. Congress, although its Upper House of Chiefs was created with features both of the U.S. Senate and the British House of Lords in mind: "We were dreaming of change, of the day when Africans would sit in parliament and would be able to buy land."[4] The ANC's hymn, "Nkosi Sikelel' iAfrika," became the national anthem for all South African blacks under apartheid. After its beginnings, the ANC dwindled until the 1930s, when a black Anglican cleric, James Calata, from the Eastern Cape, together with the president, A. B. Xuma, revived it. They produced the document "Africa Claims," a forerunner of the 1955 "Freedom Charter," demanding that all forms of racial discrimination be abolished and that colonialized peoples be allowed to pursue self-determination and be granted the right to vote.[5] With Walter Sisulu's encouragement, Oliver Tambo and Nelson Mandela (b. 1918, and a member of the royal family of the Thembu) joined the ANC and organized the Youth League. Mandela met Sisulu in Alexandra (near Johannesburg), where he went to study law after leaving his village in the Transkei at the age of 21.

While these developments occurred among black South Africans, changes were also coming about among the South African whites. The Afrikaners, organized largely as the Nationalist party and chafing under the governing English-speaking minority, finally won the 1948 national elections and took over the government. Apartheid (racial separation) became the official ideology and policy of the government; it was intended "to check blood mixture and to promote racial purity," as the minister of the interior put it when he introduced the first bill of the new government, a bill that prohibited racially mixed marriages. Again, the crudity of such phrases could also be heard in the southern United States during the same period.

Coloreds on the voting rolls in the Cape Province were stripped of their rights in South Africa in 1956, and the government declared

4. Mary Benson, *Nelson Mandela: The Man and the Movement* (New York: W. W. Norton, 1986), 26.
5. Ibid., 27–28.

instead that there were eight officially recognized ethnic groups among blacks, which in the future would have separate citizenship and their own respective "homelands," to be created by the South African government. These eight groups were the North Sotho, South Sotho, Tswana, Zulu, Swazi, Xhosa, Tsonga, and Venda. In 1960 the umbrella political groups for the blacks, the ANC and the Pan-Africanist Congress, were banned by the government, so they went underground and into exile. A cadre of laws was passed, further institutionalizing racial separation and Afrikaner power and privileges in the marketplace and elsewhere in South African society. Next, in 1984, a new constitution was enacted by parliament. That constitution cynically granted the coloreds (population: 3,127,000) and the Indians (930,000) limited political rights by creating a racially segregated three-chambered parliament, but it completely ignored the majority black population (20,600,000). Each chamber meets and legislates separately, but laws and statutes passed by the Indian and colored chambers can be vetoed by the white chamber. (The total white population in the country is about 5,000,000.) The office of state president was created along with a council that has the final say on all legislation and can break any impasse between the three chambers.

The Christian churches also reflect the cultural segregation between the early European settlers, primarily the Dutch, British, and German. The Dutch Reformed Church came with the Dutch settlers, but the present South African Dutch Reformed Church is not organically or theologically related to the Dutch Reformed Church in the Netherlands. It actually has two branches, the Nederduits Gereformeerde Kerk and the Nederduits Hervormde Kerk. The policy of maintaining a racially separated church within the South African Dutch Reformed Church began in 1881 when the Gereformeerde Kerk, the dominant of the two white Reformed churches, created the Nederduits Gereformeerde Zendingkerk (Sending or Mission Church) for coloreds for "practical" considerations. Both white Dutch Reformed churches were expelled from the World Alliance of Reformed Churches at the alliance's meeting in Ottawa, Canada, in 1982, at which time apartheid was condemned as a theological heresy and identified as a *status confessionis* (a Lutheran term meaning that a matter or condition is so severe as to be considered a deadly threat to the Christian gospel and church). The black South African leader Dr. Allan Boesak, then a Cape Town pastor in the Zendingkerk, was elected president of the World

Alliance at that meeting, a position from which he resigned in 1990.

SOUTH AFRICAN LIBERATION THEOLOGY

South African liberation theology first came to the attention of the West with the publication of *Essays on Black Theology*, edited by a South African, Mokgethi Motlhabi, and published in Johannesburg in 1972. Promptly banned by the South African government, the essays were later edited by an Africanist, Basil Moore, himself banned from South Africa, and published "in exile" in London in 1973 under the title *Black Theology: The South African Voice*. The essays in the book were culled from a series of consultations on black theology held in Johannesburg, Pietermaritzburg, the Cape Province, and other towns in 1971; the consultations had been convened in order that black South Africans might begin to interpret the significance of God and Jesus Christ within a culture shaped by apartheid, with its tyranny for blacks and privileges for whites. When the original editor of the collected volume of addresses from those consultations, Sabelo Ntwasa, was placed under house arrest after their publication, his place was taken by Motlhabi, a Roman Catholic who was acting director of the Black Theology Project, which was originally sponsored by the University Christian Movement. Writing about the essential thrust of this first statement of South African liberation theology, Basil Moore noted:

> Black Theology is a revolt against the spiritual enslavement of black people, and thus against the loss of their sense of human dignity and worth. It is a theology in search of new symbols by which to affirm black humanity. *It is a theology of the oppressed, by the oppressed, for the liberation of the oppressed.* Unless this is understood from the outset, these essays will make little sense.[6]

The similarity between early South African black theology and American black theology is not accidental. In part this is because at one of the very first seminars of the Black Theology Project, held in Dar es Salaam, James Cone, the major pioneer in American black theology, and Gayraud Wilmore, a major scholar of black religious

---

6. Basil Moore, ed., *Black Theology: The South African Voice* (London: C. Hurst & Company, 1973), ix; see also Allan Boesak, *Farewell to Innocence* (Maryknoll, N.Y.: Orbis Books, 1978).

history and thought, presented a paper on black theology and black liberation, which was listened to very studiously.[7]

South African liberation theology begins, first, with an image of salvation in Jesus Christ, who is also the sign of liberation. As one African theologian, Ndwiga Mugambi, states so clearly: "[Liberation] is not just one of the issues, but rather, all issues are aimed at liberating Africans from all forces that hinder them from living fully as human beings. In the African context, and in the Bible, SALVATION as a theological concept cannot be complete without LIBERATION as a social/political concept."[8] Allan Boesak speaks of this salvation as "righteousness" and "love": God's righteousness and love implicitly include justice for the oppressed over against the oppressor.[9]

It is important to note that these terms, *salvation, love*, and *righteousness*, are to be understood as having meaning within a concrete context. For black South Africans, that context is the one created, shaped, and nurtured by apartheid. The ideology of apartheid is based, on the one hand, on the superior power of the European minorities in South Africa and upon the fact that under the law they are treated as one; on the other hand, that ideology is based on the powerlessness of blacks — including Africans, coloreds, and Indians — who under the law are treated as separate groups. The martyred Steve Biko depicted this situation in the following terms:

> We must resist the attempts by protagonists of the Bantustan theory to fragment our approach. We are oppressed not as individuals, not as Zulus, Xhosas, Vendas, or Indians. We are oppressed because we are black. We must use that concept to unite ourselves and to respond as a cohesive group. We must cling to each other with a tenacity that will shock the perpetrators of evil.[10]

---

7. The paper is in Wilmore and Cone, eds., *Black Theology*, 463–76. For a considered appraisal of the theological task of South African liberation theology, see Theo Sundermeier, ed., *Christus, der schwarze Befreier* (Erlangen: Verlag der Ev.-Luth. Mission, 1973), 9–36. For parallels between South African liberation theology and black American liberation theology, see Josiah U. Young, *Black and African Theologies: Siblings or Distant Cousins?* (Maryknoll, N.Y.: Orbis Books, 1986); Dwight N. Hopkins, *Black Theology USA and South Africa: Politics, Culture, and Liberation* (Maryknoll, N.Y.: Orbis Books, 1989).

8. Cited in Desmond M. Tutu, "Black Theology/African Theology — Soul Mates or Antagonists?" in Wilmore and Cone, eds., *Black Theology*, 486.

9. Allan Boesak, *Black and Reformed: Apartheid, Liberation, and the Calvinist Tradition* (Maryknoll, N.Y.: Orbis Books, 1984), 7.

10. Steve Biko, "Black Consciousness and the Quest for a True Humanity," in Moore, ed., *Black Theology*, 47.

Second, the biblical story of the exodus is both a source for divine empowerment in the struggle to overthrow apartheid and a metaphor of divine sanctioned freedom and hope.[11] At the same time, the exodus is the essential clue for understanding the ministry of Jesus Christ as a ministry to the oppressed and the poor. Boesak speaks of this ministry as a liberation of whites as well as blacks in South Africa: "We are staying, so we have no Red Sea to cross. But neither do we want white people in South Africa to cross any sea. We want them to stay, but not as they are now."[12]

Third, experience and engagement are important sources, though not the norms, for liberation theology. The norm is scripture, as found in both testaments, but the experience of the people is an essential source in order to avoid the capture of liberation theology by academics and intellectuals. The latter can indeed articulate concepts and provide learned support, but the people's experience remains an important monitor for the authenticity of liberation theology in order to avoid the European tradition of a *deus remotus* or a *deus absconditus*. Liberation theology is about an engaged God and people that must be held accountable for the way it deals with matters of life, death, and empowerment in an apartheid culture. The archbishop of Cape Town, Desmond Tutu, described this correlation between the claims of liberation theology and the experience of the people in passionate terms at a conference on African theology in Ghana in 1977:

> I write after the National Party, led by B. J. Voorster [the Afrikaner prime minister], has been returned to power with a considerably increased majority, and he has already declared that there will be no significant changes in the policies of his government. And I write after the security forces of Ian Smith [white prime minister of Rhodesia (now Zimbabwe)] have recently killed over a thousand so-called terrorists (including women and children) in Mozambique. To write with an academic detachment and objectivity might please members of certain Senior Common Rooms, but it would be to discredit the-

---

11. It should be noted that the exodus is not the only metaphor for freedom and hope in South African liberation theology; the *imago dei*, the creation stories, and the Trinity are also used by some South African theologians.

12. Allan Boesak, "Liberation Theology in South Africa," in Kofi Appiah-Kubi and Sergio Torres, eds., *African Theology en Route* (Maryknoll, N.Y.: Orbis Books, 1979), 173.

ology as the pastime of those who would fiddle while their Rome was burning.[13]

A more recent exemplar of South African liberation theology is the 1985 *Kairos Document*, a text signed mostly by black clerics but also by several whites representing a number of non-Afrikaner churches. It captured the religious world's attention and reflected a liberation theology distinct in context and method from Latin American liberation theology; yet it found a strong echo in non-African Afro cultures.

Written from within the culture of apartheid, the document reflects critically on the theological models operating in the white churches of South Africa. It asks questions about the adequacy of those models for dealing with crisis and issues of injustice against black people. The theological and biblical justification of the current apartheid culture is identified as "state theology," on the one hand, and "church theology," on the other hand. "State theology" is an uncritical affirmation of the status quo in society. "It blesses injustice, canonizes the will of the powerful and reduces the poor to passivity, obedience, and apathy." It does this by using scripture, such as Rom. 13:1-7, to defend the state's concept of law and order and by exploiting fears about communism.[14]

"Church theology" is that type of theology usually favored by the English-speaking churches; those churches seek to uphold the social fabric by emphasizing reconciliation, nonviolence, and justice, without acknowledging that they themselves represent the views of simply another privileged class in South Africa. The *Kairos Document* complains that "church theology" has a naiveté about it because it neglects any hard social analysis of the actual conditions suffered by the oppressed. Further, its plea for reconciliation and nonviolence only helps perpetuate injustice: "Any such plea plays into the hands of the oppressor by trying to persuade those of us who are oppressed to accept our oppression and to become reconciled to the intolerable crimes that are committed against us. That is not Christian reconciliation, it is sin."[15]

13. Desmond Tutu, "The Theology of Liberation in Africa," in Appiah-Kubi and Torres, eds., *African Theology en Route*, 162.

14. *The Kairos Document: A Theological Comment on the Political Crisis in South Africa* (Braamfontein, South Africa: The Kairos Theologians, 1985), 3–6.

15. Ibid., 9.

Instead, the signatories opted for what they call "prophetic theology" — a biblically grounded theological method that reads the times, conducts social analysis, and then supports action that confronts apartheid and privilege. Those who practice prophetic theology are convinced that God is partisan toward the oppressed. They proclaim that "Christians, if they are not doing so already, must quite simply participate in the struggle for liberation and for a just society." Prophetic theology is connected to what they call "people's theology":

> The method that we used to produce the Kairos Document shows that theology is not the preserve of professional theologians, ministers, and priests. Ordinary Christians can participate in theological reflection and should be encouraged to do so. When this people's theology is proclaimed to others to challenge and inspire them, it takes on the character of a Prophetic Theology.[16]

Thus themes of oppression and suffering have to be a part of any biblical interpretation and model of Christ in order to speak to the South African context where black Christians live their faith: "When we read the Bible from our daily experience of suffering and oppression, then what stands out for us is the many, many vivid and concrete descriptions of suffering and oppression throughout the Bible culminating in the cross of Jesus Christ."[17] Oppression and suffering occur under tyranny, and the document identifies the system of apartheid as tyrannical and irreformable; it stands in opposition to the biblical understanding of God: "A regime that has made itself the enemy of the people has thereby also made itself an enemy of God. People are made in the image and likeness of God and whatever we do to the least of them we do to God (Matt. 25:40, 45)."[18]

At the same time the theme of liberation from oppression also has theological significance. "God is not neutral. He does not attempt to reconcile Moses and Pharaoh, to reconcile the Hebrew slaves with their Egyptian oppressors, or to reconcile the Jewish people with any of their late oppressors.... Oppression is a crime and

16. Ibid., explanatory n. 15, 2d ed.
17. *The Kairos Document*, in Willis H. Logan, ed., *The Kairos Covenant: Standing with South African Christians* (New York: Friendship Press; and Bloomington, Ind.: Meyer-Stone Books, 1988), 27.
18. Ibid., 33.

it cannot be compromised with, it must be done away with."[19] The integral relationship between justice, the social context, and doctrines or theology is a fundamental part of God-talk. For much of the church's history its doctrine and dogma have been shaped within a context located at the "top" of society. However, South African liberation theology is being shaped from the "underside" of history and society. Unlike Christian models generated from the top, black South Africans draw on their experiences of suffering, humiliation, and tribulations to shape their theology in much the same way that St. John the Divine shaped his when writing to Christians in the Book of Revelation. The enemy is identified quite explicitly, and the list of charges for supporting tyranny and suffering endured by blacks is made quite concrete.

CARIBBEAN LIBERATION THEOLOGY
(RASTAFARIANISM)

The social and economic conditions in the Caribbean that led to the emergence of an indigenous liberation theology are more complex than those of South Africa, given the geography and several types of colonialism historically at work in that part of the world. Each phase of colonialism brought with it classical European and/or North American Christianity. There is no single unifying liberation theology in the Caribbean that has captured the allegiance and support of all the region's English-, French-, Spanish-, and Dutch-speaking nations. But an indigenous faith first established in Jamaica, Rastafarianism, has spread to many parts of the Caribbean with very vocal and visible efforts aimed at cultural and religious liberation.

The cultural contributions of the Rastafarians (Rastas) are possibly more widely known than their religious tenets due to the popularity of reggae music, spread largely by the deceased Bob Marley (1945–1981) and others, and their painters, such as Ras Akyem Ramsey and Ras Ishi in Barbados. Both the music and the art highlight Rasta themes in Afro Caribbean culture and traditional religion, including the well-known Rasta "dreadlocks," which have made the Rastas both feared and notorious. Reggae itself is socially critical music, addressing both social and political problems and also moral and religious issues. Its roots lie in a number of sources: the slave legacy of drumming; Jamaica's several African-descended cults,

19. Ibid., 33–34.

such as Pocomania, Kumina, and Nyabingi; Christianity; and, of course, Rastafarianism.

Rastafarianism itself was established in Jamaica because of the religious teachings of Marcus Mosiah Garvey (1887–1940). Garvey was born in St. Ann's Bay, a small town on the northern coast of Jamaica, on August 17, 1887, to Marcus and Sarah Garvey; he was the youngest of 11 children. His father, thought to have been a descendant of the maroons, the slave freedom fighters in the various Caribbean islands, named him Marcus because he was born under the sign of Leo with the sun in the ascendancy, thus ensuring that he would be like a lion as a future leader of his people. His mother, a very religious Methodist, insisted that he be named Moses because she hoped he would be a leader like the Old Testament prophet. The father, not particularly devout and an infrequent congregant, usually showing up only at funerals, would have none of this, so the name Mosiah was added as a compromise, although Garvey never used his middle name.[20] Garvey became one of the most significant twentieth-century black leaders, and like Crummell and Blyden before him, his work spanned two continents. He began his liberation activities as a trade unionist working among Jamaica's poor and working classes. He organized the first black Jamaican political club, the National Club, which published a fortnightly appropriately called *Our Own*. However, unable to make a living wage, he departed Jamaica and journeyed to Costa Rica, where he had his "Damascus Road" experience. The U.S. corporate giant, the United Fruit Company, was expanding its agricultural holdings. Seeing the impossible working and living conditions of the blacks, and the indifference of the white supervisors, Garvey became militantly problack, since, as he put it, no white person seemed able to "regard the life of a black man equal to that of a white man."[21]

Finding little economic or political success in Costa Rica, he migrated to Panama, then soon thereafter moved on to Ecuador, Nicaragua, and other Central American countries, eventually returning to Jamaica in 1911, because he was "sickened with fever and sick at heart over appeals from his people for help on their behalf."[22] The

20. Amy Jacques Garvey, *Garvey & Garveyism* (New York: Collier Books, 1970), 2–3.
21. Cited in Edmund David Cronon, *Black Moses: The Story of Marcus Garvey and the Universal Negro Improvement Association* (Madison: University of Wisconsin Press, 1964), 14.
22. Garvey, *Garvey & Garveyism*, 7.

following year he traveled to London, where he was exposed to Africa through African immigrants and their problems, while, at the same time, witnessing the problems of other migrants. Fortuitously, while in London, he read Booker T. Washington's autobiography, *Up from Slavery*. "I read *Up from Slavery* by Booker T. Washington, and then my doom," recalled Garvey later, "of being a race leader dawned upon me.... I asked: 'Where is the black man's Government? Where is his King and his kingdom? Where is his President, his country...?' I could not find them, and then I declared, 'I will help to make them.'"[23]

Returning to Jamaica in 1914 ablaze with pan-African pride, Garvey together with some of his friends created an organization that eventually spread to New York City's Harlem, Chicago's South Side, and other major U.S. black metropolitan areas: the Universal Negro Improvement Association (UNIA), whose membership was open for "all people of Negro or African parentage." One of its prime objectives was "to promote a conscientious Christian worship among the native tribes of Africa"; however, soon the word "Christian" was changed to "spiritual." Garvey not only urged Caribbean, North American, and European blacks to return to Africa as their only place of solace and liberation; he also had a religious goal: to de-Europeanize God on the way to liberating blacks:

> If the white man has the idea of a white God, let him worship his God as he desires.... We, as Negroes, have found a new ideal. While our God has no color, yet it is human to see everything through one's own spectacles, and since the white people have seen their God through white spectacles...[we] Negroes believe in the God of Ethiopia, the everlasting God — God the Father, God the Son and God the Holy Ghost, the one God of all ages. That is the God in whom we believe, but we shall worship Him through the spectacles of Ethiopia.[24]

Before departing from Jamaica in 1916 for the United States, Garvey charged blacks there in a farewell speech "to look to Africa for the crowning of a Black king; he shall be the redeemer." His emphasis on Africa and especially Ethiopia arrested the spiritual and religious imagination of many blacks both in the United States and in Jamaica, particularly in a time of lynching, growing

---

23. Cited in Cronon, *Black Moses*, 16.
24. Cited in Randall K. Burkett, *Garveyism as a Religious Movement: The Institutionalization of a Black Civil Religion*, ATLA Monograph Series, no. 13 (Metuchen, N.J.: Scarecrow Press & The American Theological Library Association, 1978), 47.

pan-Africanism among American blacks, and severe racial discrimination in the United States. In a 1924 speech at Madison Square
Garden, he again thundered this theme: "Our desire is for a place
in the world, not to disturb the tranquility of other men, but to lay
down our burden and rest our weary backs and feet by the banks
of the Niger and sing out songs and chant our hymns to the God
of Ethiopia."

In the United States the harnessing of the pan-African religious
sentiments released by Garveyism took the form of the African Orthodox Church, founded in 1921 under the leadership of George
Alexander McGuire (1866–1934), the chaplain-general of the UNIA
and a disaffected Anglican priest. McGuire was consecrated the first
bishop of the new church. Born and raised in Antigua, McGuire
had traveled to the United States, where he had served as an assistant in several Episcopal black parishes; in Arkansas he served as
Archdeacon for Colored Work; later he served as rector of the historic St. Thomas Church in Philadelphia, the oldest black Episcopal
parish in the United States. In Africa the African Orthodox Church
developed under Daniel William Alexander, who learned of Garveyism through Garvey's newspaper, *The Negro World*.[25] In Jamaica the
African Orthodox Church took the form of Rastafarianism.

Jamaica was caught up in a class as well as a caste struggle in
the 1930s as the Depression of the United States and Europe spilled
southward to the Caribbean. Unemployment for black workers, who
made up most of the poor, was quite severe. Although Garvey was in
Jamaica at this time, having been deported from the United States
in December 1927, he failed to capture the same kind of massive
following and financial support for his organization that he had had
in the United States among poor blacks and black workers. Yet many
did hear a new message of hope and empowerment in Garvey's vision of the eschatological and redemptive role of Africa and Ethiopia
and in his schema of liberation. They were stirred uncommonly by
his rhetoric:

> At this moment methinks I see Ethiopia stretching forth her hands
> unto God and methinks I see the angel of God taking up the standard
> of the Red, the Black, and the Green, and saying, "Men of the Negro
> race, Men of Ethiopia, follow me!" It falls to our lot to tear off the

25. See the rather remarkable story of Alexander in Richard Newman, *Black
Power and Black Religion: Essays and Reviews* (West Cornwall, Conn.: Locust Hill
Press, 1987), 109–30.

shackles that bind Mother Africa. Climb ye the heights of liberty and cease not in well-doing until you have planted the banner of the Red, the Black, and the Green upon the hilltops of Africa.[26]

At the same time the Book of Revelation was and remains an important biblical resource for the Rastas, especially 5:1-5 and chapter 19:

> And I saw in the right hand of him who was seated on the throne a scroll written within and on the back, sealed with seven seals; and I saw a strong angel proclaiming with a loud voice, "Who is worthy to open the scroll and break its seals?"...Then one of the elders said to me, "Weep not; lo, the Lion of the tribe of Judah, the Root of David, has conquered so that he can open the scroll and its seven seals." [Rev. 5:1-2, 5]

> Then I saw heaven opened, and behold, a white horse! He who sat upon it is called Faithful and True, and in righteousness he judges and makes war....On his robe and on his thigh he has a name inscribed, King of kings and Lord of lords. [19:11, 16]

When in 1930 the young Ethiopian prince Ras Tafari (1891–1975) was crowned Emperor Haile Selassie, the truth of these texts was confirmed for Rastas. Their hope was kindled anew, and they recalled Garvey's admonition and vision about Africa: "Look to Africa where a black king shall arise — this will be the day of your deliverance." Furthermore, attributes engraved on the Ethiopian royal crown, "Kings of kings and Lord of lords, Conquering Lion of the Tribe of Judah," validated Old and New Testament prophecy, thereby heightening messianic expectations of liberation and salvation. Ironically, when Selassie fled to London to escape Italian occupation of Ethiopia, he let it be known that he wished no contact with "Negroes."

Selassie was seen as an incarnation of the divinity of God and the humanity of Jesus Christ as well, for God's divinity is always revealed in historical concreteness. Such sentiments are expressed still in Rasta hymnody:

> Ethiopia, the land of our Fathers,
> The land where all God's love to be.
> As the swift bees to hive sudden gather,

26. Cited in Mary White Ovington, *Portraits in Color* (New York: Viking Press, 1927), 18.

Thy children are gathered to Thee.
With our Red, Gold, and Green floating o'er us,
With the Emperor to shield us from wrong,
With our God and our future before us,
We hail Thee with shout and with song.[27]

Jamaica was identified with Babylon in the Book of Revelation, i.e., a place of bondage and suffering (although "Babylon" soon became a generic name for all countries where blacks suffer and are oppressed). The Promised Land was Ethiopia, and Rastas, the true Israelites, were agents for liberation and redemption of black people in Jamaica and elsewhere. In preparation for this liberation and return, during the 1930s poor Jamaicans were learning Amharic and trying to comprehend the basics of the non-Chalcedonian Ethiopian Orthodox doctrine that Jesus Christ is one *from* two natures, human and divine, rather than one *in* two natures, the latter being the Chalcedonian formula upheld by Catholic and Protestant churches in the West and by Eastern Orthodoxy. The Coptic Church of Egypt, the Armenian Church, and the Ethiopian Orthodox Church defend the first position, called the "monophysite position" by the Chalcedonian churches. As another sign of the intense expectations of liberation, following Selassie's coronation, drumming could be heard throughout the night in Jamaica along with the refrain, "The Lion of Judah shall break every chain and bring us the victory again and again."[28]

The progenitors of the Rastas and the first in Jamaica to interpret biblical texts with Garvey's view of Africa and Ras Tafari as the black messiah in mind were two ministers, Leonard Percival Howell and his assistant, Robert Hinds. They had read a publication called *The Black Man's Bible*, by Robert A. Rogers, which had been published during the First World War and which spoke of blacks' destiny after Armageddon. In 1932 Howell, having been abroad, sold picture postcards of Emperor Haile Selassie as "passports" to Ethiopia and preached to great crowds what sounded to the British colonists like rebellion: black Jamaicans ought to transfer their loyalty from the king of England to the emperor of Ethiopia. In 1940 he established the first Rastafarian commune at Pinnacle Estate near

27. Cited in George Eaton Simpson, *Religious Cults of the Caribbean: Trinidad, Jamaica, and Haiti* (Rio Piedras, P.R.: Institute of Caribbean Studies, 1970), 214.
28. Horace Campbell, *Rasta and Resistance: From Marcus Garvey to Walter Rodney* (Trenton, N.J.: African World Press, 1987), 77.

Kingston, which was also his headquarters. This was raided by the police in 1941, thereby only increasing the Rastas' public visibility. Both Howell and Hinds were arrested and charged with "intending to excite hatred and contempt for his majesty the King of England and those responsible for the government of the island."[29] Howell was sentenced to two years of hard labor and Hinds to one year of hard labor. Eventually, after his release from prison, the authorities arranged to have Howell committed to a mental asylum, so desperate were they to contain his teachings and contact with the black poor. In 1954 the police closed Pinnacle for good, and Rastas went underground throughout Kingston.

Early Rastafarians also identified with a fierce nationalist, anti-British group in Uganda, the Nyabingi, which preached death to black and white oppressors and practiced armed resistance against the British. (Among their membership in Africa was a member of the Ugandan royal family, Queen Muhumusa. Africa thus became a role model on several fronts for the Rastas. But Ethiopia with its ancient biblical connections and the emperor always remained the real Zion for them in the early stages.) This embrace of the concept of armed struggle with whites evoked much consternation among the political authorities on the island, particularly after an article appeared in one of the local papers in 1935 reporting that Selassie himself had taken charge of the Nyabingi movement at about the time of Italy's aggression against Ethiopia. Italy's attack was interpreted by blacks throughout the world as a racial attack by a white European state on a sovereign black state, which only confirmed mistrust of the European God and Christian religion.[30]

No doubt enormous numbers of Rastafarians felt prophecies had been fulfilled when Haile Selassie, who never denied or affirmed his divinity, thereby only heightening the mystery, made a state visit to Jamaica in August 1966. On that occasion he reputedly encouraged the Rastas to focus on liberation at home rather than returning to Africa, a message that appealed to many university students and artists like Bob Marley, Don Drummond, and Tommy McCook, and such groups as the Skatalites, a reggae group formed in 1963. (The group took its name from *ska*, a form of music in Jamaica which used Rasta drumming and lyrics and black American jazz; it was popular first among the poor.) The Rastas shifted toward more deliberate

29. Campbell, *Rasta and Resistance*, 71.
30. Ibid., 72–73.

political engagement and critique of Jamaican society in their writings, demonstrations, and especially their music. This new emphasis also coincided with the emergence of the black power movement in Jamaica, which was heavily influenced by the parallel movement in America.

The Rastas have become highly visible in Jamaica and elsewhere through (1) their liturgical life, which uses marijuana (ganja) and drumming as essential features in their ritual, and (2) their styles of dress and grooming, especially the "dreadlocks," the long, unkempt, braided hair worn by men and women. Both exhibit the double theme of rejection and metamorphosis: a rejection and at the same time a metamorphosis of white-imposed norms and values into an affirmation of blackness and Africa.

Ganja, brought to Jamaica by Indians the British imported, has been a regular feature of life in Kingston's slums, even though it has been an illegal substance since 1938. Sometimes called the "chillum pipe," "bangi," and "Indian hemp," ganja is grown and used widely in Jamaica not only for smoking but also as a vegetable, in tea, and for medicinal purposes among the poor and working classes as well as many of the elite. For the Rastas it is an important part of their "reasoning sessions" or periods for meditation, prayers, and discussions about members' visions and dreams. Biblical evidence cited for ganja use includes: "And God said, 'Behold, I have given you every plant yielding seeds which is upon the face of all the earth, and every tree with seed in its fruit; you shall have them for food" (Gen. 1:29). "And he showed me the river of the water of life...; also, on either side of the river, the tree of life with its twelve kinds of fruit, yielding its fruit every month" (Rev. 22:1-2).

At their ceremonies the "herb," also called the "holy herb" or the "sacred chalice," is smoked in a pipe or hugely rolled "joints" during drumming, chanting, and poetry recitation. At "sessions" the communal ritual for using ganja includes (1) "gracing" the ganja pipe before lighting it or taking a puff; (2) passing the pipe from left to right; (3) not leaving the ceremony until all the ganja has been consumed; (4) emptying the pipe only after all the ganja has been burned up.[31] The Rastas claim they guard against addiction by teaching their followers that ganja is to be smoked only when the

---

31. Barry Chevannes, "The Dreadlocks Rastafari" (Paper presented to the Conference on African-Caribbean Religious Expressions, Howard University Divinity School, Washington, D.C., December 11, 1986), 5.

person "is at one with himself; otherwise he will be unable to cope with the feelings produced and unable to channel them properly."[32]

The "dreadlocks," of course, are well known in West Africa among the Fulani tribes and in East Africa. For example, Masai warriors in Kenya, with whose strength as fighters the Rastas strongly identify, have always worn dreadlocks, which they dye red with a paste of fat and red clay as a sign of beauty and vanity. (Masai women shave their heads.) There are, furthermore, equivalents of dreadlocks in central and southern Africa as well.[33]

The exact origins of the name are uncertain, but it may derive from the strict Rasta discipline often referred to as "dreadful." The unkempt appearance was and continues to be a deliberate protest against the middle-class colonial standards that the Rastas claim are draining both the African spirituality and the pan-Caribbean political consciousness of Jamaicans. According to some scholars, the decision not to comb the hair was taken in the 1940s in solidarity with the outcasts in Jamaican cities and towns, whose appearances were considered offensive by mainstream Jamaicans and British colonialists:

> The issue was largely a social one, at first, because society did not accept unkempt hair. Not to comb was to declare oneself anti-social and mad, like the derelicts and outcasts, the most well-known of whom was Bagawire.... He and so many others in the then rapidly expanding city made the streets their home, scavenged around the markets, wore sackcloth and anything else they could find, and were stoned by children and shunned by everybody. Because they neither washed nor groomed, their hair grew into heavily matted locks. The debate was whether consciously to become Bagawires and thereby confront society, or to remain bearded but "decent."[34]

A split occurred over this issue in the early 1950s. One group, holding to the unkempt tradition, formed the House of Dreadlocks, and the other group, holding to changing the tradition, formed the House of Combsomes.[35]

32. Quoted from an interview in Peter B. Clarke, *Black Paradise: The Rastafarian Movement* (San Bernardino, Calif.: Borgo Press, 1987), 25.

33. For an excellent pictorial display of the different styles of dreadlocks in Africa, see Esi Sagay, *African Hairstyles: Styles of Yesterday and Today* (London: Heinemann, 1983).

34. Chevannes, "The Dreadlocks Rastafari," 7.

35. Ibid.

Others point out that dreadlocks really came into their own for the Rastas in the 1950s after they saw photographs of the Mau-Mau (Kenya) freedom fighters in their struggle for independence from the British. These warriors, sporting long, matted locks, became role models for the Rastas because they too were fighting against British colonialism, albeit mentally and emotionally, rather than militarily. The phrase "natty dread" came into vogue as an assertive and provocative phrase of freedom against colonial aesthetical standards in Jamaica. It was popularized internationally by the reggae groups, Bob Marley, and others whose songs tell of the brutalities endured by the slaves, especially the floggings, whippings, and mutilations of black flesh. Long, unmatted hair worn by the slaves was also interpreted as an act of defiance.[36]

Biblical authority cited for this Rasta tradition includes Num. 6:5-6: " . . . no razor shall touch his head; until the time of his consecration to God is completed, he remains under vow and shall let his hair grow free." But dreadlocks are also an important outward and visible symbol of the inward strength of blacks, a symbol that Rastas use as a reminder, first of all, to blacks themselves, and secondly, to nonblacks:

> The Rastafarian not only cultivates dreadlocks to resemble thereby the head and mane of the lion, the royal symbol of the vigor and enterprise of the black race, but also imitates this animal's regal, dignified walk, manifesting to others that despite enslavement and oppression he belongs to a princely race with a glorious past. Dreadlocks then are a device for stimulating a greater self-awareness, a deeper consciousness of the Rasta's origins, and also of his present condition.[37]

Obviously, as Rastafarianism matured and stabilized, different interpretations emerged about its religious, cultural, and political mission in Jamaica. Many of the differences centered around what manner of dreadlocks and grooming best witnessed to the Rastas' inward and spiritual identity. So those who sport beards and wear their dreadlocks matted, braided, and uncut are identified as the *locksmen*. There are subgroups even under this rubric. *Beardsmen* are those who do not plait their beards or dreadlocks but who wash their hair and trim it occasionally. Those wearing neither dread-

---

36. Campbell, *Rasta and Resistance*, 96.
37. Clarke, *Black Paradise*, 90.

locks nor beards are called the *baldheads*, *cleanfaces*, or "non-lock" Rastas.[38]

As Africa was replaced by Jamaica as the place for liberation in Rasta theology, a change encouraged by Selassie and reinforced by his death in 1972, Ethiopia became even more distant in people's minds. The changed emphasis reminded Rastas that they do not have to migrate to Africa, since liberation is also an interior matter; hence Africa is a metaphor as well as a geography for liberation in whatever conditions or wherever Rastas find themselves in the struggle against political and cultural oppression. Consequently, the quest for social justice and cultural integrity as African descendants in Jamaica has been translated into what can be described as a theology of liberation, paralleling a similar quest by black South Africans, although the unjust conditions in South Africa are much more odious than those in the Caribbean.

What are some of the theological hallmarks of this Caribbean religion of liberation? First, the Rastafarians identify humanity with divinity, and vice versa — God is the individual's inner person, inner reliance, and inner strength. God's name is Jah, and after Jah is Rastafari, who is Haile Selassie, King of kings and Lord of lords. Jah's spirit dwells everywhere and in all living things, as the Book of Revelation and the Psalms testify. Life's goal is union with Jah, a union more recognizable in some individuals, such as Emperor Selassie, than in others. Jah is invoked at all Rasta rituals and even in reggae music. Jah is he who surrounds as well as he who is within every living creature. To put it in Rasta terms: "Before the tree comes to this perfection, it was seed, and it was in itself. The seed was in itself. And so with us. In the beginning was the Word. The Word is the seed from which all men spring and they cannot go beyond the potentialities contained within the seed."[39]

This identity of humanity with divinity also has cultural implications: it fosters self-reliance, liberation of the black personality from neocolonial values, and autonomy, goals that the Rastas believe Christianity, as the white man's religion, violates:

38. Rex M. Nettleford, *Identity, Race and Protest in Jamaica* (New York: William Morrow, 1972), 75.

39. Cited in Sheila Kitzinger, "The Rastafarian Brethren of Jamaica," in Michael H. Horowitz, ed., *Peoples and Cultures of the Caribbean* (Garden City, N.Y.: Natural History Press, 1971), 584.

We don't business with religion! A colonial thing that! That is what
the white man bring down here to enslave the blackman!... When
we hear the bell ring at Sunday morning time for church, we think it
was the same slave bell. We take the chain off our foot and we go sit
down and hear about Je-sus![40]

A second theological hallmark of Rastafarianism is the belief
that the second advent of the messiah, who is Haile Selassie, has
already taken place, as the inscriptions on his crown and throne
witness. He is called the Elect of Jah, the Power of the Holy Trinity,
the Mediator, the Avenger, the Savior of the World; he is the black
God who has returned for the salvation of black people. Like Jesus
he comes from the lineage of David, and that only confirms his
messianic return; in fact there is no conflict between the messianic
claims of Jesus Christ and those associated with Haile Selassie.

Historical events and personalities as pointers of prophecy are
also very important for the Rastas. They claim that just as Christians
declare Jesus Christ divine and the Son of God, so they declare
Selassie divine. Many believe that those who spread these Rasta
teachings are "the vanguard of celestial selectees," "the re-incarnated
Moseses, Joshuas, Isaiahs and Jeremiahs...destined to free the scattered Ethiopians who are black men."[41] Indeed, Rastas hold that
the real Christ — as contrasted with the "preached" Christ in the
churches — is a Rasta since his mission was to redeem his people
in his time. He is not dead and did not die on the cross; rather he
overcame death and has come for the final advent in the person of
Haile Selassie. His coming signals our last days and promised liberation and deliverance. It is a liberation that can be experienced
as the person strives for unity with Jah and as witnessed in various
events.[42] As the late Jamaican Reggae singer Bob Marley wrote:

> And ain't it good to know now
> JAH will be waiting there
> Ain't it doggone good to know you all
> JAH will be waiting there
> Wait in Summer, wait in Spring

40. Cited in Jed Mays and Philip Wheaton, eds., *Jamaica: Caribbean Challenge* (Washington, D.C.: EPICA Task Force, 1979), 94.
41. Cited by Sam Brown, "Treatise on the Rastafarian Movement" (A part
of the Oral History Collection, University of the West Indies in Jamaica); see also
Nettleford, *Identity, Race and Protest*, 108.
42. Clarke, *Black Paradise*, 67.

Wait in Autumn, Winter thing
Tribe goes up, all the tribe goes down
Bring my children from the earth.[43]

Third, Africa, most especially Ethiopia, is the land of liberation
for blacks. The fact that there are oppression and injustice in the
world is due to the unfaithfulness of blacks — who are Jah's chosen
people — to their mission of liberation to other oppressed peoples.
The final deliverance or repatriation lies in Africa, the homeland
and the Promised Land of black people, whose metaphorical biblical name is Ethiopia. But Ethiopia is also the homeland of Haile
Selassie, Jah's messiah.

These notions of repatriation and homeland raise complex
questions. In light of centuries of separation between African culture
and Afro cultures in the Caribbean, obviously questions arise about
what such notions really mean. Indeed, in 1960 in response to calls
by Rastas, Prime Minister Norman Manley sent an unofficial delega-
tion of Jamaicans interested in a revived "back to Africa" movement
and theology to five African countries, Ethiopia, Nigeria, Ghana,
Liberia, and Sierra Leone; they were sent to inquire about possible
resettlement. After they returned, a "technical mission" team was
sent to deal with logistic and technical problems of immigration to
these countries, but only Ethiopia was prepared to opt for giving
land to Jamaicans wanting to migrate. A change of government in
Jamaica in April 1962 shelved the entire mission, and the new government failed to follow up even on the initiative of the Ethiopian
emperor.[44]

Fourth, the Rastas believe in reincarnation, an important link
both to African traditional religion and to their Afro cultural identity. In Africa, as we have seen, reincarnation of an ancestor can be
witnessed in a newborn child whose given personal name usually is
a testimony to the reincarnated person. This differs from the Hindu
understanding of cyclical reincarnation of the soul, with its perpet-
ual manifestation in either humans or animals; rather reincarnation
in Africa means a historical manifestation that has a chronology.
Hence believing all prophets of liberation to be black, beginning
with Moses, continuing through Jesus Christ, and ending in Haile
Selassie, the Rastafarians insist that these are really manifestations of

43. Bob Marley, "I Know," *Confrontation* (Island Records, 1983).
44. Nettleford, *Identity, Race and Protest*, 68–71.

the same person and that they — the Rastas — and the ancient Israelites are one as God's chosen people. They are the black Israelites
called to remind blacks everywhere in the diaspora of cultural and
religious liberation; they are to be reminders of political liberation
for all blacks who find themselves in various Babylons.[45]

Reggae music, a significant Rasta agent for cultural and religious liberation, has been an important apologetic for Rastafarianism
in other Afro cultures in the Caribbean and elsewhere. The name is
thought by some to derive from a 1967 Jamaican hit song sung by
the Rasta group Toots and the Maytals; the song was called "Do the
Reggay."[46] But others, including the leader of Toots and the Maytals, say the term already existed in poor Jamaican areas and meant
"raggedy, everyday stuff," which was popularized as "reggay."[47]
Early reggae promoted a deliberate connection with Africa and the
lifestyle and social critique of the Rastafarians:

> This couldn't be my home,
> It must be somewhere else,
> Can't get no clothes to wear,
> Can't get no food to eat,
> Can't get a job to get bread,
> That's why I've got to go back home.[48]

Religious themes are not separated from political and cultural
themes, as illustrated in the coupling of religious deliverance and
social goals in one of Bob Marley's popular songs, "Blackman Redemption":

> Whoa-A Natty Congo
> A Dreadlock Congo!
> Whoa-A Natty Congo,
> A Blackman Redemption...
>
> Tell you about the Blackman Redemption
> Can you dig it, Oh yeah
> A Blackman Redemption, can you stop it
> Oh! no. Oh! no. Oh! no.

45. Clarke, *Black Paradise*, 76.
46. Campbell, *Rasta and Resistance*, 134.
47. Stephen Davis and Peter Simon, *Reggae International* (New York: Rogner
& Bernhard, 1982), 45.
48. Lyrics by Bob Andy, cited in Campbell, *Rasta and Resistance*, 135.

Coming from the root of King David
Through the line of Solomon
His Imperial Majesty is the Power of Authority
Spread out, spread out, spread out, spread out
Spread out, look out. . . .[49]

Reggae passionately embraces all strata of society throughout the Caribbean and in other Afro cultures as well, be it in Africa, Europe, or the Americas, thereby endowing it as a cultural *lingua franca* that establishes identity, even though it is generally still associated with Jamaican music. To the extent that reggae helps establish a Caribbean identity, some form of Caribbean cultural liberation has already been put in motion by the Rastafarians. Even in conservative Anglophile Barbados, an indigenous art movement has sprung up largely because of Rastafarian artistic input and its embrace by some sons and daughters of the island's elite. (In fact, that island's highest art award has been won several times by a Barbadian Rastafarian, Ras Akyem Ramsey, whose paintings include many artifacts and symbols associated with the Rastafarians, including smoking ganja.)

Among the dominant "mainstream" churches in the Caribbean, the move toward a liberation theology very much resembles Latin American liberation theology and American black theology, with some Caribbean variations.[50] Institutionally the main drive toward a Caribbean liberation theology has been the Caribbean Council of Churches (CCC), organized in 1973 in Kingston, Jamaica, whose headquarters is now in Barbados. Not too dissimilar to the early theological consultations among black South Africans in the early 1970s, initial essays about a future Caribbean liberation theology can be found in a 1973 publication, *Troubling of the Waters*.[51] Also, the CCC's monthly newspaper, *Caribbean Contact*, has carried occasional articles about a liberation theology for the Caribbean context. All such efforts have addressed the primary obstacles in developing a Caribbean theology: (1) the divisive, competing structures and histories forged by the Europeans and Americans who colonized the region; these undergird the different economies and

---

49. Bob Marley, "Blackman Redemption," *Confrontation* (Island Records, 1983).

50. For example, see Noel Leo Erskine, *Decolonizing Theology: A Caribbean Perspective* (Maryknoll, N.Y.: Orbis Books, 1981).

51. Idris Hamid, *Troubling of the Waters* (San Fernando, Trinidad: Rahaman Printery, 1973); see also idem, *Out of the Depths* (San Fernando, Trinidad: Rahaman Printery, 1977).

cultures of the islands and erode most moves toward a Caribbean identity; and (2) the language barriers created by the fact that English, French, Spanish, Dutch, and Creole are spoken in the region. Many current undertakings concerned with Caribbean formation and identity are anchored in the folklore and cultural traditions of the region's African and Caribbean-Indian roots. These roots lie far beneath the ethnocentric European and Euro-American Christianity that remains a powerful force in the Caribbean.

PART TWO

An Afro Grammar of Faith

4

Christian Theology and Afro Cultures

To know God in the Christian faith is to know Jesus Christ and to know Jesus Christ is to know God. "He who has seen me has seen the Father" (John 14:9). Indeed the crucible of Christian theology is the doctrine of Christ as the final revelation of God. Karl Barth put it well when he said that christology is about the partnership between God, humanity, and the world in Jesus Christ.

Dogmatically and historically the church has insisted its doctrine of God, centered in the dogma of the Trinity, cannot be separated from its doctrine of Christ. But in trying to sort out conflicting claims about Christ, the church also dealt with the nature of God, since in its confessions and creeds it declared that God the Father and God the Son/Logos are one. Hence this connection — rather than natural inferences about the existence of God — is the starting point for knowing God in Christian theology: Jesus Christ, very God and very man, as the Nicene Creed puts it. In our review of African and Caribbean indigenous churches and traditional religions, we have examined the various beliefs and attributes that those churches and religions associate with God. The issue is whether it is possible for the Afro motifs and views of God to generate a theological model different from the inherited Graeco-Roman doctrinal models within the Christian tradition. Can an Afro model have the same theological integrity in affirming the confession of Peter: "Thou art the Christ, the Son of the living God" (Matt. 16:16), and that of St. Paul in his letter to the church in Philippi: "[Christ Jesus], though he was in the form of God, did not count equality with God a thing to be grasped, ... but humbled himself and became obedient unto death, even death on a cross" (2:6-8)?

As already noted, a guardianship much like an ecclesiastical social register has been established over the orthodox idea of God, and its authority has been affirmed and institutionalized by bishops and councils acting "under the guidance of the Holy Spirit," by writings, by theological propositions such as dogmas and doctrines, and by ancient liturgies. The overarching criterion for deciding what is most authentic and therefore orthodox has been "antiquity" or "the ancient church" or the early Church Fathers. In the Renaissance and in early social anthropology in the West, a similar criterion was used: In order to justify claims of the superiority of European culture and nationalities and of the inferiority of other cultures, particularly black African cultures, appeal was made to Greek and Roman antiquity. Thus antiquity — the Orthodox churches regard the eighth-century Ecumenical Council of Nicaea as the last ancient synodal authority for dogmas and doctrines, for example — has become a primary means of affirming this guardianship as oracle and legitimizing what is "authentic and correct," to the exclusion of non–Graeco-Roman cultures.

Dogma and doctrines about God, Jesus Christ, and the Spirit have generally been universalized with a view that there can be only one infallible, universal truth about the Christian God and God's revelation. This position was propagated by the ancient church and legatees of that church, such as the papacy and bishops in the Catholic and Orthodox traditions, and it has also been propounded, with some variations, by the Church Fathers in the Reformation tradition, by modern theologians like Paul Tillich, Karl Rahner, and Karl Barth, and by the modern ecumenical movement. Variations on this theme can be found of late in various liberation theologians, many of whom think within the Graeco-Roman philosophical framework and within the truth-claims inbred in the Western Christian tradition.

Interestingly enough, one of the first doctrines or dogmas about the Christian God authorized by the state and the bishops at the Council of Nicaea (325) was at the same time intended to be a confession of faith. Studied ambivalence and theological impreciseness in church statements about God continued in the liturgy and the hymns until the Council of Chalcedon (451) established firm boundaries of correct doctrine as well as an ecclesiastical "Social Register" for overseeing these boundaries:

> Following, then, the Holy Fathers, we all with one voice teach that it should be confessed that our Lord Jesus Christ is one and the same Son, the Same perfect in Godhead, the Same perfect in manhood, truly God and truly man;... *homoousios* with the Father as to his God-

head, and the Same *homoousios* with us as to his manhood.... This then we have done, having by a common sentence driven away the doctrines of error, and having renewed the unerring faith of the Fathers, proclaiming to all the *Symbol of the Three Hundred and Eighteen*, and acknowledging... *the One Hundred and Fifty*.[1]

Thus, Christian doctrines about God assumed a conceptual character and method of thinking more familiar in philosophical propositions and abstractions. They had their own external criteria for apologetics and internal criteria — what St. Anselm (1033–1109) called *credo ut intelligam*[2] — for judging their truth and coherence; these were largely influenced by Graeco-Roman antiquity and were amplified by subsequent Westerners. Adolf von Harnack (1851–1930) traces this heavy Graeco-Roman influence to the Alexandrian school and its first prominent student, Clement (c. 150–215):

> The Alexandrian school of catechists were of inestimable importance for the transformation of the heathen empire into a Christian one, and of Greek philosophy into ecclesiastical philosophy.... These Alexandrians wrote for the educated people of the whole earth; they made Christianity a part of the civilization of the world.[3]

The issue of external criteria for correct doctrine was finalized in the West in the Catholic doctrine of papal infallibility, which was proclaimed at the First Vatican Council (1869–1870).

But even theologians of the Protestant Reformation, alongside their insistence that all doctrines and dogmas must be judged in light of conformity to Christ and scripture, also supported the philosophical claims and assumptions inherited from the Fathers. "To hold to [the articles of faith defined in the ancient councils]," said Martin Luther (1483–1546), "is the same as holding to the Word of God." So, from the perspective of these guardians of orthodoxy, what newer churches can bring to the Christian tradition are, at best, "add-on's," not replacements or alternatives. Doctrinal

1. Cited in R. V. Sellers, *The Council of Chalcedon: A Historical and Doctrinal Survey* (London: SPCK, 1961), 208, 210. Emphasis added.

2. Jaroslav Pelikan maintains that Augustine was really the author of this proposition, not Anselm. "His speculations about the 'traces of the Trinity' in the human mind were the outstanding example of faith in search of understanding." See *The Christian Tradition*, vol. 3: *The Growth of Medieval Theology (600–1300)* (Chicago: University of Chicago, 1978), 260.

3. Adolf von Harnack, *History of Dogma*, trans. Neil Buchanan, 7 vols. (New York: Dover Publications, 1961), 2:319.

continuity and unity, often to the omission of a new confession about God, have become the mind-set through which theological contributions from many Third World cultures and churches are considered and heard, especially those from black African and Afro Caribbean cultures.

The church's use of specific vocabulary, metaphysical methods of reasoning, and concepts appealing to intellectual circles in the Greek-speaking Roman Empire of the first several centuries was intended to establish credibility and respectability among those circles regarding the truth of Christian claims about God and God's revelation in Jesus Christ. From the time of Justin Martyr (c. 100–165), who claimed that the Christian faith is a rational faith comparable to Greek wisdom, and from the time of Arius (c. 250–c. 336), who insisted that Jesus Christ as the Logos is God (but whose nature nevertheless is created and derived from God), God in Christian doctrine has been increasingly an object of speculative and philosophical discourse.

But even these metaphysical methods of argument, which have been universalized in the church's theology for all cultures, are related to the cultural conditions of the Graeco-Roman world. The pending conditions of expected political chaos, change, and disorder in the empire before and during the time of the early church had a telling influence on Greek philosophers who used their intellectual status for patriotic purposes. They complied with an imperial need and a longing for permanence, universal order, unity, immutability, and transcendence in the realm of the divine, so as to render attributes like disorder, transience, contingency, and decay undesirable on the political and historical scene. Hence, Latin American liberation theology's "contextualizing" of God and the Christian faith is not something that is entirely new; in fact, God and the Christian faith were long ago contextualized in Graeco-Roman antiquity. In the thought of many early Christian Fathers, the biblical God who created and acted in human history often bore many similarities to the One or the First Principle of early Graeco-Roman culture.[4] As Joseph O'Leary remarks about the entanglement of Christian doctrine and Greek metaphysics:

---

4. For a discussion of how Christianity interacted with the intellectual and political conditions in the first few centuries of the Roman Empire, see Charles Norris Cochrane, *Christianity and Classical Culture* (Oxford: Oxford University Press, 1944), 78–85.

Greek metaphysics had assigned a place to God long before its encounter with the biblical revelation, and the proclamation of the God of Abraham in the West has involved very complicated negotiations with this metaphysical God.... But Greek metaphysics had also a place for Christ, as a principle of mediation and totality. The Platonic ideas, the Stoic Logos, the Plotinian *Nous* have the function of uniting the many through a single cosmic intellectual principle and of mediating between the many and the one.... Thus the identification of the biblical God with the God of metaphysics made it inevitable that the figure of Christ would be identified with the mediating principle of metaphysics.[5]

The problem of how to relate Jesus Christ, the biblical preexisting Word/Logos of God ("In the beginning was the Word, and the Word was with God, and the Word was God"), to Greek philosophical ideas of the One or the divine Mind, the source and ground of all being as well as the cosmos, increasingly occupied various Christian theologians like Tertullian (c. 160–c. 220), Clement (c. 150–c. 215), Origen (c. 185–c. 254), and Athanasius (c. 296–373), not to mention Arius. As various conflicting claims about this relationship threatened the social fabric of the empire, Emperor Constantine summoned, financed, presided over, and even contributed to the First Ecumenical Council at Nicaea in 325; after all, it was Constantine who proposed the term *homoousios* for inclusion in the Nicene Declaration of Faith.

The use of Greek metaphysical concepts only made the biblical God even more foreign and a captive of an ethnocentric guardianship, so much so that the question of God being Greek is raised seriously today by cultures not shaped by Greek thought or culture, such as African cultures. Speculation about the nature of God and God's revelation, of course, did not cease with Nicaea's confession of faith, but was only made more intense by metaphysical terms like *ousia* and *homoousia*, *hypostasis* and *consubstantiality*. They also delimited experiential faith in non–Graeco-Roman cultures, effectively subordinating such cultures to a kind of intellectual illegitimacy or permanent state of underdevelopment in the tradition. A theological hegemony was established that today generates an imperialism that looks patronizingly upon these cultures as permanent intellec-

---

5. Joseph S. O'Leary, *Questioning Back: The Overcoming of Metaphysics in Christian Tradition* (Minneapolis: Winston Press, 1985), 74–75.

tual lepers, a view that is accentuated by the fact that these are, for the most part, black cultures.

In the theology of the Catholic and Protestant traditions, these enculturated methods of interpretation are continued as protocol for understanding the God of scripture. "Religion can express itself only through ontological elements and categories with which philosophy deals," said Paul Tillich (1886–1965), "while philosophy can discover the structure of being only to the degree to which being-itself has become manifest in an existential experience. Basically this refers to the idea of God."[6] This is not to overlook protests against the philosophical transformation of theology, protests by such theologians as Karl Barth (1886–1968). But even Barth was appreciative of and responsible to the tradition and its doctrines, and he thus took over this legacy as a starting point, as we see in his doctrine of the preexistent Christ as Logos, for example.

CULTURE AND THE GRAMMAR OF FAITH

The issue of non-Western cultures and their worldviews finding a place within the Christian tradition and indeed enlarging the theological horizons of that tradition without surrendering their own intellectual integrity has taken on critical significance in a post-colonial or neocolonial world in which there is an ever-widening economic chasm between the North and the South, between the developed nations and the Third World. But also at stake is the issue of liberating the cultural and theological integrity of Third World countries from the ethnocentric dominance of the West, especially as that integrity relates to ideas about the Christian faith. As the Christian faith grows in Third World cultures more and more and stagnates in those Euro-American cultures having charge of its doctrinal guardianship, the critical issue of culture and the grammar of faith takes on new dimensions quite different from previous battles about this issue (e.g., those fought between Henry VIII and the Catholic Church in the sixteenth century, between Germany and the Catholic Church in the nineteenth century, and between Barth and liberalism at the beginning of the twentieth century). The deeper issue is whether God and ways of thinking

6. Paul Tillich, *Systematic Theology*, 3 vols. (Chicago: University of Chicago Press, 1951), 1:230.

of God are so bound to Graeco-Roman metaphysical worldviews about divinity and methods of thinking that God must remain Greek.

For my purpose, culture means the complex of all institutions, customs, beliefs, languages, knowledge, laws, oral traditions, habits, conventions, and morals that socialize and form persons and ideas within a given geographical space, but which also may move across national boundaries. Culture, bound up with economic, political, and military power, has a very dominant influence on thought patterns, behavior, perceptions, and belief; it provides a person, a people, and a community with an intellectual grammar and vocabulary with which to view both the world and survival in that world. It fuels and nourishes the way persons, a community, or a people understand relationships within themselves (thereby touching upon matters such as self-esteem and purpose) and between themselves and their neighbors.

Often terms like "contextualization" and "indigenization" are used by the guilds who manage the guardianship of the Christian tradition. The terms are frequently employed in discussions about "de-Westernizing" or "decolonializing" the Christian faith in Third World cultures, but those using the terms often fail to note that the orthodox dogmas about God, Jesus Christ, and the Spirit were also contextualized and indigenized. Such terms may be interpreted negatively, as by the Vatican,[7] or positively, depending on the constituency and the power structure listening or speaking. The use of culture as the context for indigenizing even propositional Christian doctrines and tradition is put quite well in the Second Vatican Council's document on missions, *Ad Gentes:*

> The seed which is the Word of God sprouts from the good ground watered by divine dew. From this ground the seed draws nourishing elements which it transforms and assimilates into itself. Finally, it bears much fruit. . . . From the customs and traditions of their people, from their wisdom and their learning, from their arts and sciences, these Churches borrow all those things which can contribute to the glory of their Creator, the revelation of the Savior's grace, or the proper arrangement of Christian life. If this goal is to be achieved,

---

7. See *Instruction on Certain Aspects of the "Theology of Liberation,"* in *Origins* 4, no. 13 (September 13, 1984).

theological investigation must necessarily be *stirred up* in each major socio-cultural area.[8]

For many, searching for an accommodating relationship between culture, gospel, and doctrine immediately raises the specter of concepts like "adaptation" and "syncretism," all of which generate fears about "watering down the faith," "tampering with the orthodox faith tried and true," and "compromising the Christian gospel." That this accommodating relationship has already occurred and been accepted in the entire development of Christian doctrine and theology has already been demonstrated. Even examining ancient Christian liturgies as a filter through which to discover, reflect on, and test subsequent liturgies and liturgical principles in the Christian tradition is an act of exclusion for non-Westerners and cultures that now make up younger churches. The appeal to antiquity as legitimacy, of course, not only sacralizes ethnocentric liturgical forms and thought patterns of older cultures, but conveniently slights the historical fact that in the development of Catholic, Anglican, and Orthodox liturgies, various local liturgies simply were universalized by the church and made normative and operative for the liturgical life of the church in the West and the East.[9]

But syncretism (Greek: *synkretismos* [Lat. *syncretismus*], "the joining of two parties against a third," referring to the action of the divided Cretans who joined together in a common defense against the enemy) need not be thought of negatively. In fact, a reassessment of this term is in order with regard to a multicultural Christian faith no longer under the dominance of Western orthodox doctrines, especially in Afro cultures. How can these cultures have a stake in the ongoing Christian tradition and doctrines?

Here Leonardo Boff, a theologian from Brazil, is very helpful.[10] Syncretism, he points out, can mean *accommodation*, as when the traditional religion of a colonized people is adapted to the religion of the colonizers for various reasons. Such a process does not mean the religion of the colonized is wiped out or relinquished, only that

8. "Decree on the Church's Missionary Activity," in Walter M. Abbott, S.J., ed., *The Documents of Vatican II* (New York: America Press, 1966), 612. Emphasis added.
9. R. E. Hood, "Can the Prayer Book Be Comprehensive for All Cultures?" *Anglican Theological Review* 66 (July 1984): 273.
10. Leonardo Boff, *Church, Charism & Power: Liberation Theology and the Institutional Church*, trans. John W. Diercksmeier (New York: Crossroad, 1985), 89–107.

some of its elements are adapted to the religion of the dominant and more powerful social group.

However, syncretism can also mean *mixture*, in which deities and religious customs of other cultures are simply included alongside the deity and customs of the Christian religion, thereby producing a profusion of gods with sometimes different characteristics. This has happened in such places as Mexico, where the ancient folk religions of the original Mexicans have been grafted onto Catholicism without any concern for possible contradiction.

Syncretism can be a form of *translation* when religions claiming universality utilize compatible traditions and symbols of another culture to translate and communicate the essential truths of the Christian faith. In fact, this is a continuing process within the Christian tradition, which becomes suspect only when cultures other than mainstream cultures try to translate the Christian faith to those mainstream cultures. As Pope Paul VI, himself no radical, said of this process in his *Africae Terrarium:* "Many customs and rites previously thought to be eccentric and primitive, today, in light of the ethnological knowledge, show themselves to be integral elements of particular social systems worthy of study and respect."[11] The problem occurs when Christian identity is restricted to doctrinal fidelity and assent, whose oversight and definition are considered the sole turf of the guardians (bishops, councils, theologians, creeds, and dogmas). These guardians do perform the important function of recalling, preserving, and occasionally even expanding the tradition from time to time. Yet at the same time they must understand that the Christian experience "does not choose only one culture in which it is to be incarnated; every culture is worthy of the salvation won by Jesus Christ and of having that salvation proclaimed within it."[12] An arbitrariness about freezing the tradition because of division (the Orthodox churches) or exercising a sovereignty and guardianship over the tradition from a Western hierarchical model (the Roman Catholic Church) or exercising a theological trusteeship and historical paternalism (classical Protestantism and missionary churches) disregards the possibility that younger churches from ancient cultures may bring new insights into the Christian treasury of doctrines about God in Jesus Christ.

Nor is this guardianship challenged by modern Western Prot-

11. Cited in ibid., 98.
12. Ibid., 105.

estant abstractions about God. Examples of these abstractions are that God is "the feeling of utter dependence" (Schleiermacher), "the ground of all being" or "ultimate concern" (Tillich), "the One He is by veiling Himself in a form which He Himself is not" (Barth), and "the ultimate creative ground of anything that is" (Schubert Ogden). These abstractions merely reflect an intent furthered by these theologians' forebears, namely, establishing a metaphysical foundation for a universal deity as well as a unity in the godhead to explain the deification of humanity by God in Jesus Christ. Even Karl Barth — who struggled against this method through his own method of using the biblical narrative and vocabulary as a rigorous norm for theological discourse about God — continued this universalizing tendency. The issue is whether "baptized" philosophical tools of ancient Graeco-Roman culture can "translate" the Christian God in all epochs and cultures. Why should not the indigenous churches and Christians in Afro cultures "baptize" their traditional tools with a similar intent of enlarging the tradition within a universal, cross-cultural church?

SALVATION, SIN, AND DEATH IN AFRO CULTURES

On the one hand, many of the Church Fathers were resolved to defend and explain the unity of God in light of biblical claims that Jesus Christ was also God. This meant figuring out a way to speak of a *godhead* rather than simply making the acclamation of Judaism: "Hear, O Israel, the Lord our God is One." On the other hand, some of the early church theologians understood the real issue to be God as revealer of salvation; that is, they saw that the heart of the matter is the soteriological (Gk. *soteria*, meaning "deliverance," "preservation") or redemption issue so dramatically personalized in the question often posed by pietists: "Have you been saved?" Hence, Athanasius, for example, feared that Arius's avowal of a time when the Son as the Logos did not exist infringed upon and subverted God's offer of salvation and redemption in Jesus Christ. His reiteration of Irenaeus's (135–c. 200) famous words summed up his fears: "God became man in order that man might become God." That is, redemption meant a restoration to an original state and relationship with God, which could be accomplished only by God or someone sharing God's supreme and unique deity, i.e., Jesus Christ, the Son/Logos of God. Hence, for Athanasius the incarnation rather than the crucifixion revealed God's deliverance of humankind from sin and death and the relationship repaired, restored, and redeemed.

The liturgy of St. Basil in the Orthodox Church clearly exhibits this kind of spirituality, which at the same time was the source of a theology. In that liturgy we find: "... so that we may be worthy to offer to Thee this reasonable and bloodless sacrifice for our sins and the errors of Thy people." Thus in Jesus Christ God "reformats" (as in computer software) the structure of the relationship between God and God's creation: "Thus they proclaim that... as a man is 'in Christ' he is 're-elemented into,' 'trans-elemented into,' and 'commingled with' (St. Cyril) the Divine, and through this partaking of the eternal and incorruptible, is made superior to death and decay."[13]

The Greek metaphysical fear of change, potential chaos, and rebellion played an important role in shaping the Christian model of deity, which made it all the more important that the Christian God and that God's Logos, Jesus Christ, share the same deity in order to be victorious over change and rebellion. This model holds true whether it engages the christology of the ancient school of Alexandria — with its attention on salvation as a deliverance from the powers of evil and death, the result of human sin — or that of the school of Antioch — with its focus on salvation as a restoration of a divine order in history and a repairing of the breach between humanity and God through a new Adam, i.e., Jesus Christ, who replaces the old Adam of disobedience, corruption, and disorder.

Salvation in African culture carries with it the idea of empowerment as well as deliverance, rescue from a powerless or helpless situation to one of potency or power, gained through purification rites and propitiation of the divinities and the spirits. Generally there are three major situations or forces from which the African seeks salvation or deliverance: (1) daily hardships, such as crop failure due to the weather, everyday conflicts, infant mortality, and female infertility; (2) evil spirits, forces, and persons, such as witches and sorcerers; and (3) a lack of good relationships with ancestral spirits and the divinities.[14]

Salvation among the Igbo (Nigeria) even includes the concept of justice. Called *Ezi-Ndu* (viable life), God's salvation includes

---

13. Sellers, *The Council of Chalcedon*, 133.

14. Harry Sawyerr, "Sin and Salvation: Soteriology Viewed from the African Situation," in Hans-Jürgen Becken, ed., *Relevant Theology for Africa* (Durban, South Africa: Lutheran Publishing House, 1973), 133.

(1) the gift of children so that the family name will not be obliterated (a kind of immortality on earth); (2) deliverance from misfortunes, poverty, and interpersonal conflict; and (3) the promise of justice and equity.[15]

But we must be cautious about suggesting that there is a generally and mutually agreed to all-African concept of salvation. For example, John Mbiti remarks that his Kikamba tradition in Kenya has no word equivalent to the Latin or English noun for salvation. There is a verb, however, *kutangiia*, meaning "to save," "to rescue from danger or destruction, from death." The missionaries chose a noun, *utangiio*, and translated it in the Western sense of salvation, so that Christian salvation in his culture means concern only with spiritual affairs and not material or physical affairs. Hence there is much hesitation among the Christians of his culture about linking biblical teachings to social concerns because Christian salvation is supposed to deal only with spiritual things.[16]

In a study of the word for salvation among the Annang (Nigeria), it was discovered that although the word can mean "deliverance" from evil powers and misfortunes, it also can mean (1) "wholeness and peace," as occurs when persons have good relationships with their neighbors, friends, themselves, and God; (2) good health and having children; (3) liberation of the whole person, body and soul, from illnesses, demons, and psychic oppression of various kinds; (4) finding solutions to difficult problems in life; (5) affirmation of the world as the place where Jesus' promise of salvation was proclaimed. It has been the African indigenous churches rather than the missionary churches that preach and teach a God who is salvation, powerful in the face of evil forces and able to save them from such forces.[17]

A moral understanding of salvation, namely, deliverance from sin and death, is grasped by most Africans in a communal, rather than an individual, sense; that is, it is understood in terms of restoring communal stability. Sin is an offense against God and damages or erodes good family and community relationships; such damage or erosion occurs when the ancestors or the divinities are also of-

15. Cyril C. Okorocha, *The Meaning of Religious Conversion in Africa: The Case of the Igbo of Nigeria* (Brookfield, Vt.: Gower Publishing Co., 1987), 69.
16. John Mbiti, *Bible and Theology in African Christianity* (Nairobi: Oxford University Press, 1986), 161.
17. Ibid., 152–53.

fended. Salvation means acknowledging communal or individual shame (rather than guilt) via a sacrifice and offerings, thereby opening the way for the restoration of broken relationships.

> Although sin can be and is punished by either the divinities or the ancestors, we must realize that Africans believe that such sins are still regarded as offenses against God who is the Creator and Sustainer of the universe and its inhabitants, who expects His creatures to maintain good relationship with one another and with the supersensible world and on whose behalf the divinities and ancestors punish immoral deeds.[18]

J. Omosade Awolalu disputes the notion of many Western anthropologists that African society has no sense of good or evil, thereby dispensing individuals of any notion of a right morality and ethical accountability.[19] He notes that the biblical notion of covenant best characterizes African morality, understood to be a relationship between God, the divinities and spirits, the ancestors, and the human community. All sides have interrelated responsibilities that are sustained by sanctions and taboos in the community. These are the fountainheads of communal and personal morality, and their neglect or breach — which is sin — incurs the wrath or displeasure of the supreme deity and that deity's divinities:

> Africans do not have a rigid distinction between an offense committed against a person or society and one committed against Deity or divinities and spirits. There is no sharp dividing line in this regard between the sacred and the secular such as is assumed by the Western world. God is regarded as the founder and guardian of morality.... Human relationships must have moral foundations; they cannot be built on anything else.[20]

Another Nigerian theologian, Tokunboh Adeyemo, claims that sin for the African is always related to the consequences of committing an offense or violation. There are several words in Yoruba, for

18. J. Omosade Awolalu, "Sin and Its Removal in African Traditional Religion," *Journal of the Academy of Religion* 44 (June 1976): 287.
19. Ibid., 279. For Western opinions about ethics in Africa, see G. T. Basden, *Among the Ibos of Nigeria* (London: Frank Cass, 1966), 215–17; A. B. Ellis, *The Tshi-speaking Peoples of the Gold Coast* (London: Frank Cass, 1894), 10–11; idem, *The Yoruba-speaking Peoples of the Slave Coast of West Africa* (1894; reprint, Oosterhout, Netherlands: Anthropological Publications, 1970), 293–95; E. Geoffrey Parrinder, *West African Religion* (London: Epworth Press, 1949), 199.
20. Awolalu, "Sin and Its Removal," 279.

example, that point this out. Two of the words are: *gba ese*, "to take an evil power upon oneself or to follow an evil way causing instability and disorder in the community"; and *da ese*, "to create sin," to be the author of sin; doing something "rotten," totally despicable, something deadly and absurd.[21] These concepts are based on the notion that sin is an offense against the original covenant relationship with the supreme deity. But Africans do not speak of "original sin" as an abiding stain in the relationship with God that necessitates its being set aside by a savior. "Original sin" is simply noted for reference and viewed as accounting for God's withdrawal from intimate engagement in human affairs.[22]

John Mbiti has two minds about salvation and redemption in African traditional society. In his well-known work, *African Religions and Philosophy* (1969), he said that God is understood in sub-Saharan Africa as primarily a utilitarian God who provides humankind with the necessities of life such as food, housing, clothing, and children. God is also a presence among humankind on earth and provides a code of morality as well as protection. Mbiti describes such a belief as "two-dimensional": "So long as their concept of time is two-dimensional, ... African peoples cannot entertain a glorious 'hope' to which mankind may be destined."[23] The result is, according to Mbiti, that the Christian idea of salvation has the advantage of offering an escape route from the struggles of the material world, thereby having a universal appeal beyond the tribal and nationalistic needs of the African traditionalist. "Only a three-dimensional religion can hope to last in a modern Africa which is increasingly discovering and adjusting to a third dimension of time. ... Without the concept of distant future, the [world] religions would have remained, like African religions, only tribal or national."[24]

However, in his *Bible and Theology in African Christianity* (1986), Mbiti supports the idea that the biblical message of sal-

---

21. Tokunboh Adeyemo, *Salvation in African Tradition* (Nairobi: Evangel Publishing House, 1979), 52.
22. Awolalu speaks of this original relationship as a "Golden Age" when all was beautiful and peaceful, and a close link existed between heaven and earth; in that age human beings could go to heaven as they desired and return at their own wish (see Awolalu, "Sin and Its Removal," 282). John S. Mbiti says this image depicts God "supplying [humankind] with food, shelter, peace, immortality or the gift of the resurrection, and a moral code" (see Mbiti, *African Religions and Philosophy* [Garden City, N.Y.: Doubleday/Anchor Books, 1970], 127).
23. Mbiti, *African Religions and Philosophy*, 98.
24. Ibid., 99.

vation finds what he calls "fertile soil" in Africa because of at least two circumstances. First, the African traditional world is largely one of survival amid many physical and spiritual threats and dangers: "Man is very much aware of spiritual realities which impinge upon the physical realities. Human life is, to a large extent, a struggle to sail through those dangers and threats."[25] Second, the biblical view of salvation understands the struggle going on between spiritual and physical dangers: "In the New Testament there is clear attention given to sickness, disease and demon possession, as threats to life. The New Testament world clearly links the physical and spiritual realities.... In any case, the struggle in life is a clear element of the New Testament world."[26] The African indigenous churches have especially understood this aspect of African society and have incorporated it in their doctrines of salvation, particularly in pointing out the cosmic character of Christian salvation in Jesus Christ.

It is generally agreed among both African theologians and anthropologists that death is feared in Africa only when it is thought to have been caused by a curse or a violation of a sacred taboo. Some tribes have songs and sayings pointing to a struggle between the soul and death, which Mbiti cites, such as the Acholi in Uganda. Otherwise, as we shall see, death is not so much a monster or something to be feared as a passage to the ancestors, the end of a pilgrimage and the beginning of the journey "home." Death is a transition, an instance of birth into the life hereafter. "The hereafter is only a continuation of life more or less as it is in its human form. Personalities are retained; social and political statuses are maintained; sexual distinction is continued."[27]

For example, in Yoruba religion, judgment is expected at the end of this life, when the person must account to God (Olódùmarè) about how he or she has spent the time on earth; God then decides whether that person is to go to the good heaven (orun rere), "the heaven of one's father," or to bad heaven (òrun burúkú). The ultimate penance attached to the second heaven is that its wicked inhabitants are not permitted to rejoin the ancestors, which means that the soul wanders forever. This isolation from the community of the living and the dead is worse than death itself. Furthermore, according to

---

25. Mbiti, *Bible and Theology in African Christianity*, 156.
26. Ibid., 157.
27. Adeyemo, *Salvation in African Tradition*, 68.

widespread African belief wicked souls can be reincarnated only in birds or lower beasts, not in human beings.[28]

In summary, salvation for the African, as for the early Graeco-Roman Fathers, means deliverance and redemption. For the African it is not so much deliverance from the power of death or even of original sin; rather, salvation means deliverance from the evil and mysterious powers and forces that destabilize the community and the person and injure the relationship between God, the divinities, the ancestors, and the community or person. Death is therefore not seen as an evil or as the consequence of sin or disobedience to God or the supreme deity. Death is a welcomed passage for joining the ancestors, provided one dies a "good death." This is a very different mind-set from the understanding of death and sin in the Christian dogmatic tradition as embodied in the Nicene Creed and in the church's classical liturgical tradition.

28. J. Omosade Awolalu, *Yoruba Beliefs and Sacrificial Rites* (Harlow, England: Longman, 1979), 58–59.

5

God: Traditional Motifs

Mention of dialogue between traditional Christianity and other religions immediately calls to mind such religions as Judaism, Islam, Buddhism, Hinduism, and sometimes Confucianism. African traditional religions are not usually included in this litany. This is because the guardians and interpreters of the Christian tradition have historically slighted most of Africa, except Egypt, Ethiopia, and North Africa, but most certainly Africa south of the Sahara. Many have even attempted to discount ancient Egypt as being an African country. For example, during the Renaissance, as nostalgia for Greek and Roman antiquity swept through Western Europe, artisans as well as scholars tried to coopt Egyptian culture along with that of Persia, calling those cultures the "Old Orient," with the intention of separating them conceptually from Africa. This conception and deception intensified after Napoleon and the French arrived in Egypt in 1799 and determined that Egypt's "high culture" was more analogous to their perception of ancient Greek culture than to the cultures of Africa. Thus the paintings and other works about Egypt that appeared in the eighteenth and nineteenth centuries were said to refer to "oriental" themes, and the discipline of Egyptology — created in eighteenth-century France — was classified as an oriental study.

Thus Africa south of the Sahara and its traditional religions have been largely ignored as participants in interreligious dialogue. This Africa, where most of the growth and evangelism in faith is taking place, has generally been pushed aside by the theologians, ecumenicists, and others who set the agenda for that dialogue. Other than the World Council of Churches, only African religious groups have begun to correct this situation through consultations and conferences. A conference on Christianity and African culture was convened by the Christian Council of Ghana in 1955.[1] The All African

1. See *Christianity and African Culture: Proceedings of a Conference Held at*

Conference of Churches subsequently summoned a conference in Ibadan, Nigeria, in 1958[2] and also continued to deal with this matter in its assemblies at Nairobi (1962), Kampala (1963), Abidjan (1969), and Lusaka (1974). The World Council of Churches (WCC) has sponsored consultations and conferences on this subject, such as its dialogue between the Christian faith and the traditional religion of the Yoruba and Fon (Dahomey) at a 1970 UNESCO consultation in Cotonou, Benin; a dialogue on "Primal World-Views" in 1973 at Ibadan, Nigeria; and a more recent consultation in September 1986 in Kitwe, Zambia.[3]

However, for the most part African Christianity south of the Sahara has been seldom engaged for its intellectual and theological thought; rather, more usually it has been engaged as an appendage of nineteenth-century European and American missionary church history. Social anthropology with its clear ethnocentric origins, historians of religion, and the writings of missionaries have become by default the agents for uncovering and informing theologians and others about the nature and beliefs of traditional religion in Africa. Their work has been very important, yet at the same time, they have not shown much interest in emphasizing the theological nature of African traditional thought; nor have they necessarily been critical of the way such categories as "ancient" and "antiquity" have been used for organizing concepts in the history of ideas when dealing with Graeco-Roman cultures and for dismissing intellectual claims and worldviews of African cultures. The concept of "high cultures" has been largely modeled on ancient Greek and Roman thought and influenced by the Renaissance as well as by the premise that written thought is more esteemed than oral thought in the history of ideas, thus laying a basis for ranking cultures historically. In university and academic circles, dominated by Europeans or European-oriented scholars, the study of African traditional religion as a discipline both in French-speaking and English-speaking Africa did not emerge with any impact until the 1950s, even though work

Accra, Gold Coast, May 2nd–6th, 1955, under the Auspices of the Christian Council (Accra: Scottish Mission Depot, 1955).

2. See *The Church in Changing Africa: Report of the All-African Church Conference held at Ibadan, Nigeria, January 10th–19th, 1958* (New York: International Missionary Council, 1958).

3. See also A. B. T. Byaruhanga-Akiiki, ed., *Occasional Papers in African Traditional Religion*, 15 vols. (Kampala: Department of Religious Studies and Philosophy, Makerere University, 1971–73).

was going on in the 1940s in places like Fourah Bay College, University of Sierra Leone. J. B. Danquah (Ghana) had even published his important work, *The Akan Doctrine of God: A Fragment of Gold Coast Ethics and Religion*, in 1944.

GOD IN AFRICAN TRADITIONAL RELIGION

The rest of this chapter will examine the major motifs of God in the traditional religion of the various cultures of Africa in order to test their capacity as vehicles for interpreting biblical doctrines of God. The examination is also aimed at raising critical questions about maintaining a plurality of doctrines about God within the Christian tradition — with special attention given to those doctrines that lie outside the philosophical and intellectual guardianship of Graeco-Roman culture.

The systematic treatment of categories about God in African traditional religion as a discipline has been largely the work of E. Bolaji Idowu, now the retired patriarch of the Methodist Church in Nigeria, but at one time a university professor. He is considered the first systematic theologian of African traditional religion in much the same way that Origen is considered the first serious systematic theologian of the Christian church. Fortunately, Idowu's spirituality is African and therefore not likely to lead him into some of the extreme practices that Origen's spirituality impelled him to undertake.

As African theologians took charge of theological curricula in their newly independent countries — particularly after Idowu's *Olódùmarè: God in Yoruba Belief* (1963), John Mbiti's *African Religions and Philosophy* (1969), and Idowu's *African Traditional Religion* (1973) — a fresh understanding about traditionalist concepts and beliefs emerged in academic circles. These concepts and beliefs came to be seen as proper and legitimate subjects of study, but they were not engaged as a part of theological dialogue. Even today, while there are university departments for the study of traditional religion in some East African countries, such as Uganda (Makerere University) and Kenya (University of Nairobi), not to mention some of the theological colleges, on the whole most published scholarly and theological research in African traditional religion has occurred in West Africa.[4] The effect of all of this on most African Christians has

---

4. For a good summary and survey of the study of African traditional religion in French- and English-speaking African countries, see David Westerlund, *African*

been that their traditional conceptions of God have been overshadowed by those in the theology of the missionaries. As a Caribbean theologian said of the impact of the Christian church on the traditional religion of black folk in his region: God has become a foreign import to the peoples in Afro cultures. "Even the categories of our religious experiences are imports which do not reflect our cultural and native experiences. We experience God as an outsider."[5]

The traditionalist worldview — revealed in beliefs, rituals, ceremonies, stories of creation, greetings, salutations, music, dance, rites of passage, the use of herbs and medicines, the use of charms and talismans, and in notions about divinities, spirits, and ancestors — has shaped the culture and daily life of all Africans, Christians and non-Christians alike. Names of God may differ with each tribe or ethnic group and culture just as we find in the Old Testament, but both God and the general worldview throughout Africa south of the Sahara have common features regardless of the different traditions. And even though many Africans have become Christians, either in the missionary or the indigenous churches, their culture and tradition remain with them; they live on two levels, the traditionalist and the Christian.

Traditional Christian doctrines and the theological formation of missionary Christianity both display what can be described as the Graeco-Roman legacy, which is a primary feature of European and American ethnocentric churches and cultures. This legacy — especially perpetuated in such fundamental doctrines as the Trinity, the two natures of Christ, the work of the Holy Spirit, the concept of sin and salvation, and the division of flesh and spirit — in effect has become a kind of orthodox monoculture that has been universalized as a litmus test for Christianity in the Third World. The result is summed up well and somewhat passionately by Gabriel Setiloane of South Africa:

> What we cannot buy in Western theology is its inevitable dependence on Western culture, civilization, or whatever you call it. Its Greek-Roman thought-forms and modes of expression are the "swaddling clothes" that we need to tear open in order to get to Christ. . . . If theology is reflection, in African theology we try to break the seal of

Western thought-forms and culture so that we can come face to face with Christ, and in him see ourselves and others. "Selfhood" is the word used in Africa as the goal of this search.[6]

Even though African cultures have developed historically without being hostage to these philosophical assumptions and ideas, the theologically orthodox monoculture of the West (and the East) has restricted the possibility of doctrinal pluralism and a culturally pluralistic Christian faith; in so doing it has proscribed Afro cultures and their traditional religion as "primitive," "pagan," "heathen," "idolatrous," "fetishistic," "polytheistic," "animistic," and "superstitious." These rather emotional and negative assessments distract from the integrity of the traditional cultures as well as hinder their dialogue with the Christian tradition.

Created largely by Western Christians and anthropologists with certain cultural assumptions about the higher value of cultures closer to the antique Greek ideas of noncontradiction, unity, and consistency, these terms legitimized a cultural pecking order with certain claims for "higher cultures" over against "lower" or "primitive" cultures. All these cultures were measured by, among other things, their conceptions of God and being. But if *polytheism* is belief in and worship of many gods, as contrasted with many spirits or divinities; if *animism* is believing that animals, birds, and inanimate objects have souls; if *fetishism* is worship and veneration of charms, trees, sticks, and so on; if *heathenism* (from German: referring to the wasteland or heath where outlaws and vagabonds lived) means someone outside the pale of the great monotheistic world religions, such as Christianity, Judaism, and Islam; and if *idolatry* (Greek: *eidola*, an image copied from the actual god or the Greek world of Forms) means worshiping material objects identified as God or a god — if all this is so, then these terms do not accurately characterize Africans' basic understanding of God or the supreme deity in their traditional religion.

M. I. Boas points out how deep-seated these terms are in our own cultural and religious formation:

> The word pagan has little real meaning for most of us today. When we hear it pronounced, it affects most of us in a way that has been

---

6. Gabriel Setiloane, "About Black Theology," in Donald Jacobs et al., eds., *A New Look at Christianity in Africa* (Geneva: World Student Christian Federation, 1972), 2:70.

determined by school books, that is, we have a vision of the gods on Mount Olympus, a group of bearded Druids gathered around some woodland altar. . . . When we call these people pagans we simply mean that their belief was polytheistic in contrast to our own religions which are identified with monotheism, a distinction which is debatable, if not absolutely incorrect.[7]

Africans as well as Afro Caribbeans are quite clear that the multiplicity of spirits or divinities in traditional religion neither replaces nor supplants belief in one supreme God or deity, as charged by Westerners. The supreme deity is the source of power and authority within the hierarchy or pantheon of divinities and spirits. Even Yoruba, with its 1700 divinities, is clear that the *orisha* have neither existence nor power apart from Olódùmarè, the supreme God, also sometimes called Olórun and Odùduwà. As an ancient Yoruba proverb observes:

Be there one thousand four hundred divinities of the home;
Be there one thousand two hundred divinities of the market place;
Yet there is not one divinity to compare with Olódùmarè:
Olódùmarè is the King Unique.[8]

Yet even here one must be cautious in trying to fit African traditional religion into tidy, convenient Western boxes. Okot p'Bitek, the Ugandan anthropologist, protests that Western anthropologists undertake the study of African societies, including African traditional religion, partially to legitimize their field to other colleagues in the social sciences, thereby serving the needs of Western political interests and scholarship. Such studies of African religions have fallen generally into three categories: (1) studies by Christian apologists wishing to establish an attack on eighteenth- and nineteenth-century nonbelievers in Africa; (2) studies by African nationalists defensive about Western charges that African religion and cultures are "primitive," "animistic," and the like; (3) studies by missionaries desiring to establish a "dialogue with animism."[9]

7. M. I. Boas, *God, Christ and Pagans* (London: Allen and Unwin, 1961), 7f. (cited in E. Bolaji Idowu, *African Traditional Religion: A Definition* [London: SCM Press, 1973], 117–18).
8. Cited in E. Bolaji Idowu, *Olódùmarè: God in Yoruba Belief* (Ikeja, Nigeria: Longman, 1962), 55.
9. Okot p'Bitek, *African Religions in Western Scholarship* (Nairobi: East African Literature Bureau, 1970), 40.

The first group includes the work of people like Edward Tylor, E. E. Evans-Pritchard, and Geoffrey Parrinder. The second group includes the studies of Jomo Kenyatta of Kenya, Leopold Senghor of Senegal, K. A. Busia of Ghana, and John Mbiti of Kenya, now of Switzerland; these scholars wrote primarily to impress upon Europeans "that the African peoples were as civilized as the Western peoples. They dress up African deities with Hellenic robes and parade them before the Western world."[10] The third group includes the work of well-intentioned Western missionaries who have become Africanists — scholars like John Taylor, long-time student of African religion and retired Anglican bishop of Winchester, England, and Edwin Smith; these missionaries wished to engage the new African elites and intellectuals in a dialogue with Christianity. Okot p'Bitek has made the following comment about this third group: "When students of African religions describe African deities as eternal, omnipresent, omnipotent, omniscient, etc., they intimate that African deities have identical attributes with those of the Christian God. In other words, they suggest that Africans hellenized their deities, but before coming into contact with Greek metaphysical thinking."[11]

There is great disagreement among African scholars — particularly Christian Africans — about such an appraisal. But p'Bitek disputes the objectivity even of so-called scientific methods of the social sciences and theological concepts growing out of research into African societies and religion; he says these methods and concepts disguise cultural and ethnocentric interests linked to claims and boundaries of their parent Western cultures.

Concepts of God in traditional religion are shrouded in oral tradition, ceremonies, languages, proverbs, salutations, and stories, which necessitate exegesis and interpretation. Since Africans have begun to interpret their own traditions and culture theologically, and as their writings have become more available to the non-African world, interpretations of God are emerging that are different from those of the social scientists. In *Concepts of God in Africa*, even John Mbiti, employing largely Western theological categories for mostly Eurocentric readers, discovers a wide diversity of views about God's nature, attributes, and work in the natural order.

Mbiti, for one, would disclaim p'Bitek's judgment that African deities do not have attributes similar to those of the Christian

10. Ibid., 41.
11. Ibid., 80.

God. However, caution even here is warranted, for Mbiti does employ many of those Hellenized categories to describe the supreme
being of African traditional religion that are suspect for the Ugandan p'Bitek. Indeed p'Bitek called Mbiti "Africa's chiefest [sic] intellectual smuggler," who "smuggled" Greek metaphysics into the
interpretation of African divinities, while overlooking the dissimilarities.[12] Mbiti has confirmed that names in Africa are important
and tell us much about the attributes of God; he has confirmed
also that many African words that refer to God resemble or are the
same as those used to refer to the Christian or biblical God; yet
like other African scholars, even Mbiti confirms that Hellenism cannot exhaust the integrity of African notions about God. Mbiti and
others have pointed out that there is a great similarity between the
way African cultures and the Old Testament attach significance to
names. Clearly, in Africa the ideas about God are shaped by the various languages and names that are essential elements of the cultures
of African tribes and ethnic groups.

ATTRIBUTES OF GOD

What are some of the characteristics of God in traditional religion
that can be vessels for conceptualizing and interpreting the Christian
God? One about which African theologians agree is that the supreme
deity in traditional religion, regardless of his name, is *omni*: all-wise
(omniscient), ubiquitous (omnipresent), all-powerful or almighty
(omnipotent), and beyond the beyond (transcendent). But having
used this Greek prefix, I am also aware of the danger of Hell300nizing the African supreme being. "African peoples may describe their
deities as 'strong' but not 'omnipotent'; 'wise' not 'omniscient';
'old' not 'eternal'; 'great' not 'omnipresent.' The Greek metaphysical terms are meaningless in African thinking.... [Modern] Western
Christian anthropologists are intellectual smugglers. They are busy
introducing Greek metaphysical conceptions into African religious
thought."[13] Nevertheless, wanting to address both Western and African theologians, I think using *omni* is a risk worth taking for the
sake of constructing an Afro alternative to the traditional Greek
metaphysical model for God-talk. Because of the diversity and richness of the various African languages and tribes, using this Greek

12. Cited in David Westerlund, *African Religion*, 62.
13. p'Bitek, *African Religions*, 88.

concept pragmatically allows for a kind of familiar *lingua franca* or medium that can be used to communicate to Westerners an understanding of African models of God.

Divine Ubiquity

The first *omni* attribute is that God knows, sees, and hears everything because God is the owner of everything. Thus, the Akan tribes in Ghana call God several names: Brekyirihunuade, "He who knows or sees all"; Abommubuwafre, "One who is the Consoler or Comforter providing salvation"; and Nana Nyankopon, "Grandfather Nyame who alone is the Great One."[14] The Barundi in Burundi name God Indavyi, "Watcher of everything," and Rushoboravyose, "He is not surprised by anything," while the Luo in Kenya have a name for God, Wang' Chieng', which means "Eye of the Sun."

In Yoruba God is named Olódùmarè, believed to come from *Ol*, meaning "owner of" or "lord of," *Odo*, meaning "chief head" or "a very large and deep pot" or "of superlative quality and worth," and *mare*, derived from Yoruba legends about the rainbow (*Imi Oshùmarè*), which is believed to be a sign of the ancient covenant and bond between the supreme deity and its creature; in Yoruba *mare* thus means stability or that which remains. Another layer of Yoruba tradition says *mare* derives from the expression signifying uniqueness, as in *Arè*. Thus, according to Idowu, God in Yoruba is one who is unique and in covenant with humankind, one who is supreme, "incomparable and unsurpassable in majesty, excellent in attributes, stable, unchanging, constant, reliable."[15]

The Igbo (eastern Nigeria) call God Chukwu, from *chi*, "source being or spirit," "personal guardian spirit," as well as "destiny"; and *ukwu*, meaning "great," "without dimensions." Hence Chukwu means the great source of being or spirit,[16] but also the great source

---

14. John S. Mbiti, *Concepts of God in Africa* (London: SPCK, 1970), 327.

15. Idowu, *Olódùmarè*, 36.

16. *Chi* has several derivations and meanings, which can be confusing to the Westerner. The context determines how this word is rendered. Hence it may mean "supreme being" as in the Igbo sayings *Okike kere onye bu Chi ya* (One's creator is one's God) or *Chi ma onye oga enye ma onye oga enye amaghi* (God knows to whom he will give, but the person who will receive does not know); it can mean "a personal guardian spirit" as in *Ebe onye dara ka Chi ya kwaturu ya* (When a person falls it is his or her personal guardian spirit who pushed him or her down); and it can mean "fate" or "destiny" as in *Agbataghi Ajo Chi n' uzo olu* (You cannot escape bad fortune by cleverness) (see Emefie Ikenga Metuh, *God and Man in African Religion: A Case Study of the Igbo of Nigeria* [London: Geoffrey Chapman, 1981], 22–23).

and controller of destiny in the universe.[17] Appropriately, Igbo believe that every person is also born with a *chi*, which shapes the person's character while on earth but returns to Chukwu at death. Thus *chi* signifies a dependence on the supreme deity but also a soul that is the image of Chukwu and that sustains and nurtures the human person during his or her earthly life. At the same time, *chi* serves as a personal guardian spirit bringing prosperity as well as obstacles to the person.[18]

An Ashanti (Ghana) name for God is Onyankōpon, roughly rendered "the unique great one to whom one can take petitions and requests for counsel." A proverb says: *Wope aka asem akyere Onyankōpon a, kã kyere mframa* (If you wish to tell anything to the supreme deity, tell it to the winds).[19] Another name among the Ashanti is Ananse Kokroko, "the Great Spider, the All-wise one." The Yoruba call him *'A-rinú-róde Olluùmò okàn*, "the One who sees both the inside and the outside (of the human being)." Thus the idea of the supreme deity knowing and seeing everything is very pervasive in all African traditional religion.

A second *omni* characteristic of God is ubiquity. An Igbo proverb says: *M̀madù naàbò bàa izú. Chukwu si, 'Ỷâ mè àtó* (When two persons talk in secret, God says, "I make a third").[20] The Kono of Sierra Leone speak of God as Yataa, "the One you meet everywhere." Mbiti draws our attention to the practical application of this attribute, as when someone is wronged by another, he or she may say "May Yataa see this person" or "Yataa will see him," meaning the violator cannot escape God's presence since God is everywhere.[21] The Ewe in Togo express God's ubiquity thusly: "The lizard says that unless Mawu (God) is tired, he will never go hungry," indicating that God's providential care not only is everywhere, but also sustains and cares for even the reptiles of the earth as well as human beings.[22]

17. Ibid., 24.

18. J. Omosade Awolalu and P. A. Dopamu, *West African Traditional Religion* (Ibadan: Onibonoje Press and Book Industries, 1979), 40; Elizabeth Isichei, *A History of the Igbo People* (New York: St. Martin's Press, 1976), 25.

19. Cited in R. Sutherland Rattray, *Ashanti Proverbs* (Oxford: Clarendon Press, 1976), 24.

20. Cited in Elizabeth Isichei, *Igbo Worlds: An Anthology of Oral Histories and Historical Descriptions* (Philadelphia: Institute for the Study of Human Issues, 1978), 283.

21. Mbiti, *Concepts of God*, 5–6.

22. N. K. Dzobo, *African Proverbs: Guide to Conduct Vol. II* (Accra, Ghana: Waterville Publishing House, 1975), 173.

The Ila of Zambia speak of God as Mutalabala, meaning "to be in all ages, everywhere and at all times"; God has a "nowhere and nowhen," meaning that God's presence is without a fixed location or time.[23]

God's ubiquity is also witnessed in specific objects and events in some cultures, such as the Kikuyu in Kenya, where God's presence is linked with certain sacred mountains, e.g., Mount Kenya, although the precise place of God's dwelling is not known. The Sonjo (Tanzania) have a mountain called Mogongo jo Mugwe, "the mountain of God,"[24] while the Nyakyusa, also in Tanzania, call God Kalesi, "the one who is everywhere present," especially in sexual intercourse between a man and his wife that results in the conception of a child.[25]

God as all-powerful is an equally important attribute in traditional religion, for power is a significant part of the ethic in many African cultures, though this is not mean, ruthless, and unbridled power. In the Fon culture of Benin (formerly Dahomey), a paramount parent of Haitian Voodoo, Nana-Buluku is the supreme God with power and authority over the two gods in charge of creation and the natural order, Mawu, who is both female and the moon, and Lisa, who is both male and the sun. Frequently the supreme deity is called Mawu-Lisa. Their subordination to the power of the supreme deity is attested to by the fact that their respective jurisdictions were assigned to them by the more powerful Nana-Buluku.[26]

In a Yoruba legend, the 1700 divinities, weary of God's rule, conspire to challenge God in order to weaken God's absolute power and authority. They demand that he retire in sixteen years so they can take control of the earth and the natural order. God (Olódùmarè) had heard of their plan beforehand, but nonetheless agrees to their proposal with one amendment. The divinities ought first to test for 16 days how it would feel to have full charge and then he and they can consult again after this trial period. They agree and as soon as they leave, Olódùmarè turns off all the cosmic machinery operating the universe, so that everything comes to a standstill. After eight days, the divinities are totally frustrated and powerless. Nothing

23. Mbiti, *Concepts of God*, 8.
24. Ibid., 7, 275.
25. Ibid., 8.
26. Melville J. Herskovits, *Dahomey: An Ancient West African Kingdom*, 2 vols. (New York: J. J. Augustin, 1958), 2:10.

functions: the heavens do not yield rains, rivers cease to flow, even the sap in the trees has a bad taste. So they return to Olódùmarè, confess their folly, and acknowledge God's supreme authority and power. God laughs at them and immediately turns on the cosmic machinery so that everything functions properly again. The bewildered but chastened divinities leave the supreme deity singing God's praises in a song that is still sung in Yoruba today and that was mentioned above: "Be there one thousand four hundred divinities of the home;... / Olódùmarè is the King Unique."[27]

The Shona of Zimbabwe have two names for God that testify to God's power: Chipindikure, "the One who turns things up-side-down," and Chirozva-mauya, "the One who has power to destroy completely." These are not dissimilar to the idiom about the supreme power of God over the plans of humankind: "Man proposes and God disposes." Mbiti comments that God as almighty in some cultures is also associated with natural phenomena; for instance, the Kiga (Uganda) call God Kazoba, "the One who makes the sun set," and Rugaba, "the One who gave everything on this earth and can take everything away," a natural reaction for a people living near the equator where the seasons and the rhythm of the sun coming and going are the same year in and year out.[28]

Finally, there is the divine *omni* trait that I call "beyond the beyond." That is, the one God is beyond all that the human mind can fathom and is beyond all to which the natural order can lay claim. But this is not a beyondness in the Greek sense of God as an absolute transcendent "being beyond being," unstained by our corporeal realm in a perfect, immutable, unchanging realm. This beyondness is not like that which we find in Plato's famous fable of the charioteer and the winged horses riding toward the realm of pure wisdom; it is not even similar to that of the Logos that mediates between the eternal unchanging One, which is beyond, and the transient changing many, which are earthly. The traditionalist understanding of God's beyondness includes at the same time God's ongoing communion with us and the rest of creation in concrete, anthropomorphic ways, with which we can identify. Nowhere is this brought out better than in the creation stories of the various cultures and ethnic peoples and tribes.

For example, the Bushongo or Bakuba tribe in Zaire, whose

27. Cited in Idowu, *Olódùmarè*, 55.
28. Mbiti, *Concepts of God*, 11, 331.

oral tradition dates back to the fifth century A.D., refer to God as Bumba. Bumba at the beginning of creation saw only water. One day he was in awful pain and belched up the sun, thereby suddenly providing light everywhere. The sun's heat dried up the water, however, revealing the edge of the world, sandbanks, and reefs. The pain did not cease, so Bumba belched again, this time creating the moon and the stars. That separated the day into day and night, with each sphere (sun and moon) now having its own light. Bumba belched again and birds, beasts, and insects came forth. With another heave, humankind was created. But it was the creatures created by Bumba that finish the creation, not Bumba: the primordial birds create other birds, the crocodile creates the snakes and the iguana, the beetle creates other insects, and so on. When creation was complete, Bumba inspected everything and gave humanity possession of the land, while at the same time affirming the kinship between the animal world and the human world.[29]

The Igbo of Nigeria, also an ancient culture, understand God to have created humankind in the beyond, in God's own heavenly realm. The first human was called Eri or Nri (depending on the Igbo region telling the tradition). This primordial being, this superhuman, landed at Aguleri or Enugu-Ukwu, both of which are villages in Anambra State in present-day Nigeria. Finding the earth waterlogged and unfit for human habitation, Nri/Eri appealed to Chukwu to send an Awka blacksmith to blow his bellows on the waterlogged earth to dry it out. This was done and the earth became dry, so Nri/Eri married and had children, thus populating the dry land.[30]

Another Igbo creation myth says there were other primordial beings in the sky with Chukwu, though these were below Chukwu in rank and status, much like the angels in the Christian tradition who function as heavenly messengers for God. One of Chukwu's favorites was Edo, a female divinity known for her industry and

29. Barbara Sproul, *Primal Myths: Creating the World* (San Francisco: Harper & Row, 1979), 44–45.

30. Isichei, *Igbo Worlds*, 22–25. Because of his special relationship to Chukwu in Igbo traditional religion, the king of the Nri, a priestly clan in northern Igboland, receives tribute from the subtribes and ethnic groups. He is thought to have special powers from Chukwu to affect the fertility of the soil and to absolve anyone of an abomination against a divinity. He is also the final authority, much like the College of Arms in England and the Levites in the Old Testament, in settling disputes about conflicting traditions among the Igbo (See Metuh, *God and Man in African Religion*, 5).

initiative. As a sign of his grace and favor, Chukwu gave Edo a piece of his scepter, which was made of *nzu*, a kind of white chalk, and a small clay pot of water. Edo then took the *nzu* and the water toward earth. But her exuberant spirit took her beyond the earth and she soon became disoriented and lost, and she left a trail by breaking pieces from the *nzu* and scattering them all over. Eventually Chukwu found Edo tired and lonely, so he sent her a companion for conversation and errands. Chukwu then populated the earth himself by putting the broken pieces of chalk into the water pot, pulling out different pieces, and giving them names. He blew on them and made them live. In Nnewi in modern Nigeria, Edo is the most honored divinity and her festival is observed by women every seven years and by men every nine years, when all sons and daughters of the area, regardless of religion, return home from wherever they are in the world, if possible, to celebrate the *Ikwu-Aru Edo* — "rededication of body and soul to Edo."[31]

The Zulu of South Africa refer to God's beyondness as *Unku-lunkulu*; God is "the one who dwells in the sky" after first dwelling on earth. God ascended to heaven on a spider web because of human misconduct.[32] God's "beyond the beyond" is affirmed in such Zulu proverbs as: "Who can plait a rope for ascending, that he may go to heaven?" This suggests that it is impossible to get to God's beyond.[33] However, daily prayers, personal names, and sayings establish communion with God in the beyond.

The Ila tradition (Zambia), whose name for God is Shikaku-namo, "the Besetting One," illustrates God's beyondness and covenant in a legend about a woman searching for God to cure her of a life-long affliction, for which she held God responsible. She built one tower after another to heaven, only to have them tumble down. She then went from one country to another until she reached the ends of the earth where, she thought, heaven touched earth, for surely the supreme deity would be there. This plan too was fruitless. As she told people on the way what her goal was, they said to her an expression still found among the Ila today: "In what do you differ from others? The Besetting One sits on the back of each of us and we cannot shake him off," which means that while God is beyond

31. Awolalu and Dopamu, *West African Traditional Religion*, 57–58.

32. Alice Werner, *Myths and Legends of the Bantu* (London: George G. Harrap & Co., 1933), 21.

33. The sentence in the original is: *Ubani ongapot' igoda lolulupuka aye ezul-wini?* (see ibid., 61).

this life, God is also at the same time on the back of every human being at all times.[34]

Divine Creator

In addition to the *omni* attributes of God, a second general attribute is God as creator. There are variations among African cultures about God's being the original, absolute creator as in the Christian and Greek traditions. God is acknowledged as the supreme creator, but God also is a vulnerable creator, because in some cases he makes mistakes as creator. For example, in the creation stories of the Mande (Mali) in Central Africa, God or Mangala first tried to create a seed, but it was a failure. So he tried again, this time making twin seeds and other seeds contained in what is called the "egg of God," the "egg of the world," and the "placenta of the world." The twin seeds were the progenitors of humankind as well as the fish and beasts of the earth. One of the twins, Faro, was sacrificed to atone for some treachery of his twin, Pemba, against God. His body was scattered all across space, and where it fell on earth, trees and vegetation grew.[35]

Likewise, God as creator is sovereign but not an absolute sovereign, since he delegates his power to other divinities who can also create, as in one Yoruba version of creation. According to this tradition, which comes from the sacred city of Ilé-Ifè, Olódùmarè sent Orìshà-nlá (or Obàtálá), whom he had instructed in the craft, to create humankind and its environment. But Orìshà-nlá got intoxicated from palm wine, and while working in a drunken state, created misshaped clay figures with the result that many of them had deformities, such as crooked backs, missing legs and fingers, shortened arms, bent backs, etc. Yet he could not give them life; even he needed to call on the supreme God to breathe life into these clay figures. The gift of life was the grace and favor of God alone. After he wore off his drunken stupor, he saw his misdeeds and vowed never again to drink palm wine. To this day in Yoruba, the blind, lame, and the handicapped seek the help of Obàtálá when they have special needs or are in trouble of any kind.[36]

34. Mbiti, *Concepts of God*, 13.
35. Sproul, *Primal Myths*, 66–67.
36. Harold Courlander, *Tales of Yoruba Gods and Heroes* (New York: Crown Publishers, 1973), 19–20. Courlander says that the watery marshes and oceans were under the domain of the female deity Olókun, not under the supreme deity. Awolalu, himself Yoruba and Christian, identifies Olókun as a male divinity (see J. Omosade

Thus, God creates from nothing, *ex nihilo*, but God also creates from something already existing and fashions it as a grand organizer. Always connected with creation is the gift of life which God alone gives, even to the work of his intermediaries and divinities. The three Ila (Zambia) names for God's activity, for example, derive from three verbs: *Chilenga*, from the verb *kulanga*, meaning "to originate," "to be the first one to do something"; *Lubumba*, from the verb *kubumba*, meaning the molding of pots by the potter; and *Shakapanga*, from *kupanga*, meaning "to arrange things," "to put things order," "to construct something (like a house)." God is the supreme deity who originates things, shapes and constructs them as finished products.[37]

Other cultures place the earth above and heaven below; these may or may not have been created by God, but again God alone is owner or lord of the entire cosmos. The Bambuti (Congo) say creation began with dust and dirt falling from the earth above into God's food during mealtime. Tiring of this annoyance, God ordered the divinity of lightning to find God a new abode in earth rather than in heaven. This divinity split earth and traveled on the upward part, where he found an abode for God and the moon at the same time. In the Bambuti tradition, the closest cosmic object to God is the moon rather than the sun, and creation began with earth and heaven, followed by the creation of lightning, the chameleon (who figures prominently in a number of African creation stories), water, trees, humans, and animals. Mbiti points out that the following items and phenomena are also important in Bambuti culture: the Ituri forest, the many tropical storms with much lightning and thunder, the tributaries of the Congo River, and animals that are an important source of food.[38]

Divine Pastoral Care

Finally, there is the attribute of divine pastoral care, which is intimate to God's nature and is revealed in God's relationship with the animal and plant kingdoms as well as with humankind. Many anthropologists and historians of African religion have mistaken the absence of temples or iconography to the supreme deity in traditional religion to mean that God is always distant and unconcerned

Awolalu, *Yoruba Beliefs and Sacrificial Rites* [Harlow, England: Longman, 1979], 48). Olórun (Olódùmarè) rules the heavenly domain.
    37. Mbiti, *Concepts of God*, 46, 283.
    38. Ibid., 49–50.

for humanity and the animal world, that the African God is *deus incertus* or *deus remotus*. One Englishman active in colonial Nigeria described God in the Yoruba tradition in the following way:

> The native says [God] enjoys a life of complete idleness and repose
> ... and passes his time dozing or sleeping. Since he is too lazy or too
> indifferent to exercise any control over earthly affairs, man on his side
> does not waste time in endeavoring to propitiate him, but reserves
> his worship and sacrifice for more active agents.[39]

However, as one Yoruba theologian points out, God's several names in such social conventions as personal names, daily greetings, colloquial expressions, and expressions of thanksgiving are evidence of his continuing active presence in African culture. This often escapes Westerners, unfamiliar with the subtlety of African cultures. "To the travellers [Yoruba] say *'Mo fi Olórun sin ó'* ('I pray God may go with you') and to those going to sleep *'K'Olórun shó wa mójú ó'* ('May Olórun watch over us till daybreak'). He who can watch over somebody sleeping cannot Himself be said to be sleepy, idle or remote. He who can deliver somebody from an unexpected danger cannot be disinterested."[40]

Idowu adamantly takes Westerners to task for asking Africans questions about their experience of God's remoteness and presence, noting that such questions are awkward for Africans to answer: "In African thought, Deity is absolutely essential and cannot be disregarded: the notion of a god as so transcendent that he is not immanent is alien to African belief.... Africans are explicit about the divine rulership and absolute control of the universe."[41] However, African traditional religion is also quite clear that anthropomorphic descriptions of God's pastoral character do not determine or exhaust God's nature. The supreme deity may be atop a hierarchy as in Yoruba or more of a first among a host of divinities as in other cultures, but God is always understood to be the sovereign King of kings and Lord of lords in all realms, heavenly and earthly, and therefore is without equals.

The pastoral care of God is especially apparent in those cultures where God is mother or mother and father, as in matrilineal cultures, such as the Nuba (southern Sudan) where God is called Masala, "the

39. A. B. Ellis, *The Yoruba-speaking Peoples of the Slave Coast of West Africa* (1894; reprint, Oosterhout, Netherlands: Anthropological Publications, 1970), 36.
40. Awolalu, *Yoruba Beliefs*, 17.
41. Idowu, *African Traditional Religion*, 160.

great mother." Feminine traits are appealed to in sayings and prayers to God: "Masala gave birth to the world," indicating Masala both created or mothered the world and also cares for her creation in time of need. Likewise, the Ovambo in Namibia say, "The Mother of pots is a hole in the ground; the Mother of people is God."[42]

Among the Fon, as already noted, God is commonly referred to as Mawu, the generic name for Mawu-Lisa, Mawu being the female element in the deity and Lisa the male. Mawu as female is mother, gentle, and forgiving, while Lisa as male is considered robust and ruthless. Mawu rules over the moon and thus is associated with the coolness of night. This is significant because in Dahomean culture wisdom is associated with coolness — a wise person is one who has matured and is without the compulsiveness (heat) of youth. As the moon sheds coolness, so does Mawu exemplify wisdom in the world, whereas the heat of the sun over which Lisa lords is connected with strength:

> During the day when [Lisa] reigns, men are condemned to toil and strive, to feverishness and anger, for his symbol is heat. But during the night when Mawu reigns, it is cool, and men sleep and refresh themselves after the day's work. It is then that the pleasures of life are enjoyed by mankind — dancing and story-telling and love-making. So it is said that "when Lisa punishes, Mawu pardons."[43]

Interestingly enough, when the Catholic missionaries wrote a catechism for the Fon, God was translated as Mawu, and Jesus was translated as Lisa.

It is also important to understand God's pastoral nature within the context of the African kinship system and extended family. Biological terms like "father" and "mother" are much more inclusive than in the industrialized West, with its more restricted nuclear family models, gender politics, and nursing home welfare system for the discarded elderly. An Ashanti proverb says this quite well: *Nuipa uhiña ye Onyàmé mma, obinye asase ba*, "All men are the children of God; no one is a child of the earth."[44] The Bambuti even call God "Grandfather" and "Great Father" when praying to him because they have no precise name for the creator of the universe.[45]

42. Mbiti, *Concepts of God*, 92–93.
43. Herskovits, *Dahomey*, 103.
44. Cited in Rattray, *Ashanti Proverbs*, 28.
45. Mbiti, *Concepts of God*, 92.

(The names convey how high the wisdom and especially the authority of the elderly are held in all African cultures.) Also the role of grandfather and grandmother are associated with judiciousness and concern for the welfare of the younger and less experienced members of the family and community. Likewise a grandfather is a living symbol of ancestral lineage and communal customs and traditions. His wisdom is consulted when there is a need for counsel, certainty, and resolving disputes, which means that the village or community expects exemplary conduct from the grandfather as well.[46]

God's pastoral care also extends to the animal and plant worlds. The Zulu believe cattle were created in the same place as humankind — on the one hand, they were created for food and sustenance, but, on the other hand, they were also created as God's special possession. Curiously, unlike the many other African cultures where being struck by lightning is a sign that a taboo has been violated, in Zulu culture if lightning strikes cattle, it is a sign of a blessing for the village where it occurred: "God has slaughtered for himself among his own food. Is it yours? Is it not the Lord's? He is hungry, he kills for himself."[47]

The chameleon is a favorite animal in many African traditions and is associated with God's pastoral care. In these traditions the chameleon generally acts as a kind of Angel Gabriel, as a messenger from the supreme being sent to announce special events. In one strand of the Yoruba tradition, God sends the chameleon to inspect Obàtálá's or Orìshà-nlá's work on earth and directs the chameleon to return with a report. The chameleon does so and recommends that the work continue. In the Zulu tradition the chameleon is sent by Unkulunkulu to earth to tell humankind that it will not die. On the way the chameleon strays, gets fascinated with some fruit, and fails to return to God (Unkulunkulu), who subsequently sends a lizard after the chameleon with a new message, namely, that humankind will die. The lizard does as directed and returns to the dwelling place of God before the chameleon. Finally, the chameleon completes his mission and tells humankind that it has gained immortality. But people do not believe him, saying that the new word of the lizard has preceded his old word. Thus in spite of his closeness to God as a chief messenger, even the chameleon's word and authority de-

46. Harry Sawyerr, *God: Ancestor or Creator?* (London: Longman, 1970), 8.
47. Ibid., 99.

pend on God's graciousness and favor. When that is withdrawn, even God's messengers no longer are authentic bearers of good news.

THE RELIGIOUS WORLDVIEW OF AFRICANS

Traditional religion has shaped a worldview that is pervasive in the socialization and formation of Africans, whether they be Christians, non-Christians, or traditionalists. This fact has been expressed very well by John B. Taylor. The primal worldview functions in different ways within traditional religion itself, and though some may have abandoned the inheritance of their fathers and mothers with no new faith to replace it or may have taken on some form of the Christian faith in Africa, no Africans can forsake their culture. "It may well be that across much of the primal world there is a broad similarity in certain attitudes to the natural environment and its resources, to human society, to the most significant or critical human experiences associated with birth, puberty, marriage, sickness or death, and to human well-being and the forces which oppose it."[48]

J. Omosade Awolalu expresses this communion between traditional religion and culture even more graphically:

> Young taxi drivers on Nigerian roads still offer sacrifice to Ogun, the god of iron. Farmers in Yorubaland do not eat of the new yam until they have ceremonially brought home the yam and have first presented it to Orisa-Oko [the divinity in charge of agriculture and farming operations]. It is no exaggeration that no day passes by at Ilé-Ifè without, at least, one traditional festival being observed either in honor of a divine or an ancestral spirit. And it is no exaggeration either that no night passes by at Abeokuta (where Christianity was first established in Yorubaland) without sacrifice being placed at a road junction, or near a stream or at the foot of a tree or at a dunghill.[49]

Thus we can say that in spite of the many variations and thoughts about God in African cultures, there are indeed some common beliefs and assumptions about the supreme deity: (1) God is real, concrete, and not philosophically abstract; (2) God is unique, incomparable, and absolutely supreme among all the deities and

---

48. John B. Taylor, ed., *Primal World-views: Christian Involvement in Dialogue with Traditional Thought Forms* (Ibadan: Daystar Press, 1976), 5.

49. J. Omosade Awolalu, "Continuity and Discontinuity in African Religion: The Yoruba Experience," *Orita* 13, no. 2 (December 1981): 12.

divinities, though not necessarily immutable; (3) God is the absolute lord of the universe who keeps the universe going at all levels, even when delegating authority to the divinities or spirits, since only God can give the breath of life to animals, plants, and humankind alike; (4) God is one, even though God is identified by different tribal names; (5) God is just but also righteous, as illustrated in the beliefs about the wrath of the supreme deity, humanity incurring judgment, and the need to maintain a good relationship with God through the observation of traditions and taboos.[50]

Furthermore, the continued observance of festivals in Africa is an important testimony to the continued presence of God in modern African culture. As Awolalu contends, claims by some European anthropologists and others that African traditional religion is dying out because fewer people are practicing it or have abandoned it are not supported by evidence. Rather, the continuing occurrence of and attendance at festivals are evidence of the vitality of traditional religion:

> Generation after generation of Africans have passed away, and the festivals have not reduced in number; neither has the enthusiasm with which they have been celebrated and still are being celebrated diminished in any way.... The sophistication and urbanization and Western education do not discourage the inhabitants of [Ibadan] from worshipping the spirit of Oke-Ibadan. Who is the reigning paramount chief at Ondo [a state in modern Nigeria] that will neglect the annual festival of Ogun or the ruler of Oshogbo that will not observe Osun Festival and yet will expect the subjects to cooperate with him?...[They] are observed in honor of some divinities and spirits who lend support to the maintenance of peace in the society.[51]

The worldview of African traditional religion about God and God's relationship to African culture is summarized very well in the Igbo tradition of Mbari houses. Erected to honor particular divinities (spirits), much in the same way that chapels are built in Western Christendom to honor a saint or in thanksgiving for a favor or blessing, Mbari houses are built by the community, not by an individual, in thanksgiving for a blessing. In the middle of the house's space is an oversized mud statue of Ala, the earth mother, sitting on a throne with a child on either side. Other divinities sit in other parts of the space; these other divinities include the divinity of thunder,

---

50. Idowu, *African Traditional Religion*, 149–65.
51. Awolalu, "Continuity and Discontinuity in African Religion," 11.

Amadioha; the river divinity, Ekwunoche; the divinity of fertility in women; an agricultural divinity; a divination spirit, such as Agwunsi; various local spirits; and even a representation of a latecomer on the African scene, the European colonialist, depicted either coming up from a hole in the ground (which indicates he came from nowhere into African society) or as an officer looking down on the African scene from an upstairs window.

Here we have the mystical, mythical, and experiential of the old and the new African worlds: the several kinds of spiritual beings, an unbroken continuity between the material and the spiritual orders, a hierarchy of beings, and a dynamic interaction between these beings and the community.

> There is a continuous exchange between all the beings... irrespective of the class of being (visible or invisible) to which they belong. Men can be possessed by spirits and spirits sometimes incarnate themselves in visible form. Men can influence the deities and the spirits through sacrifices, prayers, and spells. Conversely, the deities can intervene in human affairs to bring order and blessings, or they can upset the human order whenever their laws are not obeyed.[52]

The result is that most Africans do not understand faith as being assent to Christian doctrines or a series of creedal statements to be recited, renewed, and affirmed by a subjective individual or personal religious experience of Christ. What is lacking for Africans in such a tradition are the communal expressions for finding authentic being and identity as an African Christian. To be without a community or cut off from the tribe and its customs means alienation for most Africans. To cite Mbiti again:

> [Africans] trust... that [the supreme being] will bring them rain, deliver them from trouble, accept their prayers and sacrifices, give them children, and so on. African peoples are not spiritually illiterate, but the word "Faith" in its technical sense seems somewhat foreign to them. To assert, however, that they have "no faith" in God would be absolute nonsense, and there are no atheists in traditional African

---

52. Metuh, *God and Man in African Religion*, 56. The first description of Mbari houses and art in English was written by the Yoruba art scholar Ulli Beier, *African Mud Sculpture* (Cambridge: Cambridge University Press, 1963), 15–43. Although the precise etymology of the concept is still uncertain, *mbari* can mean (1) "creation," (2) "the act of creation," (3) "renewal," and (4) "regeneration." See Herbert M. Cole, "The Survival and Impact of Igbo Mbari," *African Arts* 21, no. 2 (February 1988): 54–65.

societies.... This search after [the supreme being's] attention is utilitarian and not purely spiritual; it is practical and not mystical....
[They] do not seem to search for him as the final reward or satisfaction
of the human soul or spirit.[53]

53. Mbiti, *Concepts of God*, 219.

6

Christ:
A Son Out of Egypt

It is not the Christian God who causes problems for Afro cultures; it is the Christian Christ. Or perhaps more precisely, it is those Christian dogmas and doctrines that are derived from Graeco-Roman (Latin) sources — dogmas and doctrines that have built-in philosophical worldviews and assumptions about God — that baffle and often appear as a kind of cultural imperialism in theological clothing.

Yet earlier, ante-Nicene notions of Christ's significance were more fluid and open. They may even have included a direct link between Jesus and Africa through the reference to Egypt in Matt. 2:15: "Out of Egypt have I called my son." Biblical scholars tell us that Matthew lifts the phrase "out of Egypt" from Hos. 11:1 and Exod. 4:22 to show how Jesus "fulfills what the Lord had spoken by the prophet" and to draw a parallel between Jesus and Moses.[1] Further, in the wider Hellenistic environment in which Matthew's Gospel was received, the reference to Egypt may also have called to mind Egypt's role as a refuge for people escaping despots and tyrants, Egypt's black and multicolored populations,[2] its legendary

1. Scholars give essentially two alternative interpretations of this reference to Egypt in Matthew's birth narrative: (1) it refers to the link between God's deliverance of the Jews from bondage in Egypt and the promised restoration to be ushered in by the Messiah; (2) it refers to Egypt allegorically, as in Rev. 11:8, which refers to Egypt as the place where the dead are buried and links it to the crucifixion ("Out of death have I called my son"). See, e.g., Ulrich Luz, *A Commentary, Matthew 1–7*, trans. Wilhelm C. Linz (Minneapolis: Augsburg, 1989), 146.

2. As Egypt was traditionally known as a place of refuge for people escaping despots and tyrants, it could indicate hope and deliverance from Romans. Raymond Brown maintains that this more likely ancient understanding of Egypt as a place for refugees escaping despotism rules against those insisting that the Holy Family actually went into Egypt via the Gaza Strip, which lay within the empire. See Raymond Brown, *The Birth of the Messiah: A Commentary on the Infancy Narrative in Matthew and Luke* (Garden City, N.Y.: Doubleday and Company, 1977), 203.

status as a place where religious concepts about gods and spirits originated,[3] and its reputation for astrological speculation about a new, messianic age.[4]

In this way the deep Jewish traditions of liberation and messianic hope may have connected with the deep religious yearnings of the wider Hellenistic milieu. The partnership of God with Israel, which continues and is fulfilled in Jesus, now embraces all humankind. Its theological depth is made more poignant in the Letter to the Philippians: "Therefore at the name of Jesus every knee shall

In the Old Testament, Ethiopia, not Egypt, is treated as the place of and symbol for African blackness — a convention continued in the early Church Fathers, for instance in Origen's commentary on the references to Ethiopia and blackness in the Song of Songs. And some scholars dispute the color of the inhabitants of Egypt. But their work might well distract from the fact that Egypt, as an African country, had inhabitants who were black as well as variations of black. Upper Egypt, which is actually its southern part, was and continues to be the territory dominated by blacks, Kush and Nubia (modern northern Sudan) being instances of this. The Egyptians themselves called their country *Kemit*, meaning "black," although some Westerners say this refers to the color of the soil rather than the people. *Kam* is a Hebrew word meaning "black," "burned," "heat," and the word may very well have been derived from the Egyptians, among whom the Hebrews lived some 400 years as slaves. See Cheikh Anta Diop, *The African Origin of Civilization: Myth or Reality*, trans. Mercer Cook (Westport, Conn.: Lawrence Hill and Co., 1974), 7.

At the same time, not to be overlooked is the testimony of Herodotus, one of the few Greek scholars who actually visited and wrote about Egypt and Africa. Journeying to Egypt in the fifth century B.C., he found a population whose land had been occupied and ruled by foreigners for a number of years — the Assyrians (briefly in 671 B.C.) and Persians (525–404). Impressed but at the same time surprised by the color of the Egyptians, even with their variations produced from intermarriage and mulatto offspring, Herodotus blamed their blackness or darkness (compared to the Greeks) on the heat. Likewise, he also described the citizens of Colchis as being originally Egyptian because they had black skin (*melanochroes*) and wooly hair and had been circumcised. Hence in the Roman Empire in the first century A.D., Egypt connoted particular social and ethnic conditions.

3. According to a work attributed to the Greek satirist Lucian (c. 115–200), who was greatly interested in early Christianity, Egypt was regarded in Syria, Assyria, and Palestine, as well as by the Greeks, as the origin of religious concepts about gods and spirits, their own established places of worship, and yearly religious festivals. The Egyptians were also considered to be the first to reveal the holy names and sacred stories of the gods. See Harold W. Attridge and Robert A. Oden, eds., *The Syrian Goddess (De Dea Syria) Attributed to Lucian* (Missoula, Mont.: Scholars Press for the Society of Biblical Literature, 1976), 11.

4. Matthew's association of Egypt with Christ the new Messiah possibly had a radical apologetic goal, namely, connecting the Messiah with popular astrology of the time. Egyptian astrology and its zodiac were known throughout the Roman Empire, as Martin Bernal points out in his provocative book on the African and Asian roots of Greek classical civilization (see Martin Bernal, *Black Athena: The Afriasiatic Roots of Classical Civilization* [New Brunswick, N.J.: Rutgers University Press, 1987], 1:126, 129). Belief in the equinoxes was known to be widely circulating among all segments of the populace in the empire by 50 B.C.

bow, in heaven and on earth and under the earth, and every tongue shall confess that Jesus Christ is Lord, to the glory of God the Father" (2:6-11).

Doctrines of Christ within the Christian tradition have generally moved in two directions: from above toward humankind or from humankind toward above. Christology from above usually emphasizes God's deity or divinity, while christology from below tends to emphasize God's humanity. The first embraces philosophical conceptions about deity as sovereign, omnipotent, transcendent, perfect in every way, absolute, sinless, and not subject to the contingencies of time or history. This kind of christology frequently neglects the activity of Christ as a man. God's intervention in our human time and history in Jesus Christ is viewed as the reconciliation of a sinful humanity and a righteous God. Christ is indeed *vere Deus*, who shares God's deity as it is described above. As divine, Christ is not a secondary or subordinate deity or Greek demiurge, hence the philosophical term *homoousios* and the emphasis in the Nicene Creed: "Light from light, true God from true God, begotten not made, of one Being with the Father." To not have the same deity or divinity as God Almighty meant Christ could not truly be our salvation; he could not be the one who restores and overcomes the separation of all of humankind and the cosmos from God. Doctrines about incarnation and ascension are very important for this view of christology, although this is not to say that some of the other doctrines connected with Christ, such as redemption and the crucifixion, are neglected altogether.

The second direction in christology usually focuses on what theologians like to call the anthropological attributes, that is, Christ's earthly engagement in our human condition. This kind of christology frequently neglects the majesty of Christ as divine. He was born of a woman, suffered as all human creatures suffer, and died as all humanity must die. He was subject to all the sinfulness of the human condition without exception. In Jesus Christ, God is submitted to human sin. Jesus acts as our mediator, our intercessor, while he is also God. But in dying on the cross, he at the same time was triumphant over sin and thereby provides us with new life, yet also reveals what our true humanity is. Christ is *vere homo*. The classical doctrines of the cross and the resurrection are important for this direction in christology, although again the other doctrines are not totally neglected.

Sometimes these two directions have led to further abstraction,

so that theologians speak of the two *natures* of Christ: his deity and
his humanity, and the two *states* of Christ: his humiliation and his
exaltation. Yet both directions intend to highlight human salvation
and God's reconciliation from above toward us: "who for us men
and for our salvation, came down from heaven."

As is well known, the emphasis in the Nicene Creed on Christ
being "begotten, not created" and "of one being with the Father"
was designed as a consensus among the bishops to refute the claims
of Arius, the fourth-century monk from Africa, and the Arians.[5] It
was also in part an act of deference to the political wishes of the emperor and in part a securing of boundaries for understanding Jesus
Christ's theological identity. The separation of humankind and the
cosmos from God through sin was considered so grave that only the
supreme deity of the eternal God could overcome it. This separation
felt by the Fathers at Nicaea is captured very well in the prayer for
blessing the baptismal water used in the Eastern Orthodox tradition:

> But do thou, O Master of all, show this water to be the water of
> redemption, the water of sanctification, the purification of flesh and
> spirit, the loosing of bonds, the remission of sins, the illumination of
> the soul, the laver of regeneration, the ren.wal of the Spirit, the gift
> of adoption to sonship, the garment of incorruption, the fountain of
> life.[6]

Christology underwent yet another revision in the Reformed
theology of John Calvin (1509–1564), who emphasized Christ as
prophet, priest, and king. Although John Chrysostom did speak of
the three dignities of Christ as king, prophet, and priest, Calvin
developed this doctrine systematically. In his 1545 revision of the
Institutes, the prophetic office of Christ is understood as being
comprised of preaching the gospel regularly — it involves interpreting God's will and witnessing to the power of the Holy Spirit
among us; the priestly office involves Christ's own holiness, sacrifice, and intercession, through which we are made acceptable to

---

5. Some recent scholarship points out that Arius was more concerned about
some Fathers employing Greek metaphysical claims that true deity is immutable and
unchangeable than with unity or disunity in the godhead. He was concerned that such
an emphasis might endanger the doctrine of salvation in Christ, effectively removing
the Son from the vicissitudes of time and change in the human realm where moral
and ethical choices are made (see Robert C. Gregg and Dennis E. Groh, *Arianism —
A View of Salvation* [Philadelphia: Fortress Press, 1981], 29).

6. *Baptism* (New York: The Orthodox Church in America, 1972), 51–52.

God in spite of our sin; and the kingly office involves Christ being God's guarantee of our union with God and our triumph over evil, Satan, and death. Karl Barth revised this threefold doctrine in his concept of Jesus Christ as Lord (God in Jesus Christ humiliated as a servant), as servant (humankind in Jesus Christ exalted as Lord), as witness (the prophets and word of God verifying the reconciliation between God and humankind), but with some caution:

> What is the humiliation of Jesus Christ? To say that He is lowly as a man is tautology which does not help us in the least to explain His humiliation. It merely contains the general truth that He exists as a man in the bondage and suffering of the human situation, and is to that extent actually lowly. But the peculiar thing about the humiliation of Jesus Christ... is that in Him God Himself humiliated Himself — not in any disloyalty but in supreme loyalty to His divine being.[7]

As we have seen in African and Caribbean traditional religion, God as the supreme deity is alone the guarantor of life and coherence in the human community and the cosmos, even in those traditions where God is not the sole creator of all parts of the cosmos. Thus theologically the Afro traditionalists affirm the supreme god as one who reigns over a cosmos that includes not only humankind, but also spirits, divinities, ancestors, and other forces in animate and inanimate beings. Since the Christian God is known primarily through Jesus Christ, two essential issues to investigate are: (1) the relationship of Jesus Christ to creation and therefore his cosmological significance, and (2) his relationship to humankind and therefore his redemptive or soteriological significance.

With the exception of the Eastern Orthodox tradition, which duly gives great emphasis to the first issue, the types of colonial Christianity brought to sub-Saharan Africa and the Caribbean were European and North American varieties, which largely emphasize the second issue: human redemption, justification, sanctification, and personal salvation, thus de-emphasizing the cosmos and nature. But a christology, at least for Afro cultures, has to emphasize the good and evil forces and phenomena in the heavens and nature as well. To this extent, as we have already seen, Christ must

7. Karl Barth, *The Doctrine of Reconciliation*, vol. 4/1 of *Church Dogmatics*, trans. G. W. Bromiley (Edinburgh: T. & T. Clark, 1956), 134.

be understood as the Lord who affects (1) human sin and righteous living, a major concern in East Africa with its revival tradition;
(2) the "natural" world of divinities, spirits, and evil forces, a major concern in West Africa; and (3) political and social liberation
forces, a major concern in South Africa and the Caribbean. This is
not to say that these concerns do not have a cross-regional significance for all cultures of Africa and the Caribbean; neither does this
mean that such a christology has no significance for the Western
church.

In the Nicene Creed, for example, Jesus Christ is called not
only Lord, but also the Word of God; he is not only God in the
flesh, but also is begotten of God; he is the very source of life and the
beginning of all creation even before there was a creation; he is the
one through whom all things in creation were created, who brought
and brings salvation, restoration, and healing to the cosmos and the
human community. He is also depicted as living in historical time
and in the human condition. Regarding this matter, Afro traditional
cultures raise serious questions about (1) the adequacy of constru-
ing the Christian faith primarily as a historical faith, an attitude
engendered by thinking about and explaining historically the person
and ministry of Jesus Christ (the historical-critical approach), which
modern biblical scholarship largely fuels, and (2) the adequacy of
universalizing such historical thinking, which has dominated Western theological thought since Gotthold Lessing (1729–1781) and
the Enlightenment.

A long discourse on the history of intellectual ideas in modern
Christian thought would take us afield. It is worth noting, however,
that Lessing greatly influenced modern Christian thought by directing it to read history back into scripture; this movement came to
its peak in the nineteenth and twentieth centuries' quest for the historical Jesus lurking behind the Christ of faith. Religious belief for
Lessing was a part of a maturing historical process that he claimed
lacked firm, revealed, universal truths to which a reasonable religious person could assent as a Christian. According to Lessing, there
is thus no logical connection between the events of Jesus' life and
the truths of church doctrine about that life: "Accidental truths of
history can never become the proof of necessary truths of reason."
In an essay summarizing his thoughts about divine revelation and
orthodox Christian truth, Lessing wrote: "If God held all truth in
his right hand and in his left the everlasting striving after truth, so
that I should always and everlastingly be mistaken and said to me,

Choose with humility, I would pick on the left hand and say, Father grant me that; absolute truth is for thee alone."[8] This motif may be really the great divide separating the worldview of Western Christianity from that emerging among Christians in Africa and the Caribbean, thereby making all the more urgent arguments for doctrinal pluralism in understanding Jesus Christ and the cosmos without the imprimatur of Western Graeco-Roman metaphysical guardianship.

BOUNDARIES OF CHRISTOLOGY

The people who make up the Christian church come from a vast array of cultures, but the church's grammar and vocabulary regarding Jesus Christ have been drawn from but a few cultures. This contradiction obligates us to reinterpret and reshape the church's christological grammar and vocabulary.

The grammar of christology during the early centuries of the church reflected the mind-set of both the emperor and the bishops regarding the definition of boundaries of "true Christianity." This is shown very clearly in the "Definition of the Faith" agreed to at Chalcedon:

> Our Lord and Savior Jesus Christ, as he was establishing his disciples in understanding of the faith, stated, "My peace I leave with you, my peace I give to you" (John 14:27), in order that no one should speak differently from his neighbor about the teachings of true religion, but that, on the contrary, the proclamation of the faith should be exhibited as the same for all.[9]

Christ is to be understood, accordingly, as complete in his deity, the same deity as God's. Yet Christ is also complete in his humanity, hence the dogma of the two natures. The Fathers at Chalcedon believed this dogma to be the minimal boundary for unity in the church, which they thought could be accomplished by the power of parliamentary procedure. They believed their vote on the matter could dispel all error and disunity: "By unanimous vote we have driven away the teachings of error, and we have renewed the inerrant faith of the Fathers." We know, of course, that this vote

8. Cited in Paul Edwards, ed., *The Encyclopedia of Philosophy*, 4 vols. (New York: Macmillan Publishing Co. and The Free Press, 1967), 3:445.
9. Cited in Richard A. Norris, Jr., ed. and trans., *The Christological Controversies* (Philadelphia: Fortress Press, 1980), 155.

did not end the controversy about christology within the church;
the controversy continues, and today the debate should be open to
contributions from Third World cultures.

Barth rightly reminds us that the ecumenical councils of
Nicaea and Chalcedon were writing guidelines for understanding
the existence and action of Christ, not cementing stones for constructing an abstract doctrine of his "person": "In Himself and
as such the Christ of Nicaea and Chalcedon naturally was and
is a being which, even if we could . . . explain his unique structure conceptually, could not be proclaimed and believed as the
One who acts historically because of the timelessness and historical remoteness of the concepts."[10] But even a conceptual picture
of Christ cannot be separated from the intention of God in him,
namely, to establish a new partnership with a wayward humanity
and cosmos.

If the creeds are the minimum boundaries, but not the final
limits, for christology, can they be translated into concepts that can
be understood in African and Caribbean cultures whose worldviews
have been strongly influenced by African traditional religion and its
New World descendants? Is this simply a question of syncretism
even in the broader understanding of that term? Or might there be
alternative doctrines of Christ's divinity and humanity that move
outside these metaphysical boundaries of a christology that furthers
a God who is Greek?

CHRIST AS THE ANOINTED ONE

A number of titles and ascriptions for Christ in the New Testament
are theologically and culturally significant as to how the early Christians thought of him and his ministry. An important one that strikes
immediate familiarity in Afro traditional cultures is Christ as Messiah (Hebrew: *masiah*, "an anointed person or thing"). However,
the Greek word *christos*, first used in the Septuagint (285 B.C.–
c. 100 B.C.) to translate the Hebrew *masiah*, was adapted by the New
Testament Christians to include both titles (Christ and Messiah) as
designations for Jesus. The new technical title of *christos*, signifying
the one who has been anointed with oil and given a divine character,
suggests that the Christian translators wanted to point to Jesus' deity or divinity, since *chriein* in Greek simply means "to pour or rub

10. Barth, *Church Dogmatics*, 4/1:127.

[oil or ointment on a person]." The New Testament scholar C. F. D. Moule makes an interesting point regarding Jesus' attitude toward the titles of Messiah and Christ. He notes that in Mark 5:30 Jesus tells the disciples to keep his being the Christ a secret. Jesus does not refuse the title of Christ in this text or in the rest of the New Testament; rather he tells his disciples in this instance not to tell others that he is the Messiah.[11]

Anointment in Israel conferred special authority and a holiness as gifts from God on a person for a royal or kingly task. This authority was accentuated by the coming of the divine Spirit upon the person, who then became the possession of God in a unique way, like Saul, David, and Samuel. Neither the authority nor the power could be transmitted or handed down by the one anointed. When he or she died, a new person had to be anointed. As God's anointed sharing in the holiness of God, this person was to be protected as God's possessed and listened to, as we see in David's refusal and hesitancy to usurp Saul's authority, even though David was God's anointed as well as Saul (1 Sam. 24:7, 11; 26:9, 11).

Yet anointment was not unique to Israel. It certainly existed in Canaan well before Israel's kingship was established and possibly in Damascus as well.[12] Also, in Israel's tradition priests as well as kings were anointed (see, e.g., Exod. 40:12-15; 29:4-9; Lev. 4:3, 5, 16), and both were endowed with a sacred authority and permission to perform certain religious acts. As such the king or priest was a *masiah*, a messiah, "an anointed person." But *christos* was used deliberately to designate a *divine* task, as contrasted with a kingly or priestly task.[13] This meaning probably emerged with heightened expectations in the first-century Hellenistic Jewish community in Palestine, burdened by the conquest of Pompey and thinking of God's ancient promise, as in the apocryphal Psalms of Solomon, where the long-expected savior is identified with the Messiah: "Thou, Lord, has chosen David to be king over Israel, and thou hast sworn to him concerning his seed for all time, that his kingdom shall never cease from before thy face" (Pss. of Sol. 17:4).

When Jesus stands before the Sanhedrin, he is called the Mes-

11. C. F. D. Moule, *The Origin of Christology* (Cambridge: Cambridge University Press, 1978), 33.

12. Roland de Vaux, *Ancient Israel*, 2 vols. (New York: McGraw-Hill, 1961), 1:104.

13. Moule, *The Origin of Christology*, 32.

siah (Mark 14:62), and he does not deny it. Eduard Lohse, the German New Testament scholar, points out appropriately:

> In the multiplicity of its messianic images, Judaism did not know of an anointed one of God who becomes the friend of tax collectors and sinners and in dying takes upon himself the guilt of the world. But the Christians believed in the crucified and resurrected Messiah as the living Lord. Nevertheless, belief in the Messiah is never spoken of in Judaism; belief, as confidence in the truth of God's word, is rather one good work among many in the life the devout.... Hence the Messiah will be the executor of salvation, not its ground, meaning or content.[14]

So the authority of Jesus as the Christ/Messiah indicates his uniqueness as God's anointed and his deity and thus his power that supersedes all other powers and forces.

Authority conferred by anointing is important in the traditional religions of Afro cultures. In Haitian Voodoo oils and ointments created by *houngans* or *mambos* for anointing a devotee confer on the devotee an empowering authority for performing daily tasks. He or she may also derive authority by "inheriting" a *loa* or spirit from a father or mother, but the anointing confers and recognizes that authority as authentic. Also, as the result of anointing, the *houngan* or *mambo* is expected to be wise in family affairs and problems, a good manager of his or her own personal life, politically savvy (since the civil authorities can have an effect on the holding of Voodoo ceremonies), skilled as an intercessor or mediator in civil or private conflicts, and most especially knowledgeable about the rituals for healing and evoking the *loa*.

At the initiation of new devotees of Voodoo during *kanzo*, a ceremony conferring a status second only to that of *houngan* or *mambo*, anointing has a special meaning. After the candidate has made confession to a Catholic priest in a church and to a Voodoo priest or priestess, he or she is bathed and stretched out on a bed of mombin leaves, an emblem of ancestral mother Africa, and the palm branch of the Ayizan tree, Ayizan also being the name of the spirit exorcising evil and the mother of spiritual purification and birth.[15]

---

14. Eduard Lohse, *The New Testament Environment*, trans. John E. Steely (Nashville: Abingdon, 1976), 193.
15. Maya Deren, *Divine Horsemen: The Living Gods of Haiti* (New York: Documentext, McPherson & Co., 1953), 221.

Then the body is anointed with oil once or twice a day for four days. Oil is again used to anoint the hands of the initiate before he or she handles and kneads boiling-hot dough during the *bulé-zin*, "boiling pots" ceremony. Afterwards the anointed must pass their anointed hands and legs through fire, not as an act of courage, but rather as a sign that they as the anointed ones now have superior power, good health, good luck, and wisdom.[16]

Likewise, in Trinidadian Shango new devotees are anointed with olive oil after being possessed by the *orisha*. A sweet oil is used to seal that person's loyalty to a particular *orisha* in a "head-washing" ceremony. During the annual festival in Shango, possessed persons are calmed down by anointing the face, neck, and chest with oil.[17] Therefore, in many Afro Caribbean cultures, anointing bestows a sacred character and authority upon a person. It is a powerful metaphor, and it is associated with Jesus Christ's role as God's Messiah. In Afro Caribbean cultures, that association helps establish Christ as a uniquely powerful and efficacious being with peculiar authority in the world.

CHRIST AS LORD OF THE HEAVENS

Still another significant attribute of Jesus Christ for Afro cultures is his lordship; he is *kyrios*, "Lord." Christ's lordship is not simply an academic question as for many Westerners; instead in African and Afro Caribbean cultures it has urgent practical and religious implications for the cosmos with its divinities and good and malevolent spirits. Hence, his triumph over the cosmos as well as sin finds a resonance in Afro cultures, even in the United States. That triumph is announced in 1 Cor. 8:5-6:

> For although there may be so-called gods [*theoi*] in heaven or on earth — as indeed there are many "gods" and many "lords" — yet for us there is one God, the Father, from whom are all things and for whom we exist, and one Lord, Jesus Christ, through whom are all things and through whom we exist.

We must not assume, however, that this understanding of lordship with its emphasis on Christ's obedience, death, and exaltation

16. Alfred Métraux, *Voodoo in Haiti*, trans. Hugh Charteris (New York: Schocken Books, 1972), 208.
17. George Eaton Simpson, *The Shango Cult in Trinidad* (Rio Piedras, P.R.: Institute of Caribbean Studies, 1965), 48–50.

on the cross was the definitive theology of *kyrios* for all the early Christian communities. We know there was great diversity of teaching about his lordship, some of which emphasized its cosmic impact more than the Pauline stress on its human or anthropological impact. For example, in the Gnostic Gospel of Truth (c. 136–140), thought to have been written by the second-century African Valentinus of Egypt,[18] the Coptic text reads:

> Since the Father is unengendered, he alone is the one who begot him for him[self] as a name, before he brought forth the aeons, in order that the name of the Father should be over their head as lord, that is the name in truth, which is firm in his command through perfect power.... The Son is his name.... The name, therefore, is that of the Father, as the name of the Father is the Son. [38:30b–39:1, 20, 25][19]

The similarities to Philippians 2 (also second-century) are striking: the Gospel of Truth speaks of the preexistence of the Name; Phil. 2:6 speaks of the preexistence of Jesus Christ. Both declare his lordship over creation and all the forces and creatures in creation. It is God, called "the Father" in the Gospel of Truth, who not only confers the name "Lord," but is also at one with the Son and exalts the Son. And there is little doubt that both of these Christian communities used the word "Lord"[20] to affirm both the divinity and the authority of God Almighty in Jesus Christ, who reigns over all of creation, seen and unseen, which the author of the Gospel of Truth calls "aeons."[21]

---

18. See Jacqueline A. Williams, *Biblical Interpretation in the Gnostic Gospel of Truth from Nag Hammadi*, Dissertation Series, no. 79 (Atlanta: Scholars Press, 1988), 4–5.

19. The Gospel of Truth, in Harold W. Attridge and George W. MacRae, eds. and trans., *Nag Hammadi Codex I (The Jung Codex)*, The Coptic Gnostic Library (Leiden: E. J. Brill for the Institute for Antiquity and Christianity, 1985), 113.

20. Williams says because the Jewish reverence for God's name (YHWH) was protected by a taboo forbidding speaking it, all sorts of alternatives sprang up, including the Greek word *kyrios*, "Lord," which was a carry-over from the Hebrew. Hence "Lord" referred to the divine name — an exalted name carried by Jesus Christ in Philippians and by the Son in the Gospel of Truth. But for Valentinus, unlike Paul in Philippians, the Name is given the Son at his begetting in his preexistent state. Thus his cosmic lordship is as significant as his earthly lordship (see Williams, *Biblical Interpretation*, 161).

21. "Aeons" is the Gnostic term for a complex spiritual world that in many cases functioned like the divinities in African traditional religion, except that the Gnostics, unlike the traditional religion either of Africa or the Caribbean, also understood Christ to have been an aeon uniting with the man Jesus and thus bringing about redemption of humankind through a special knowledge (*gnosis*).

Thus the cosmic victory in Christ's lordship was an important teaching in various early Christian communities along with the teaching about his victory for humanity. His lordship is certainly linked to his resurrection, or what Barth aptly calls the Yes of God, already prefigured in the No of God on the cross. Rom. 14:9 verifies this when it says: "for to this end [our adoption by God as God's own] Christ died and lived again, that he might be Lord both of the dead and of the living." Any African would understand the "dead" to include the ancestors and the "living" to include the spirits and other powers in animate and inanimate objects as well as humanity.

Moule points out the crucial link existing between Christ's crucifixion and resurrection and his lordship. It was not that Jesus after death would return to his former life or even to his former spirit in reincarnation, as many first-century Jews believed about their great spiritual heroes and forebears; rather the early Christians believed that Jesus Christ as Lord had gone beyond his old self and beyond death into life eternal before temporal history had begun and would reign within that history that still continues. "If he is the Lord of the End, is he not Lord of the Beginning also? Once he is recognized as God's agent in the consummation, it is not a big step to find in him the Mediator of God's initial creation also."[22]

Toward this end, the Letter to the Colossians, particularly its famous hymn of thanksgiving (1:12-20), is helpful in constructing a christology about Christ's lordship that speaks to the Afro worldview. The Christian community is implored to give thanks to God (a continuation of the Hebrew tradition of confessing the wonderful acts of God in the world and giving God praise because of these acts).[23] But it is an act of confession and praise to God *through* Jesus Christ: "do everything in the name of the Lord Jesus, giving thanks to God the Father through him" (Col. 3:17). Therefore, God, creator of creation, intimately linked to Christ as Lord of creation, is affirmed through this giving of thanks, this act of confession and praise.

God's mighty acts in creation are enumerated: deliverance (rescue) from the rule (ruling power) of darkness (*skotous*), placing us (in the sense of moving mountains or transplanting a people to another

22. Moule, *The Origin of Christology*, 154.

23. Eduard Lohse, *Colossians and Philemon*, trans. William R. Poehlmann and Robert J. Karris, Hermeneia Commentary Series (Philadelphia: Fortress Press, 1971), 34.

land) under his Son's lordship, forgiving our sins. The meaning of
the word *darkness* is not explicated, although Jesus uses the same
word at his arrest: "When I was with you day after day in the temple, you did not lay hands on me. But this is your hour and the
power of darkness" (Luke 22:53). Paul's mission in Acts is also described as turning the Gentiles "from darkness to light and from the
power of Satan to God" (Acts 26:18). We do know that the struggle
between the kingdoms of light and darkness was a dominant theme
in early Judaism and Christianity, as seen in Revelation, the Letter
to the Ephesians, and in the writings of many of the Fathers (e.g.,
Clement, Chrysostom). Although usually interpreted morally, the
term *darkness* also has extratemporal and cosmic significance, such
as in the phrases "darkness below the sea," "the darkness of chaos,"
and "the darkness of the underworld and domain of evil spirits."[24]

Hence, the lordship of Christ is joined with deliverance from
forces and spirits that Afro cultures believe are active and can be
identified in this earthly life as evil and magical, without maligning
their belief in good spirits and divinities. Nor are these magical or
evil forces necessarily independent of Christ's lordship. Isa. 45:7 says
that God created both light and darkness and is the sovereign Lord
of both: "I form light and create darkness, I make weal and create
woe, I am the Lord, who do all these things." The psalmist calls God
the sovereign of darkness (Ps. 105:28). The New Testament refers
to Christ as the *ikon* ("image") of this same God, the first-born of
all creation; all things in heaven and on earth, visible and invisible,
are created through him and in him (Col. 1:16).

Lohse suggests that "just as darkness designates those who are
lost, light characterizes the rule of Christ, which here and now shapes
the life and conduct of those who are baptized."[25] This deliverance is
a liberation for the new life in Christ, our redeemer and emancipator,
and from the captivity of sin and cosmic powers. Hence Christ as
Lord and "first-born of all creation" (*prototokos*) links creation and
crucifixion, made all the more evident in Col. 1:20: "through him
to reconcile to himself all things, whether on earth or in heaven,
making peace by the blood of his cross." This is the foundation of
doctrines of atonement in the Christian tradition.

---

24. William Bauer, *A Greek-English Lexicon of the New Testament*, trans.
William F. Arndt and F. Wilbur Gingrich (Chicago: University of Chicago Press,
1957), 765.
25. Lohse, *Colossians and Philemon*, 38.

But the passage also joins Jesus' lordship in creation to his being "first-born from [of] the dead [*ek ton nekron*]," which is particularly pertinent to the Afro worldview with regard to death and the ancestors. This attribute may be referring also to his resurrection, particularly when recalling 1 Cor. 15:20: "Now is Christ risen from the dead, and become the first-fruits of them that have fallen asleep." It is interesting that few Western exegetes have done much with this phrase except to say that it refers to Christ's resurrection ushering in a new life, a new order for humankind, so that death no longer need be feared. But is death feared in Afro cultures?

Homer (before 700 B.C.?) used *nekron* to mean those no longer alive. In classical Greek death was understood as a virtue because it affects only the body and in so doing frees the soul. It was considered natural as life is natural, that is, a given to be accepted. The concept of death in the first century A.D. can be sketched only from extant Greek and Roman fragments from intellectual circles and Jewish funeral rituals, both of which, however, are carry-overs from the classical period.

But it is quite clear that the New Testament writers feared death as a phenomenon, as a destructive power whose true nature is revealed by Jesus Christ, who brings in return a life that the Book of Common Prayer calls "perfect freedom." How this fear of death developed is not clear. The fear of death did prevail in many Greek intellectual circles during the first century; these intellectuals thought that preparation for death included reading philosophy, thereby preparing the soul for communing with the eternal through contemplation, once it was released from the material body.[26] Unlike classical and Hellenistic Greek thought, the New Testament and early Christians did not consider death to be natural, but rather viewed it as an aberration, a consequence of straying away from or disobeying God's purpose; that is, it was a consequence of sin (John 8:21; Rom. 6:16). Although early Hebraic thought did not speculate about death's origins, the story of creation in Genesis 2-3 ("for the day that you shall eat [of the tree of the knowledge of good and evil] you shall die") suggests that, theoretically, had our primal parents not violated God's taboo, death would not be a part

---

26. For a summary of views about death in ancient Greece, see Jacques Choron, *Death and Western Thought* (New York: Collier Books, 1963), 31–80. For an investigation of early Christian attitudes toward the dead, see Philippe Ariès's massive *The Hour of Our Death*, trans. Helen Weaver (New York: Alfred A. Knopf, 1981), 29–92.

of our condition and history. But there never was a time in human history, according to Paul, when death was not: "Therefore as sin came into the world through one man and death through sin, and so death spread to all [humanity] because all sinned.... Yet death reigned from Adam to Moses, even over those whose sins were not like the transgression of Adam, who was a type of the one who was to come" (Rom. 5:12, 14).

Consequently, death (*thanatos*) is held up as an enemy of God (1 Cor. 15:26); indeed it is the last rupture in the present creation before God reveals the new heaven and the new earth (Rev. 20:14). Death signifies that which is perishable, thereby rendering it unable to enter the imperishable kingdom of God: "For the trumpet will sound, and the dead [*nekroi*] will be raised imperishable, and we shall be changed.... When the perishable puts on the imperishable ... then shall come to pass the saying that is written: 'Death is swallowed up in victory.' 'O death, where is thy victory? O death, where is thy sting?'" (1 Cor. 16:53-55).

In his grand vision of the last times, St. John the Divine says that at that time when human history and time as we now understand them will be no more and Jesus Christ returns to render judgment on all creatures, living and dead, then even the sea, Death, and Hades shall yield up their dead (Rev. 20:13). Hades, the universal burial place for all the deceased unless they died at sea, and Death, even as enemies of God in the last days when God's universal resurrection and judgment occur, will surrender their captives to Christ, thereby acknowledging his lordship.

The notion of death as a journey through perils and terrors was a Jewish and classical Graeco-Roman legacy that came to be a part of Christian burial rituals. In Roman culture, the corpse was buried with a coin, believed to be Charon's fee for taking the dead soul across the Styx, the river in the underworld, on its journey to the dwelling place of the dead. This custom was transformed by the Christians into a description of protective Christian virtues in life, such as good works, baptism, faith, and participating in the Eucharist (the Last Rites), which was given to the dying. Stories also circulated about early Christians asking to be buried with the Eucharist in their mouths, thought to be a throwback to Charon's coin.[27]

---

27. Geoffrey Rowell, *The Liturgy of Christian Burial* (London: Alcuin Club/ SPCK, 1977), 14.

Nevertheless, perhaps because of this prevailing fear of death, Christ's death was seen as disenfranchising its authority because his death overcame sin, the source of death, and thereby fortified Christian hope. Death, therefore, made sense only in the light of the new life and new possibilities revealed in the crucifixion and resurrection of Christ: "Therefore, if any one is in Christ, he is a new creature; the old has passed away, behold, the new has come. . . . For our sake he made him to be sin who knew no sin, so that in him we might become the righteousness of God" (2 Cor. 5:17, 21). Thus, for New Testament Christians, just as Christ is the one through whom God has created the world and humanity, so also he is the one through whom God defeats the terror of destructive powers like death: "Fear not, I am the first and the last, and the living one; I died, and behold I am alive for evermore, and I have the keys of Death and Hades" (Rev. 1:17-18).

As seen previously, death in Afro cultures is generally not something to be feared, but a transitory rupture to be greeted. If it is a "good death," it evinces a return and reunion with the dead and the ancestors. In Haiti, for example, the corpse is dressed in new clothing, and a rosary, soap, a comb, a handkerchief, and face powder are among the items placed in the casket beside the corpse. Money is not among the items, not only because Haitians are so poor, but also because it is believed that if the dead soul has money, he or she will return and take over the rest of the meager wealth of the family. Prickly plants called *hoholi* are placed in the coffin to prevent body snatchers from stealing the corpse for black magic rites at night. Very important are the wakes held on the night of death for dead adults and children alike, generally inside the house. Prayers are said either by a "bush priest" (*prêt' savanne*) or a Catholic priest, after which friends and relatives submit their own petitions to the dead. They ask him or her to speak to a deceased mother or to help the family farm have a good harvest. But outside people sing joyously, children play, and a storyteller entertains with special stories and chansons.[28] Furthermore, on the night following the burial, a *mange mort* (a dinner for the dead) is held as testimony to the deceased enjoying the felicity of the ancestors, where he or she will be in a position to be a guardian for the family and the community. A table is laid out with crockery, cutlery,

28. Melville J. Herskovits, *Life in a Haitian Valley* (New York: Octagon Books, 1975), 206–10.

and various foods for the dead as a sacrifice and at the same time as a petition for continued guardianship and benefaction from the dead.

At the same time, death proffers opportunity for the dead to return reincarnated in a newborn child in the family. Zulu traditionalists in South Africa bury their dead in a squatting position, symbolic of the fetal position of the embryo in the mother's womb, and the place of burial is called the *navel*, indicating hope in rebirth or being "born again" into the family through reincarnation.[29] Yet unlike some Asian religions, reincarnation does not mean endless rebirth after rebirth of the soul in different forms of life, be they plant, animal, or human. In African religion reincarnation occurs only in the family of the deceased, but the *soul* is not reincarnated. It remains in the community of ancestors. For this reason, ceremonies for the dead may last several days, as we have seen in Jamaica and Trinidad, because a "right" or correct burial insures proper arrival at the place of the dead. One plantation owner in Jamaica observed a slave burial and noted at the "covering" of the body:

> [Then] the body is put in the Ground; all the while they are covering it with Earth, the Attendants scream out in a terrible manner, which is not the Effect of Grief, but of Joy; they beat on their wooden Drums, and the women with their Rattles make a hideous Noise. After the Grave is filled up, they place the Soup which they prepared at the Head, and a bottle of rum at the Feet.[30]

The Igbo in Nigeria — like people in parts of Jamaica who conduct Nine Night wakes — have a "second burial" that occurs sometime after the first burial ceremonies in order to make certain that all the proper rituals were carried out, thereby insuring a good relationship between the dead and the living, especially if the deceased should become an ancestor. The idea of "going home" and rejoining the ancestors was common to all the slave communities regardless of the various tribal origins and geography. The Igbo, for

---

29. Kofi Asare Opoku, "Death and Immortality in the African Religious Heritage," in Paul and Linda Badham, eds., *Death and Immortality in the Religions of the World* (New York: Paragon House, 1987), 15.

30. Orlando Patterson, *The Sociology of Slavery: An Analysis of the Origins, Development and Structure of Negro Slave Society in Jamaica* (Rutherford, N.J.: Fairleigh Dickinson University Press, 1967), 196.

example, say the deceased has "gone home" or "gone to the land of the spirits."[31]

This African remnant or survival was also found in American slave burial customs, even after some slaves had converted to Christianity. At burials slaves would sing folk spirituals that spoke of hope for going home. Death was often addressed in these spirituals as "the Great Deliverer." The people would call: "Come down, Death, Right Easy."[32] After the funeral, there was usually much eating and festivity. Often these ceremonies, however, were suspended in order that a "second funeral" could take place some days, weeks, or even a year after the corpse had been interred. Many regarded the second funeral as the *real* funeral and the first as only a "burial." The second funeral acted as a link between the living and the dead and had as its bases the concepts of an afterlife and an eventual deification with the ancestors. The mortuary art and decorations found on slave graves, such as broken water pipes, upturned flowerpots, mirrors, broken glass, dishes, even headlights on tombstones (to illuminate the way as the deceased's soul travels to the glory of the next world), were intended to make the spirit feel at home in its new life. As a slave song reminded the mourners: "Put a pone of co'n bread way down in my hand / Gwine sop on the way to de Promised Land."[33] A woman who had slaves on a South Carolina plantation observed: "The colored people do not fear death; on the contrary, they invest it with a kind of solemn religious exultation, and the majority of them certainly regard the Lord as a warm personal friend. It would seem as if the black man, after ages of trembling worship before his evil deities, turned joyfully to the Christian's God, as one willing to befriend him."[34]

31. S. T. Basden, *Niger Ibos: A Description of the Primitive Life, Customs, and Animistic Beliefs of the Ibo People of Nigeria* (New York: Barnes and Noble, 1966), 282 (cited in Patterson, *Sociology of Slavery*, 198).

32. *The Negro in Virginia*, comp. Workers of the Writers' Program of the Work Projects Administration in the State of Virginia (New York: Hastings House, 1940), 76.

33. David R. Roediger, "And Die in Dixie: Funerals, Death and Heaven in the Slave Community, 1700–1865," *The Massachusetts Review* 22 (Spring 1981): 163–83. For a discussion of African survivals in the burial customs of black Americans, see Robert Farris Thompson's essay on black mortuary art in cemeteries, "The Structure of Recollection: The Kongo New World Visual Tradition," in *The Four Moments of the Sun: Kongo Art in Two Worlds* (Washington, D.C.: National Gallery of Art, 1981), 181–203; see also idem, *Flash of the Spirit: African and Afro-American Art and Philosophy* (New York: Vintage Books, 1984), 128–58.

34. Mary A. Waring, "Mortuary Customs and Beliefs among South Carolina Negroes," *The Journal of American Folk-Lore* 7 (1894): 318–19.

Having now established some of the attributes of the traditional religion's attitudes toward death and lordship of the cosmos, we can now return to our consideration of Christ as Lord of the heavens and of nature. According to Colossians, Jesus Christ is not the first-born in a network of created beings. As the preexistent head, the first-born, he has a primacy that establishes his dominance over all elements and powers. This includes, as the psalmist says, "all that hath breath" and all that hath not breath; it includes the angelic powers and the principalities; all have been created through him and for his benefit. If Ernst Käsemann is correct that the original reference to Christ in Col. 1:18 ("he is the head of the body, the church") meant that he was the head of the cosmos ("church" was inserted later), then his primacy over nature and the cosmos was also of major concern for the early Christians.[35] Christ as first-born means that even what we call "natural" is liberated by the grace of God. As Dietrich Bonhoeffer put it, in the light of Christ the so-called "natural world" has validation only from Christ: "Christ Himself entered into the natural life, and it is only through the incarnation of Christ that the natural life becomes the penultimate which is directed toward the ultimate."[36] Consequently, even evil forces and magical powers used in black magic and witchcraft are under the governance of Christ, very God of very God, or as Col. 1:19 understates it so well: "in him all the fullness [*pleroma*] of God was pleased to dwell."

Karl Barth calls evil powers and principalities under Christ's lordship *nothingness* (*das Nichtige*), that which God rejected, that which God does not will, the chaos of creation. This does not mean that such powers and forces have no significance and can be ignored by Christians or do not matter to God. They are real just as death is real; but the force of their harm is blunted by the victory of Jesus Christ on the cross and in the tomb:

> Nothingness is a factor so real that the creatures of God, and among His creatures man especially, in whom the purpose of creation is revealed, is not only confronted by it and becomes its victim, but makes himself its agent.... The issue in this whole history is the repulse and final removal of the threat thus actualized. And God Himself is

35. Ernst Käsemann, *Essays in New Testament Themes*, trans. W. S. Montague (London: SCM, 1964), 150–53 (cited in Lohse, *Colossians and Philemon*, 42–43).
36. Dietrich Bonhoeffer, *Ethics*, trans. Neville Horton Smith (New York: Macmillan Publishing Co., 1955), 145.

always the One who first takes this threat seriously, who faces and throws Himself against it. . . . As He affirms and elects and works His *opus proprium*, the work of His grace, God is always active in His *opus alienum* as well. And He is always holy. Therefore He always wills that His creature should be holy. He wills to take part in its conflict.[37]

Christ's lordship also includes triumph over demons, which, as we saw, were adopted by the New Testament from popular Judaism as manifestations of evil, as well as the causes for sickness and mental disorders, a belief also in African and Afro Caribbean cultures. Origen in his dispute with Celsus struggled with the authority of demons (*daimones*: "lesser gods"), a concept known in oriental biblical and classical Greek religion, in light of Christ's lordship. Celsus called Christianity an untrue religion, since its followers refused to worship the emperor as a god. He claimed that such conduct subjected Christians to the charge of being traitors and unbelievers or atheists, because the invisible guardians called *daimones*, lesser gods but nonetheless gods, were believed responsible for the appointment of rulers and for all that takes place on earth.

Origen agreed with the classical view about the governance of the world being in control of invisible guardians; but mindful of the biblical concept, he declined to call them *daimones*; rather he called them angels.[38] Angels are good, but *daimones* are evil. Yet even Origen conceded that demons can be used by God to carry out certain divine judgments. It was because the demons (*daimones*), believed to lie behind the authority of the emperor, were called "gods" by the pagan intellectuals, said Origen, that Christians could not swear an oath to the emperor. Thus, while accepting the ancient cosmology about the existence of demons in the created realm, Origen and the early Fathers replaced their authority with that of the angels, thereby relegating demons to the realm of opponents of God rather than divine agents. "While [first-century] Christians could insist that it was the God and Father of our Lord Jesus Christ who appointed the emperor, they did not deny that the emperor was under the guardianship of a *daimon*, and this belief had no small significance for the Christian problem

37. Karl Barth, *The Doctrine of Creation*, vol. 3/3 of *Church Dogmatics*, trans. J. W. Edwards et al. (Edinburgh: T & T Clark, 1958), 352–53.

38. Origen, *Against Celsus* 8.32 (cited in Clinton Morrison, *The Powers That Be: Earthly Rulers and Demonic Powers in Romans 13:1-7* [London: SCM Press, Ltd., 1960], 85).

of 'honoring the emperor' without being involved in a religious recognition."[39]

Because of Christ's cosmological victory as Lord, Colossians affirms boldly that not only has he reconciled sinful humankind to God; Christ has also reconciled an alien cosmos to himself: "to reconcile to himself all things in earth and heaven, making peace by the blood of his cross" (1:20). This includes personal fears and anxiety about evil spirits that may inhabit animate and inanimate things of nature, such as the spirits that dwell in the trees and the shrines. Hence, Afro cultures understand very well the significance of Jesus' retort to the Pharisees in Luke 19:40; after the Pharisees scold him for not refuting his followers' claims about him as the Messiah, Jesus replies, "I tell you, if these were silent, the very stones would cry out." That is, the lordship of Jesus Christ is such a total lordship in nature and the cosmos that even the spirits believed to dwell in the rocks — a reference in line with African traditional cosmology — acknowledge his lordship. Within the Haitian worldview, this rather powerful apologetic of Christ's lordship is viewed as including Christ's power over even zombies and black magic.[40] "The old has passed away, behold, the new has come" (2 Cor. 5:18).

For an Afro christology, therefore, the cross of Christ is not solely an event revealing God's humiliation and our justification and exaltation, important as these doctrines are in the Christian tradition. With regard to the worldview in traditional Afro cultures, the cross becomes primarily an event in a two-act drama. In the first act, God in Jesus Christ undergoes the same death suffered by humankind, with all its suffering, seriousness, and mourning. In the second act, Jesus Christ triumphs in his resurrection from the dead, but not as an ancestor or even chief ancestor, but as God who defeats the troubling powers and forces in the cosmos. As Barth said, "God gives himself, but he does not give himself away." God acted against himself as God on the cross, but God never ceased to be God, Lord of lords and of humankind. "What took place on the cross of Golgotha is the last word of an old history and the first word of a new."[41] Or as a hymn in the Cherubim and Seraphim

---

39. Morrison, *The Powers That Be*, 90.
40. See an ethnobotanist's experiences and findings about zombies in Haiti in Wade Davis, *The Serpent & the Rainbow* (New York: Simon and Schuster, 1985). Unfortunately the book was trivialized and sensationalized in a Hollywood film.
41. Barth, *Church Dogmatics*, 4/1:176.

Church (Nigeria) puts it: "The Satan's Kingdom fall / All creatures now burst forth with joy / The Father glorify."[42]

CHRIST AS HEALER

The major ministry of ritual leaders and priests in Afro traditional religions is healing: healing by faith, herbal medicine, and other remedies. In the Caribbean and in Africa, many turn to these leaders as a primary source of health care and healing. Others engage them after having no satisfaction with Western medicines and physicians. We have seen the important role faith healing plays in the African independent churches, where it is practiced at each service. Herbal or folk medicine maintains that the origin and root cause of ailments may be physical, spiritual, or human. If physical, then a knowledge of plants and herbs is called for. If spiritual, meaning a disjointedness between the person and the divinities, then a knowledge of traditional religion and its ceremonies is called for to eliminate the condition, thereby restoring the person to sound health. If human in origin, then knowledge of superior powers to overcome the evil powers causing the illness is called for. Paul Tillich once wrote that contrary to the West's individualistic approach to the healing of private ailments and neuroses, the biblical approach sees healing and health as a part of the cosmic order: "A symptom of the cosmic disorder is the enmity between the different parts of nature and between man and nature. The order of nature, called the 'covenant' between God and 'the beasts of the field,' is broken, and the result is chaos and self-destruction."[43] This is also the insight in the African and many parts of the Afro Caribbean worlds — sickness has to do not only with individualistic physical ailments, though these are not to be overlooked; it has to do also with cosmic morality.

Within this tradition, therefore, a christology of Jesus Christ as healer strikes a familiar chord for Afro cultures, whether in Africa, the Caribbean, or parts of black American culture. In one of the Twi hymns of a Ghanaian African indigenous church, Jesus is called the "Great Doctor":

---

42. *Holy Hymn Book of the Universal Cherubim & Seraphim Organization* (Lagos: Boladele Brothers, n.d.), Hymn 90.
43. Paul Tillich, "The Relation of Religion and Health," *Review of Religion* 10, no. 4 (May 1946): 349.

A woman is struggling with a difficult labor,
and suddenly all is well.
The child, placenta and all, comes forth
without an operation. He is the Great Doctor!
When he reaches a town, all its secrets are laid bare.
He is the one who digs a plantain shoot
and lays it on bare rock in the morning:
by evening it is full grown with clusters so heavy
they cannot be carried by men in their prime.
Ntafowayifo: Wonder-worker![44]

It need not be recounted how Jesus early on in his ministry revealed his healing powers, as in Mark's Gospel, for example, where
he healed a man of an "unclean spirit" in the synagogue in Galilee
(1:21-28). After synagogue he went home with the brothers Simon
and Andrew, where he healed Simon's mother-in-law (1:29-31). By
evening word of his healing powers had so spread that even people
possessed with demons (*daimonizomenous*) came to the house to be
healed by him (1:32-34).

Healing was more of a central part of Jesus' ministry than his
calling for moral conversion, although this is not to be slighted.
Morton Kelsey in his informative *Healing and Christianity in Ancient Thought and Modern Times* recalls that almost 20 percent of
the Gospel narratives deal with Jesus' healing; Kelsey counts 47
separate instances of mental and physical healing alone. Hence, it
will not do to pass this part of his ministry off as "prescientific"
mythology, as some modern biblical and medical scholars are wont
to do.[45]

Ailments needing relief varied from a simple fever (Peter's
mother-in-law; Matt. 8:14; Luke 4:38) to leprosy (Mark 1:40; Matt.
8:2; Luke 5:12; 17:11) to blindness (Mark 10:46; Matt. 9:27; 20:30;
Luke 18:35) to paralysis (John 5:3-9) to demon possession (Mark
9:14; Matt. 12:22; 17:14; Luke 9:38; 13:10). Jesus' healing powers
became so well known that apparently a tradition arose — similar
to certain traditions in Afro cultures — associating him with conjuring. The Jewish Talmud tells the story of how Jesus of Nazareth was

44. *Jesus of the Deep Forest: Prayers and Praises of Afua Kuma* (Accra: Asempa
Publishers, 1981), 14. *Ntafowayifo* is Twi for "one who performs magical or wonderful deeds."
45. Morton Kelsey, *Healing and Christianity in Ancient Thought and Modern
Times* (New York: Harper & Row, 1973), 54.

hanged on Passover Eve because he was accused of practicing conjuring or sorcery, meaning he healed with the aid of evil or magical
spirits rather than God.[46]

Furthermore, not to be overlooked is the fact that Jesus claimed
faith healing to be a sign of the kingdom of God. When the disciples
of John the Baptist inquired whether Jesus was the Messiah whom
the Jewish people had longed for and who had been promised, he
recited the tradition of Isaiah as proof that the kingdom of God
had indeed already been realized in him. At the same time he linked
healing to ministry among the poor: "Go and tell John what you
hear and see: the blind receive their sight and the lame walk, lepers
are cleansed and the deaf hear, and the dead are raised up, and the
poor have good news preached to them. And blessed is he who takes
no offense at me" (Matt. 11:4-6).

Even when Jesus commissioned his disciples to continue his
ministry, healing was to be a constitutive part of it: "He gave them
authority over unclean spirits, to cast them out, and to heal every
disease and every infirmity" (Matt. 10:1). Likewise, when he sent
them off on assignment, he instructed them, "heal the sick, raise
the dead, cleanse lepers, cast out demons" (Matt. 10:8; cf. Mark
6:7; Luke 9:1-2). And the disciples had success in this area, according to Luke, for they returned rejoicing: "Lord, even the demons
are subject to us in your name," whereupon Jesus cautioned them,
"Nevertheless do not rejoice in this, that the spirits are subject
to you; but rejoice that your names are written in heaven" (Luke
10:17).

Significantly, this link between anointing and healing in Christ
as a sign of divine authority strikes a strong chord in the Afro
worldview, as we noticed already. Kelsey rather wisely points out
that Christ's claim of divine authority (from the one God) demar-
cated his healing from the ancient Greek understanding of healing.
There were Greek deities and cults for healing, including those of:
Apollo, source of epidemics, whose priests healed by mystical methods, such as *incubation*, using dreams and sacrifices; Hecate, whose
potions caused death; Cybele, daughter of Minos, deified because
she healed colds and the flu in children; Hera, goddess of childbirth; Aesculapius, chief deity of healing in Homer's *Iliad* and the
Hippocratic Oath, deified because as a human he used herbs for
healing wounds.

46. Ibid., 57.

We also know of the medical schools in ancient Greece, that of Pythagoras (b. 575 B.C.) in Crotona, which trained physicians and surgeons, and that of Hippocrates (c. 460–370 B.C.), father of modern scientific medicine, who proposed that disease and illness had physical causes stemming from internal bodily disturbances rather than external agents such as demons. However, even he also acknowledged divine causes of illnesses for which he could find no physical cause. He accepted the benefits of charms, amulets, and talismans in healing when he was uncertain about why healing took place after his methods had failed.[47]

Jesus as God's anointed, sharing God's divinity, according to scripture, announces that healing also has cosmic and divine roots: "Sickness and demon possession were considered prime evidences of evil in the world. By dealing with them as the Messiah, the agent of God, Jesus laid the attitude of God toward sickness out on the counter where all could see it."[48] In Acts, Peter confirms this bond between Christ and healing: "You know the word which [God] sent to Israel, preaching good news of peace by Jesus Christ (he is the Lord of all) . . . how God anointed Jesus of Nazareth with the Holy Spirit and with power; how he went about doing good and healing all that were oppressed with the devil, for God was with him" (10:36, 38).

Exactly how one becomes a healer in Afro cultures varies: a divine calling, a legacy from one's father or mother, an apprenticeship, being anointed in an indigenous church. In the United States, during slavery, the black preacher was often also a healer and exorcist, the latter role based on believing evil spirits to be the cause of mental disorders, which had carry-overs into the white world. Slaves who knew herbal medicine were consulted by whites and rewarded when their advice benefited the white population, as was the case in South Carolina in 1751. The state legislature gave a slave his freedom and an annual stipend for life because he healed many whites of snakebite.[49]

In the Caribbean and Africa folk healing almost always has to do with religion (an exception is the case of herbal medicine in some of the French-speaking islands, the American Virgin Islands,

---

47. George Gordon Dawson, *Healing: Pagan and Christian* (London: SPCK, 1935), 71.

48. Ibid., 59.

49. Herbert M. Morais, *The History of the Negro in Medicine* (New York: Publishers Company, 1967), 13.

and the Bahamas; in those places herbal medicine is not linked to religious ceremonies). Prayers and certain rituals are combined with herbs for healing remedies. George Eaton Simpson notes that in Trinidad there are three types of healers — the Shangoists (followers of the Afro traditional religion of Shango), the Shouters (members of a Christian, African-oriented religion), and conjurers, also called "circle people." Both the Shangoists and Shouters are known for their knowledge and power in the spirit world, with the Shouters known for invoking the Holy Spirit for healing. Even conjurers have to consult spirits, albeit evil ones, to afflict a person's enemy.[50]

The tradition of herbal, faith, and magical healing runs deep in Afro cultures, no doubt a legacy of African traditional religion. The fact that healing includes consulting spirits both good and evil has resulted often in some confusion both within Afro cultures and outside those cultures between faith healing (consulting good spirits or Christ) and conjuring (consulting evil spirits). Those who practice the latter — sometimes called "juju" doctors in African cultures and "Hoodoo" or "root" doctors in black American culture — are those who use charms and magic. It is not unusual to see classified notices in black American newspapers advertising "healers," "spiritual healers," "faith healers," and "spiritualists." Zora Hurston did some field work in the black South in the 1930s; there she discovered that the "Hoodoo doctor" was considered a conjurer who practiced "roots," meaning having knowledge of certain herbs and plants that could inflict injury upon one's enemy, although not all the root doctors were Hoodoo doctors. And indeed some Hoodoo doctors also practiced folk medicine for healing purposes.[51]

Traditional healing in Afro cultures does not mean that Western medicine and techniques are neglected in those cultures or that there is a general mistrust of them. On the contrary, both are utilized; however, in many rural areas, where medical facilities are often few or nonexistent, but also in some urban areas, Western medicine has been found to come up short, even in some black communities in the United States. The church — in its Catholic and its more restrictive Protestant form — has been a defender of a Christianized

50. The summaries of various Caribbean anthropological studies dealing with healing are found in Michel S. Laguerre, *Afro-Caribbean Folk Medicine* (South Hadley, Mass.: Bergin & Garvey, 1987), 54–55.

51. See Zora Neale Hurston, *Mules and Men* (1935; reprint, Bloomington, Ind.: Indiana University Press, 1963), 183–89; see also Laguerre, *Afro-Caribbean Folk Medicine*, 53.

Western Hippocratic legacy and has thus looked suspiciously on traditional healing in Afro cultures, usually labeling it "superstition"
or "fetish," or the work of Satan. It also confuses faith healing uti-
lizing good spirits with conjuring using bad spirits. In Catholicism
counteraction against such practices usually has taken the form of
statues and medals of saints, exorcism and pogroms, whereas in the
Protestant tradition it has taken the form of exorcism by much praying and preaching damnation on practitioners. Yet because of success
with traditional herbal and faith healing, people in Afro cultures find
little contradiction in attending churches of missionary Christianity
in the day and consulting the healing powers of the spirits through
the drums and chanting of traditional religion at other times.

Much of the negative feeling of Westerners toward traditional
methods of healing has to do with perceptions of "possession" and
demons. It will be helpful to examine these perceptions critically
and in light of New Testament texts. As to modern Westerners' suspicions about traditional healing we can begin by saying that they
are based on (1) the lack of a clear understanding of the spirits
and divinities, generally thought to be demons, in the traditional
religions of Afro cultures, and (2) a suspicion of nonscientific and
nonphysical explanations for illnesses. We have examined some of
these matters in earlier chapters, but the perception of all spirits
and divinities as demonic needs some attention. The phenomenon
"possession" conjures up a negative meaning among Christians; it
is associated with demons or something satanic. Because possession
will be examined in the section on the Spirit, suffice it to say that
possession in neither ancient nor modern Afro cultures is simply
"emotional," "neurotic," or "psychological." Otherwise, the next
step would be to assume that proper education or psychological
therapy of some kind would deal with the issue personally. In Africa
and Afro Caribbean cultures, possession entails forces, both good
and evil, that cannot be contained by ordinary human therapy or
medical technique; hence one seeks wisdom and skills from a traditionalist priest/leader, a prophet in an indigenous church, or the
extraordinary healing powers of Jesus Christ.

Nor are these forces dealt with by "spiritualizing" them, as
though they are imaginary figments of an unenlightened mind or
an unredeemed sinful soul. Good and evil forces are real even in
the material sense. They affect people visibly and reveal themselves
in various kinds of external behavior, most of which are not harmful. When good spirits and forces possess the souls and bodies at

a ceremony, not subject to the control of ordinary means or the persons themselves, the link between the world of spirits and the living reaches its desired, highest form of communion. But when bad spirits do so, it is undesired and harmful. Possession reveals for believer and nonbeliever alike the mastery of the spirits over matter. As one writer comments about Haitian Voodoo: "Deification, therefore, does not consist in the spiritualization of matter; on the contrary, the ceremony of *retirer d'en bas de l'eau*, which is itself the ritualistic reversal of the rites of death, restores the disembodied soul *to* the physical, living universe. . . . The Haitian is an eminently realistic, reasonable man. His loa must share the needs as well as the privileges of life; to have great power is to need great energy."[52]

The word in the New Testament that most influenced Western Christian understanding of spirits is *daimonion*, a derivative of *daimon*, from which come our words "demon" and "demonic." *Daimonion* occurs some 11 times in Matthew's Gospel, 13 times in Mark, 23 times in Luke, and 6 times in John's Gospel. Paul's First Letter to the Corinthians mentions it 4 times, 1 Timothy once, and it occurs 3 times in Revelation. The word translated "spirit" is *pneuma*, but when a spirit is spoken of as evil and in the plural, or is linked to an illness, then "demon" or a derivative is preferred by the writers, as for example:

> As they were going away, behold a dumb demoniac [*daimonizomenon*] was brought to him. And when the demon [*daimonion*; KJV: devil] was cast out, the dumb spoke, and the multitudes marvelled, saying, "It was never to be seen in Israel." But the Pharisees said, "He casts out demons [*daimonion*] by the prince of demons [*daimonia*]." [Matt. 9:32-34; cf. Mark 1:32-34]

Daimon, as used in reference to the Greek pantheon of gods, is thought to have first been used by Homer to mean "an unknown superhuman factor" in our human world.[53] A *daimon* was a supernatural power, force, or divinity that affected and determined particular acts, situations, circumstances, and experiences in our world. Others, however, think the Greek poet Hesiod (c. eighth century B.C.) first used the expression to mean the souls of the dead who act as guardians and protectors of humans as well as distributors of

---

52. Deren, *Divine Horsemen*, 32–33.
53. Gerhard Kittel and Gerhard Friedrich, eds., *Theological Dictionary of the New Testament*, trans. G. W. Bromiley, 10 vols. (Grand Rapids, Mich.: Wm. B. Eerdmans, 1964), 2:2.

prosperity and wealth. They clothe themselves in darkness in order to be able to walk around the earth undetected and unseen.[54]

Eventually in the Greek world the popular idea developed that souls of the dead were in fact more powerful than the living and could take control of (possess) a living human being. Thus Sophocles (c. 496–406 B.C.) used *daimonizesthia* to describe possession by a *daimon* ("demon"), which did not mean an evil spirit, which is what we would customarily associate with being "possessed." Greek philosophers divinized this popular notion of demons; in the *Phaedo* and the *Republic* Plato wrote of demons acting as intermediaries between gods and human beings, even though the demons were inferior to the heavenly gods. In the *Politics* he says every demon has its own sphere of responsibility as well as the task of looking after people within a particular sphere as its flock. Thus, in popular Greek belief by the time of Plato, a demon was a spirit of the dead that had supernatural powers, the ability to possess a person, and the ability to appear at particular times in the material world and natural phenomena.[55]

Popular Judaism of the Hellenistic period revised the concept of *daimon* to mean something negative. The revision went in two directions: (1) demons were placed under the authority of Satan or Belial as a special order of angels under Yahweh; they were thought to serve as Yahweh's angels of vengeance with the mandate to inflict punishment and wrath on sinners and disbelievers; (2) demons were revised into apostate angels who rebelled against God, entered the natural world, and caused havoc and mischief among God's creation. They were described as angels of fire, snow, and famine, phenomena that bring retribution and devastation upon humankind.

Certainly by the time of the Septuagint, *daimon* ("demons") had already become a term for heathen gods and spirits destructive to humankind, rather than beneficial intermediaries between humanity and the gods, so that the Septuagint, wanting to uphold the honor due the biblical God alone, resisted using the word *daimon* in relationship to God. In Jewish apocryphal literature, the rabbis portray demons as beings "fallen" from God (Gen. 6) and seducers of people, tempting them to witchcraft, idolatry, war, and hatred.[56] They are bonded to Satan and in the Testaments of the Twelve Patri-

---

54. *Encyclopedia of Religion and Ethics*, s.v. "Demons and Spirits (Greek)."
55. Kittel and Friedrich, eds., *Theological Dictionary*, 2:8.
56. Ibid., 2:12–16.

archs (Test. XII), a distinction is made between the spirits of Belial and the Spirit of God. This suggests to some that demons in rabbinic Judaism became the scapegoat theologically and conceptually, so that evil becomes an essential characteristic of spirits outside the Spirit of God.[57] Still it is interesting to note that even the demons in the Gospels know Jesus. When he rebukes a demon-possessed man, he also rebukes the demon responsible (Luke 4:33-39); when he heals several people of diseases, he forbids the demons to speak because "they knew he was the Christ" (4:40-41).

It is clear that the biblical worldview about the powers of demons parallels traditional Afro worldviews about the powers of other divinities and spirits in the universe. The issue is whether one has to accept the biblical cosmology of possession as being essentially evil or under the power of demons to understand the power of Jesus Christ as healer. In other words, is there a built-in cultural and even religious imperialism against possession that has been sacralized by Jewish and Christian theology? And do such claims thereby blight and demonize possession as a form of communication with good spirits and divinities in Afro cultures?

Appropriately enough, the healing power of Christ witnessed in the New Testament included not only mental disorders and illnesses, but also physical illnesses. Thus, he healed leprosy, withered limbs (Mark 3:1; cf. Matt. 12:9; Luke 6:6), blood diseases (Mark 5:25; cf. Matt. 9:20; Luke 8:43), blindness, even a man's ear (Luke 22:49). He contravened the popular view at the time that ill health was the result of sin and punishment from God. He repudiated any notion that a blind man's infirmity was caused by his own trespasses or those of his parents: "It is not that this man sinned, or his parents, but that the works of God might be made manifest in him" (John 9:3).

Therefore Jesus Christ as healer establishes an immediate cultural link to Afro cultures; many certainly in Africa and the Caribbean can understand and even identify with Jesus as healer. The supreme authority of his healing is established in his being God's anointed and Lord over all spirits and forces, good and evil, which we see as a major part of his ministry. The fact that as healer he can even command the evil powers and spirits, something no traditionalist priest can do, is a telling commentary of Christ's victory, since these evil powers and spirits do exist within the cosmos and

57. *The Interpreter's Dictionary of the Bible*, s.v. "Demons, Demonology."

are known in the human community. As the hymn of an African independent church in Ghana testifies to this cosmic victory over evil powers:

> Should the devil himself become a lion
> and chase us as his prey,
> we shall have no fear;
> Lamb of God!
> Satan says he is a wolf —
> Jesus stretches forth his hand,
> and, look: Satan is a mouse![58]

THE LIBERATOR AND THE LIBERATED

The center of Karl Barth's doctrine of justification is Jesus Christ as the judge judged: taking our place, Jesus takes on God's judgment for us. God in divine freedom was able to be both judge and the judged in Jesus Christ, and did so without contradiction. As such, God subjected himself in Christ to the threat of the No of his own wrath and judgment against a sinful humankind. At the same time that God rendered judgment on sinful humankind through Jesus Christ, God also liberated humankind from the power of sin and Satan, thereby revealing in Jesus Christ what Barth calls our true humanity. Thus the basis for understanding humanity is Jesus Christ, not man or woman, biology or psychology, for true humanity is redeemed humanity even with its sinfulness. Our given vocation, therefore, is living truly liberated and free because of Jesus Christ and our obedience to God's will.

This paradigm is useful also for understanding Jesus Christ as the liberator and the liberated, which addresses Afro cultures caught in the evil circumstances of South African apartheid and Caribbean postcolonial captivity of black souls, at least as claimed by the Rastas and their many supporters. The major motif in both areas is liberation: political, religious, and cultural, intended to free blacks as well as whites to be fully human. On the one hand, South African liberation theology depicts Jesus Christ in much the same way as the Latin American and black American liberation theologies: He is the Son of God who identifies with the poor, the underprivileged, the lowly; he is the liberating Jesus who is intent on ending the plight of the

---

58. *Jesus of the Deep Forest*, 18.

oppressed; he reveals a new hope and thereby empowers the poor. As the Reformed South African minister Allan Boesak puts it: As the royal man, he summoned the lowly to claim their own humanity.[59]

Claiming one's humanity within the context of South Africa means affirmation of a *black* humanity, because blackness has traditional, political, and cultural meaning for identity and love of self. This is also the message of Rastafarian liberation theology. Liberation God-talk in Afro cultures, therefore, has to do with an indigenous Christian faith that terminates the colonial legacy of the self-contradiction of locating salvation primarily in European and American ethnocentric interpretations of the Christian faith, where God always seems to be of Graeco-Roman descent. Again Boesak points to South African society:

> The standard Afrikaans-English dictionary (*Het Groot Afrikaans/ Engels*) still teaches students that the correct translation of "black person" is *swartnerf* ("black vein") or *swartslang* ("black snake").... Black children, furthermore, must use the same dictionary and must learn that the English word "gentleman" is translated into Afrikaans by the word "white man" (*witman*). When you, furthermore, discover that "gentile" is defined in terms of "respectable," "civilized," "loving," and "skillful," then both the meaning of the word and its implications are very clear.[60]

But Christ also reveals a new creation (1 Cor. 5:17), linked to baptism. In baptism one establishes a community with Christ and a community with forgiven sinners, including whites, which has an "earthly" character for black South Africans: "Man does not wait to be transformed into a new man in heaven; it takes place here on earth."[61] This new creation, which is the redeemed community, includes justice on earth, a justice that will break through the white claims of biblical authority for apartheid and break down the sinfully conceived barriers between blacks and Afrikaners in the current community. "Who can she be, the Bride of the Lamb?" reflects a South African black on Rev. 21:9. "The Bride of the Lamb is not, as one may expect, the 144,000 elect ones, the perfect number indicating those who are saved.... She is not the angels, or the saints who have

---

59. Allan Boesak, *Black and Reformed: Apartheid, Liberation and the Calvinist Tradition* (Maryknoll, N.Y.: Orbis Books, 1984), 13.

60. Ibid., 16–17.

61. Manas Buthelezi, "The Theological Meaning of True Humanity," in Basil Moore, ed., *Black Theology: The South African Voice* (London: C. Hurst & Co., 1973), 99.

suffered so for the sake of the Lamb. The Bride is not the church but the world, the holy city.... Ultimately, God's concern is not simply a pure church but a purified world, a new creation."[62]

While Rastas will not be drawn to the message that Christ as liberator also sets the terms for the liberated, their own theology of liberation revealed in their music has penetrated the soul of Afro traditions throughout the Caribbean, Africa, and the Americas. Archbishop Desmond Tutu once wrote that as we believe in one Lord, Jesus Christ, even in South Africa and the Caribbean, our cultural separation must not keep us separate but rather must be an opening for sharing with others the *historical* possibility for creating a new humanity. "Our explication of the gospel must be universal enough to include the material conditions in which people are forced to live. There is only one history, one Creator, and one Lord and Savior Jesus Christ."[63]

However, Jesus Christ as liberator also affects structures and social forces in South Africa and other such oppressive societies. Col. 1:15-23 offers political aspects of christology, aspects that often have been "spiritualized." In Col. 1:16, the author addresses "principalities" (*archai*) and "powers" (*exousiai*). In Greek the prefix *arch-* pointed to power being held by an organization or officeholder in that society. When combined with other words, the word established a vocabulary describing almost every political, religious, or civil functionary in the empire. So *archon*, for example, which means "incumbent," applied to the emperor as well as the mayors (*archontes*) of Greek towns. But also the term most likely included the context of Jewish Palestine that was divided into areas under *hyperarchoi*.[64] Hence this term, linked to political and social power and its structures, was also used to portray cosmic forces and powers, which in turn are linked to Christ.

At the same time, "authority" and "powers" (*exousia*) in Greek also point to visible, concrete human structures of power with a delegated or conferred authority from a higher authority to make decisions and to act. So, significantly, Christ is identified as the one

---

62. Allan Boesak, *Comfort and Protest: Reflections on the Apocalypse of John of Patmos* (Edinburgh: Saint Andrews Press, 1987), 135.

63. Desmond Tutu, "Black Theology/African Theology — Soul Mates or Antagonists?" in Gayraud S. Wilmore and James H. Cone, eds., *Black Theology: A Documentary History, 1966–1979* (Maryknoll, N.Y.: Orbis Books, 1979), 476.

64. The rather incisive interpretations of this term are found in Walter Wink, *Naming the Powers: The Language of Power in the New Testament* (Philadelphia: Fortress Press, 1984), 13ff.

in whom all authority (*exousiai*) has been created. Like cosmic forces both good and evil, so also human political structures and author- ities are at the service of God and not outside God's dominion. Their purpose is to serve Christ, and when these authorities violate this purpose, Christians should remind them of their own seal of authority and purpose.[65]

The supreme service of the Christian community in the midst of the civil community, wrote Barth, is to remind the latter of its mandate under God and to summon it to that mandate when it breeds injustice or makes Godlike claims through political forces like totalitarianism. The state — the civil community — is, like the church, not a part of the order of creation, but of the covenant be- tween God and humanity; standing under God's grace, the state has a mandate of obedience for furthering peace and justice. The state belongs ultimately to Jesus Christ and serves him and its redeemed citizenry.[66]

Hence, the authority (*exousiai*) of the state is legitimized and sanctioned finally by its service to, not violation of, humankind. The fostering of injustice — whether it be apartheid or other forms of captivity that mar and stifle blacks' and whites' expression of re- deemed humanity — cannot be a legitimate function of statecraft. The source of legitimized civil authority is Jesus Christ himself, "who is the head of all rule (*arches*) and authority (*exousias*)" (Col. 2:10). And if "rule" here refers to rituals and beliefs, which may presume a sovereignty of their own, then the state has no ultimate authority to identify its politics with God's will and expect ultimate loyalty from its citizens.[67] If the state does so, then the church has the task of preaching and acting in order to show such a function an affront both to ultimate loyalty due God in Jesus Christ and to the state's mandate from God, be it in South Africa, Nazi Ger- many, or the United States. Such claims by the state "delegitimize" it theologically, and earn it justifiable opposition from Christians and others. As Jesus reminded Pilate, "You would have no author- ity (*exousian*) over me unless it had been given you from above" (John 19:11).

Jesus Christ, God's revelation of true humanity, is not only the liberator but at the same time is the liberated. Jesus as the liberated

65. Ibid., 64.
66. See R. E. Hood, "Karl Barth's Christological Basis for the State and Polit- ical Praxis," *Scottish Journal of Theology* 33 (June 1980): 223–38.
67. See Wink's rendering of this passage in *Naming the Powers*, 79.

one serves as a model for the liberation of both the so-called natural order and the human community. This is of great importance for Afro christology because community in the African view provides a people and persons with identity. Community embraces, however, the living and the dead, as we have seen, and also sinner and redeemed, white and black, whose proper role in the advancement of justice has been revealed by and in Jesus Christ, *vere homo*. In the reconciling act of God in Christ, no human society is a lost society since the "natural" cosmos has been redeemed, even if our time is provisional time until the final liberation takes place in the coming of Christ.

This reconciliation may be better understood in classical terms like *justification*, which was revealed at the crucifixion and affirmed at the resurrection of Christ. Justification is not simply God's judgment on sinful humanity and individual persons, whose sin created an adversarial relationship over against God. Nor is justification simply God's pardon as judge, a pardon that happened "once for all." Nor can it be assumed that the Reformation's understanding of the concept — its claim being that justification means that Jesus Christ ended the adversarial role between sinful humanity and God — is the primary way Paul conceived the function of the term in Romans.

Justification in Romans also has to do with emancipating or liberating humankind from the bondage and slavery of sin in order that human beings might know true freedom in God as the freed, as the liberated: "We know that our old self was crucified with him so that the sinful body might be destroyed, and we might no longer be enslaved to sin. For he who has died is freed from sin . . . and having been set free from sin, [you] have become slaves of righteousness" (Rom. 6:6-7, 18).

Nor is justification restricted to the Christian community. That it now knows true liberation through Christ's justification and partnership actually means that the Christian community is mandated to preach and act in solidarity with the entire human community and a wayward creation: Jesus Christ as true humanity reveals and models true freedom as the liberated, thereby freeing up the Christian community to venture forth boldly often in uncharted waters and engage in concretizing new visions of a new creation within the human community where political authorities and evil spiritual powers reign. Jesus Christ as the liberated one models how the members of this new community are to be "fools" for the sake of a righteous and just society. Justification in Christ provides both security and insecurity, the security of eventual victory, the insecurity of oppression and setbacks. To quote Allan Boesak:

> "New" freedoms degenerate into slavery before we know it, and how often do we turn the joys of liberation into the desperation of a new tyranny. We seem cursed with the cynical wisdom of Ecclesiastes 1:9: "There is nothing new under the sun."[68]

---

68. Boesak, *Comfort and Protest*, 131.

7

Spirit and Spirits: Pneumatology and Afro Cultures

The traditional worldview in African and Caribbean cultures — where the Christian faith presently thrives — is spiritual. At the same time, spirits or divine intermediaries in those cultures, variously described as divinities or gods, are the tools most used by the church in the West and the East, mainstream and fundamentalist, to dismiss Afro cultures as superstitious, polytheistic, heathenish, fetishistic, and animistic. In modern thought, spearheaded by René Descartes (1596–1650), spirits have become suspect because experience and natural reason are the means for verifying truth claims. Although Descartes himself understood God as one of the three constituents of the world ("a substance infinite, eternal, immutable, independent, omniscient, omnipotent, by which myself and all other things have been created"), he said that matter and mind provide us with tools for testing and verifying what he called the "self-evident truth" of a claim. Nothing is true that the individual does not recognize to be true. In effect, what the Christian tradition calls Spirit was transformed into what Descartes called the mind, which is the motor of the intellect. This change was really the demythologization of spirit, which thereby endowed mind/spirit with material causality.

British empiricism, directed by John Locke (1632–1704), Anglican bishop George Berkeley (1685–1753), and David Hume (1711–1776), the Enlightenment, and modern psychiatry furthered suspicion of religious phenomena such as spirits because the self-evident truth of spirits could not be rationally explained. But as Paul Tillich comments, originally spirit meant a presence with powers and dynamism beyond rational and emotional categories. Modern thought reduced spirit as a real, vital dimension in and beyond the human experience. The effect is that spirits in modern thought are

183

considered little more than a bit of amusing folklore. All this has
taken a toll on Christian theology, for "without knowing what spirit
is, one cannot know what Spirit is."[1]

Understanding the spirits is certainly crucial for understanding the African and Caribbean worldview as well as the traditional
religion that has shaped it. Most African and Caribbean cultures, as
we have seen, are clear about being under the jurisdiction of God,
variously called the supreme deity or the High God. But spirits,
which are under God's jurisdiction, provide a means of dealing with
misfortunes, anxieties, no-way-out situations, and sickness. The relationship of spirits to the biblical view of the Spirit and the dogmatic
view of the Holy Spirit is an issue for Christian theology, since the
Holy Spirit is, according to the doctrine of the Trinity, a part of
God.

That the cosmos is occupied, if not partially governed, by
forces and spirits beyond the Holy Spirit is apparent in both Old
and New Testaments. The question is: How are these acknowledged
spirits related to the tradition of the Holy Spirit? And is the Holy
Spirit, mentioned in the New Testament and in early statements
regarding the Trinity, the same as "the Spirit" in both testaments?
Likewise, with regard to spirit possession, so characteristic of African traditional religion and its New World derivatives, is there a
substantial distinction between being possessed by the Holy Spirit
(such as occurs in black and Holiness churches in America, in traditionalist churches in the Caribbean, and in churches involved in
the charismatic movements) and being possessed by a good spirit
or divinity in Afro cultures?

Is it possible to have a hierarchy of spirits that would allow for
an accommodation of the Holy Spirit, such as the Egyptian Christians called the "Tropici" (fourth century) proposed, namely, that
the Holy Spirit, though higher than other spirits, be thought of as
exercising oversight as the "ministering spirit"? In view of the charge
of "worship of dead spirits" against Afro traditionalists, is there a
difference between the worship of God or the supreme deity, on the
one hand, and veneration of ancestral spirits, together with offerings
and sacrifices to divinities and spirits for penance or assistance, on
the other hand?

---

1. Paul Tillich, *Systematic Theology*, 3 vols. (Chicago: University of Chicago
Press, 1963), 3:22.

THE BIBLICAL TRADITION

Spirit in both testaments can mean a "breeze," a "wind," a "move-ment of air," as in Gen. 1:2b: "The Spirit [*wind* in the Hebrew] of God was moving over the face of the waters," and John 3:8: "The wind [*spirit* in the Greek] blows where it wills, and you hear the sound of it, but you do not know whence it comes or whither it goes; so it is with every one who is born of the Spirit." In the latter passage, Jesus makes a play on words, since the same Greek word (*pneuma*) can mean both "wind" and "spirit."

Furthermore, as we know, there are a number of associations between God and Spirit in the Old Testament, as in the phrase "the Spirit of God"; it is the Spirit that inspires the prophets (1 Sam. 10:6-10), arouses people to frenzy (and thus is assessed to be evil and negative [1 Sam. 16:14-16, 23; 19:9; 1 Kings 22:21]), stirs up aggressive energy in the leaders of Israel (Judg. 3:10; 14:6; 1 Sam. 11:6), and reveals the presence of God (Ps. 139:7). In the New Testament the Spirit is, moreover, linked with various sorts of beings such as angels, souls of the dead, and souls of the redeemed (Heb. 12:23).

Paul, of course, distinguishes between the Spirit of God and the spirit of humankind (1 Cor. 2:12; Eph. 2:2) and between the flesh and the spirit (Rom. 8:4; Gal. 5:16-24) as well as making other similar distinctions (1 Cor. 2:5; 2 Cor. 3:6). Furthermore, spirits as beings permeating all human affairs have political significance, as is shown when Paul speaks of the *exousiai* in Romans 13 and 1 Cor. 15:24. New Testament scholars have pointed out that this notion of Paul's reflects the belief of his day that there is a correspondence between the world of spirits and the world of politics: "The rule of the Roman Empire was the simultaneous integrated endeavor of spiritual and human authorities," but all came under the lordship of Jesus Christ.[2]

The Spirit is handled differently in the Gospels of the New Testament, largely reflecting the legacy of rabbinic Judaism. In Mat-thew and Mark there are 23 sayings about the Spirit, 14 of which speak of "unclean spirits" or something similar, meaning "demons" or "demonic" forces. The other references, however, speak of the

---

2. Clinton Morrison, *The Powers That Be: Earthly Rulers and Demonic Pow-ers in Romans 13:1-7* (London: SCM Press, 1960), 25; see also Oscar Cullmann, *Christ and Time: The Primitive Christian Conception of Time and History* (Philadelphia: Westminster Press, 1950).

Spirit as a characteristic of God's power. Additionally, in the three synoptic Gospels, Jesus himself says little about the Spirit. Mark does remark that the Spirit came upon Jesus at his baptism and immediately drove him into the wilderness, where the devil tempted him (1:9, 12). Matthew says the Spirit was linked to Jesus at his very conception (1:18).

On the other hand, in Luke-Acts and John, Jesus is connected quite explicitly with the Spirit. Luke, like Matthew, links the life-giving power of the Spirit with Jesus' conception: "The Holy Spirit will come upon you [Mary]...; therefore the child to be born will be called holy, the Son of God" (Luke 1:35). Hence even in his mother's womb Jesus possesses the Spirit, which he sends forth after his resurrection (24:49). The Spirit, a sign of the new age in the church given in the sacrament of baptism (Acts 2), is not dependent on baptism for its empowering or activity. It came like a mighty wind at Pentecost on those gathered and looked like tongues of fire, possessing or overtaking all present with such an impressive force that they began to speak in tongues (Acts 2:2-4). John recalls that Jesus promised to send the Spirit (of truth) as a comforter and counselor for his disciples after his death; from the African viewpoint it is significant that this Spirit "will not speak on his own authority, but whatever he hears he will speak" (14:15-25; 16:7-15). This resembles African religion's belief that God delegates authority to spirits and divinities.

In 1 Peter 1:12 the Spirit is identified as the Holy Spirit that inspires preachers of Christ: "...by those who preached the good news to you through the Holy Spirit sent from heaven," whereas 3:19 says Christ between his crucifixion and resurrection, while in Hades, preached to "the spirits in prison," who were there because of disobedience before and during the life of Jesus. New Testament scholars dispute just exactly what this latter passage means; some suggest that the phrase refers to fallen angels mentioned in Gen. 6:1-4, while others say they are the spirits of the disobedient who died in the Flood (Gen. 6:12f.) or the powers of evil over whom Christ as redeemer is triumphant.

The early Christian communities absorbed the concept of Spirit circulating in the surrounding, dominant Graeco-Roman cultures; the concept was a part of popular Judaism, which was influenced by those cultures and Persian religion, with its emphasis on cosmological conflict between the powers of good and evil. In Greek culture the word *pneuma* meant several things: "wind," as in nature but also in the divine; "breath," that which is inhaled and exhaled by humans and animals; "life," the Spirit being the agency and sign of living; and "soul," along with Spirit the principle of life, which is freed from imprisonment in the body at death, and returns to higher realms from whence it has come.[3] The latter concept is one of the sources of Greek dualism, which encumbered the Church Fathers when they tried to shape Christian doctrine by fitting together contemporary philosophical concepts and biblical thought.

The Hellenistic Jewish philosopher Philo (fl. 20 B.C.– A.D. 40) and the Greek translation of the Hebrew Bible, the Septuagint, heavily influenced the understanding of Spirit in first-century Judaism. Spirit, translated as *pneuma* in the Septuagint, during Philo's time meant something permeating all of matter, both animate and inanimate. But Philo said it also meant other things: it distinguishes humans from beasts, is a gift from God (the *pneuma Theou*), and inspires the prophets to prophecy. "The *pneuma* which represents the rational soul is an impress of the divine power, but the *pneuma* which man receives as a morally striving rational being is also an emanation of the divine nature."[4] The question is: What is the difference between the two spirits discussed by Philo? The Septuagint associated *pneuma* with ecstatic prophecy and God's Spirit for the first time, an assertion that has some parallels in Afro traditional religion.[5]

Spirit in the Revelation of St. John the Divine (c. 95–98) takes on a different meaning altogether — one that is closer to an understanding of spirit in African traditional religion. The Spirit is power-giving. It is the motor that makes visions possible (17:3). It speaks to the community rather than the individual, although the latter is not ignored: "I was in the Spirit on the Lord's day, and I heard behind me a loud voice like a trumpet saying, 'Write what you see...'" (1:10). The similarity between this Hellenistic oriental view and the African traditional view is especially noticeable in the mandate of the seven spirits, intermediaries between God and Christ. They stand before God's throne with the angels, so they are not fallen, and act as messengers of God throughout the earth and to humankind. "The fact that the spirits are regarded as angels is no longer a difficulty.

---

3. Gerhard Kittel and Gerhard Friedrich, eds., *Theological Dictionary of the New Testament*, trans. Geoffrey W. Bromiley, 10 vols. (Grand Rapids, Mich.: Wm. B. Eerdmans, 1968), 6:334–39.

4. Ibid., 6:374.

5. Alasdair I. C. Heron, *The Holy Spirit* (Philadelphia: Westminster Press, 1983), 32.

The two terms are often interchangeable.... The angel is a mediator between God and men who intercedes for men and presents their prayers to God."[6]

At the same time, in Palestinian Judaism, out of which the early Christian communities arose, "spirit" also came to include evil spirits and demons, particularly in the apocryphal writings about the end of history and time. Evil spirits, whose authority was Satan, were believed to dwell in the created world below the higher world of spiritual beings, steadily threatening humankind with witchcraft, evil, and distortions of God's intended creation. We have inherited this meaning of demons; for us, the word *demons* has come to mean beings who are negative and disobedient toward God and are intent on marring God's creation; and we have come to associate these beings with heathenism or paganism. The classical Greek term *daimon*, meaning a supernatural power or divinity in the natural world, turns up only once in the New Testament: in Matt. 8:31, although there are many derivatives, as we noticed. In Hebrew the corresponding term for such intermediaries between God and humankind is *mal'akim*, messengers of God (Gen. 19:1); they are used by God (Yahweh) for inflicting vengeance on enemies (2 Kings 19:35; Ps. 35:5f.) and creating disorder in the natural realm (2 Sam. 24:16).[7]

Perhaps the best summary of the traditional Christian attitude toward spirits, good and bad, is 1 Cor. 10:19ff., particularly v. 20: "I imply that what pagans sacrifice they offer to demons and not to God. I do not want you to be partners with *daimoniois*.... You cannot partake of the table of the Lord and the table of the *daimoniois*." The question is whether the New Testament's rabbinic-derived cosmology about spirits, which are thought always to be evil and therefore a distortion of God's creation and purpose, is such a fundamental part of Christian faith that African and Afro Caribbean cultures, whose view and experience of spirits do not correspond to this theological negation, have to underwrite it as necessary for Christian faith.

Is the Holy Spirit of doctrine necessarily the Spirit of scripture? Is it thinkable for the Spirit, or even the Holy Spirit, to have a beneficial and mutual relationship with other spirits, particularly good spirits? Even if we recognize the lordship of God in Jesus Christ over good and evil spirits, might there not still be in the Christian

6. Kittel and Friedrich, eds., *Theological Dictionary*, 6:451.
7. Morrison, *The Powers That Be*, 11.

tradition a place for a pluralism of beliefs about the Spirit and the spirits in the cosmos, as in the African tradition and its New World descendants? In other words, is there a built-in cultural imperialism about the unity of God and Spirit, which has been sacralized by biblical theology and past Christian doctrine? That there is tension is clear. The critical question for pneumatology is whether in the midst of this tension an alternative theology about spirits and the Spirit — a theology that is both biblically and doctrinally faithful to God's revelation in Christ — can emerge. Can there be a meeting of the church's *tradition* and the African tradition? One African scholar has stated the tension quite well:

> The New Testament is extremely aware of the spirit world and its nearness to the human world.... Africans know only too well that spirits exist and form an essential part of man's spiritual environment. The Gospel in Africa must address itself to the spirit world as well and not to the human world alone.[8]

THE DOGMATIC TRADITION

Within the tradition the theological concept of the Spirit and the Holy Spirit has been eclectic at best. The Spirit and Holy Spirit were largely topics for pious devotion during the early centuries of the church rather than grist for focused theological debate comparable to the attention given to christology; rather, theological consideration of the significance of the Spirit began on a note of expediency: it became necessary to harmonize New Testament references with the dogmatic defense of the Holy Spirit. The renewal of interest in modern times in mainstream churches, particularly in America and the mission field, has come about because of Pentecostalism and the charismatic movement, although the Spirit has long played an important role in American black religion. While the Holy Spirit as such is almost absent from the Gospels, it does play a more prominent role in the Acts of the Apostles, in Paul's letters, and in the Book of Revelation, as we have noticed.

Nonetheless, most theologians concede that the biblical notion of the Spirit is not meant to function in the same speculative way as the dogmatic notion of the Holy Spirit, the third "person"

---

8. Swailem Sidhom, "The Theological Estimate of Man," in Kwesi Dickson and Paul Ellingworth, eds., *Biblical Revelation and African Beliefs* (London: Lutterworth Press, 1969), 103.

of the Trinity. Nor was there agreement among theologians of the early Christian church about the nature, status, and function of this Holy Spirit. It was God as Father and God as Son (or Logos) that preoccupied them for the most part, as they sought to demonstrate that Christian wisdom was superior to pagan wisdom about creation and cosmic powers. The exception was such groups as the second-century Montanists, who paid a good deal of attention to the divinity of spirits. Although originating in Asia Minor, Montanism quickly spread in ancient northern Africa, whose worldview paralleled the traditional, sub-Saharan African view about the divinity of spirits. Even Tertullian, who was from northern Africa, was persuaded by the Montanists' views and joined them for a while.

However, Tertullian eventually distanced himself from the Montanist views. He became the first "approved" (orthodox) theologian to identify the Holy Spirit as God. He makes this identification in his *Against Praxean*, where he states that the godhead is a single divine "substance" that has three separate but coexisting and continuing "persons," called Father, Son/Logos, and Spirit. Origen, who likewise was an African from Egypt, also worked on the emerging doctrine of the Holy Spirit. Yet both identified the Holy Spirit as a created being rather than a "begotten" or uncreated being, albeit existing from eternity with the divine. Very little systematic work was done about the nature of the relationship between the Spirit and God, and hence its development remained deliberately undefined and imprecise for the early part of the dogmatic tradition.

But in the fourth century Athanasius set out to take up the challenge by trying to prove that the Spirit is indeed fully divine with the Father and the Son in the godhead. To claim otherwise for him undermined his inherited Greek philosophical legacy of true divinity and deity as unchanging, immutable, and indivisible. For Athanasius, for the Christian God to lack these attributes meant that God would have the vulnerability of God's creatures, since they were created *ex nihilo*, "from nothingness," and thus changing, mutable, and subject to death. The Spirit, sent by the Son, sanctifies and empowers us, so that we become "partakers" of God. To be able to do this, the Spirit, which Athanasius also called the Holy Spirit, has to have the same divine nature and stuff (*homoousios*) as God: "The holy and blessed Triad is indivisible and one in Itself. When mention is made of the Father, the Word is also included, as also the Spirit Who is in the Son. If the Son is named, the Father is in the Son, and the Spirit is not outside the Word. For there is one single grace which is fulfilled from the Father through the Son in the Holy Spirit."[9]

Basil the Great (c. 330–379), first using the phrase "Holy Spirit" in the title of a work (*On the Holy Spirit*), in 375 attacked the party called the "Macedonians," who argued that the Holy Spirit was not divine. Relying both on scripture and oral tradition moving around the church at the time, he defended the Holy Spirit as being of the same stuff as God the Father and God the Son. But he also claimed that the Spirit has a function in creation much like that ascribed to Christ in Colossians: "It is through the Spirit that all the dispensations are carried out — Creation, the Old Covenant, the Incarnation in all its circumstances, the ministry of the Church, the future Advent."[10] The Spirit is not God, who is eternal and "unbegotten," or from God in the same way as the Son, who is eternal but "begotten" by God; rather it "proceeds" *from* God (John 15:26) like breath from God's mouth. Although Basil was searching for language compatible with scripture, even he declined to identify the Holy Spirit outright with God, although he and the other Cappadocians, Gregory of Nyssa (c. 330–395) and Gregory of Nazianzus (329–389), did write and preach endlessly about its inclusion within the godhead. Their influence was apparent in later orthodoxy, which identified the Spirit in scripture with the Holy Spirit and declared it coequal with God as Father and God as Son (*consubstantiality*) in 381 at the Second Ecumenical Council at Constantinople. Hence, the Holy Spirit became a part of the Christian God more by reasonable induction than explicit biblical deduction.

The peculiar view of the Holy Spirit in the West, "the double procession," found in the Western version of the Nicene Creed ("We believe in the Holy Spirit...who proceeds from the Father *and* the Son"), originated with Augustine trying to go inside the godhead to conceive how the Spirit got there in the first place and how it functioned. He concluded that it was of the same stuff as the Father and the Son and existed always, but at the same time was generated or "proceeded" from both within the godhead itself, hence the phrase "double procession." This idea about the unity of God not only strained belief in only one God (monotheism), but also rendered God more abstract and complicated and reinforced

9. *Ad Sarapionem Orationes* 1.14 (cited in J. N. D. Kelly, *Early Christian Doctrines*, rev. ed. [New York: Harper & Row, 1978], 258).

10. *De Spiritu Sancto* 39 (cited in J. F. Bethune-Baker, *An Introduction to the Early History of Christian Doctrine* [London: Methuen & Co., 1958], 219).

the guardianship of Graeco-Roman cultural thought via the church's professional theologians, many of whom were bishops. The abstraction and complication are apparent in passages such as the following:

> And it is proved by many other testimonies of the Divine Word, that the Spirit, who is specially called in the Trinity the Holy Spirit, is of the Father and of the Son: of whom likewise the Son Himself says, "Whom will I send unto you from the Father...." And so we are taught that He proceeds from both, because the Son Himself says, He proceeds from the Father. And when He had risen from the dead, and had appeared to His disciples, "He breathed upon them, and said, Receive the Holy Ghost," so as to show that He proceeded also from Himself.[11]

This doctrine was anchored in Western Christendom at the Council of Toledo in 675. The Spirit was declared inseparable, but (notwithstanding a good deal of rhetoric to the contrary) was still not quite equal in status or attributes: the Father is eternal, not born, since this would mean a lessening of his immutable character; the Son is eternal but also was born; the Holy Spirit has eternality and no birth, but proceeds from both the Father and the Son. At a previous synod meeting also at Toledo (in 589) the *filioque* ("who proceeds from the Father and the Son") phrase was officially added to what we popularly call the Nicene Creed in the West, but it was not added to the version of this creed in Eastern Orthodox churches. Von Harnack speculates that this usage in fact was already circulating in Spain prior to the synod, but came to be identified as the *fides catholica* because of the language of the so-called Athanasian Creed.[12] This revised Nicene Creed became a part of the liturgy in the West when the Holy Roman Emperor Charlemagne (c. 742–814; emperor: 800) used it at his chapel in Aachen. The Council of Florence in the fifteenth century regularized this revision, saying that the Holy Spirit does in fact originate from the Father and the Son, which are all within the one God.

Such language only encouraged further speculation and philosophical explication, struggling to make rational sense of a nonrational biblical concept that was quite concrete in the Old Testament and quite active and dynamic in the New Testament. In this sense

---

11. *On the Trinity* 15.26, in Whitney Oates, ed., *Basic Writings of Saint Augustine*, 2 vols. (New York: Random House, 1948), 2:871.

12. Adolf von Harnack, *History of Dogma*, trans. Neil Buchanan, 7 vols. (New York: Dover Publications, 1961), 4:133–35.

the additional theological speculation by people like Peter Lombard (c. 1100–1160) and Thomas Aquinas (c. 1225–1274) really brought about what can be called a "disembodied Spirit," since the Spirit's character and the nature of God became increasingly more distant, incomprehensible, and incoherent in relation to the concrete situation. The Orthodox theologian Vladimir Lossky, commenting on the increasingly protective stronghold around the Spirit erected by academic and dogmatic theologians as the only authentic guardians of the tradition, wrote: "This is a sort of Caesaropapism of the scholars, which might succeed in imposing its authority over the Church, if tradition were not for Her a living reality of revelation of the Holy Spirit."[13]

THE AFRICAN TRADITION

Yet the question still to be explored is the relationship between the Holy Spirit in Christian dogmatics and the spirits in the African tradition and Afro cultures. E. Bolaji Idowu observes that while the conception of spirits is not always as tidy and precise as some would like, nonetheless they can be explained: spirits are present as "shades or vapors which take on human shape; they are immaterial and incorporeal beings" that can assume many kinds of shapes in inanimate natural objects like trees, rivers, mountains, etc., or in natural phenomena such as thunderstorms, rainbows, and the earth; they can commune with humans through their presence in these objects and phenomena or through the possession of persons.[14]

Spirits are everywhere in the cosmos as a part of the *omni* attribute of the supreme deity and are manifested for good purposes and evil purposes.[15] Geoffrey Parrinder, a British Africanist, claims Africans pay so much attention to spirits because of their power to influence their lives. However, he rather shortsightedly restricts the concept mostly to spirits in natural forces, such as the sun and the moon, storms, earth, and water, and he thereby reinforces the

13. Vladimir Lossky, *In the Image and Likeness of God* (Crestwood, N.Y.: St. Vladimir's Seminary Press, 1985), 72.

14. E. Bolaji Idowu, *African Traditional Religion: A Definition* (London: SCM Press, 1973), 174.

15. See Chapter 4, above.

charge that Africans worship inanimate objects and hence reinforces the charge of "animism."[16]

In addition to ancestral spirits and the spirits of the dead (whose role is similar to those in popular Greek thought during Plato's times and popular Jewish thought during the first century B.C.), there are other spiritual categories in African traditional religion: "born-to-die" spirits, ghost-spirits, guardian spirits.

"Born-to-die" spirits are wandering spirits, which, in a pact with other mischievous spirits, return to their community on certain days and dates, seek out the wombs of pregnant mothers to be born in order to die, and eventually make the woman infertile, unless certain rites are done to protect her and to prevent a recurrence of this situation in the woman's womb. "Sometimes, the spirit may be made to 'decide' to break the pact with its spirit-companions and remain a human being on earth."[17]

"Ghost-spirits" are also wandering spirits who have been shut out of the community of the spirits of the dead because their corpses have not been buried properly; this category also includes the wandering spirits of those who died a "bad death" or of those who lived evil lives on earth. They wander eternally around the earth and may occupy rocks and trees.[18]

Finally, there is the guardian spirit, what the Germans picturesquely call a *doppelgänger*, and what in English is called a person's "double." These spirits indicate that the root of the person's personality either becomes two entities, one of which functions as that person's spiritual counterpart or double, or operates as a separate entity. The double of a husband, for example, may do mischief to his wife or may benefit her and the children. Thus in most parts of Africa there are "cults of the double," whereby people make offerings and sacrifices to the double at the foot of a known sacred tree or at the intersection of two roads.[19]

Although the popular mind sometimes confuses spirits with

16. Geoffrey Parrinder, *African Mythology* (New York: Peter Bedrick Books, 1982), 69–83.

17. Idowu, *African Traditional Religion*, 175.

18. This belief in wandering ghost-spirits can also be found in black American culture, particularly in the Sea Islands in South Carolina and Georgia (see William R. Branscom, "Acculturation among the Gullah Negroes," *American Anthropologist* 63 [1949]: 49).

19. Ibid., 177. In Jamaican Kumina one "catches" a person's "duppy" at a cottonwood tree, although a "duppy" is understood to be the person's soul (see Chapter 2, above).

divinities, the other type of good spirits in African religion, Idowu distinguishes between them, albeit not too precisely. Unlike spirits, divinities are entities that were "begotten" rather than created, to use language of the creed. Nevertheless, they are derivatives of God the supreme deity and are dependent on God for their authority and sovereignty. This characteristic of being begotten rather than created, however, does not mean a diminishing of their power in human and natural affairs.

This relationship between the divinities and God is seen in the art of Susanne Wenger, a European who chose to live among the Yoruba in Nigeria and to take up their religion. Wenger depicts divinities (*orisha*) as partial representations of Olódùmarè, since each *orisha* is the universe viewed from a particular angle. Olódùmarè is the sum total of everything in the universe:

> If you sit in this Oshun forest, you know this forest exists through its multiple forms, through the immense variety — an unorganized beauty where every detail is tremendously strong.... But there is really no hierarchy. And our immense surprise about this divine variety — that is Olódùmarè.[20]

Furthermore, different localities and tribes often have different names for the divinities, but their function is the same. They too are often associated with some force or object in the world of nature that is especially pertinent in the local area. They have their own portfolio like ministers in a cabinet, but God is the monarch, not a constitutional prime minister. In their role as intermediaries, they are the accustomed channels through which people approach God, and their roles also include keeping the other spiritual forces in balance; they are approached by offerings and sacrifices of thanksgiving or personal contrition. But these roles of spirits and divinities do not mean that God in the African society is distant and disinterested in human affairs: "The correct interpretation of the positions of the divinities is that they constitute only a half-way house.... While man may find the divinities 'sufficient' for certain needs, something continues to warn him that 'sufficiency' is only in Deity. [Theologically] the divinities are only means to an end and not ends in themselves."[21]

Yet few Africans would say that they "believe" in the divinities with the same kind of urgency that Western Christians evince when

20. Cited in Ulli Beier, *The Return of the Gods: The Sacred Art of Susanne Wenger* (Cambridge: Cambridge University Press, 1975), 34.
21. Idowu, *African Traditional Religion*, 171.

saying "I have faith in God" or "I believe in Jesus Christ" or when speaking of "faith" and "belief" as an ultimate commitment. This is well illustrated in Yoruba. Ulli Beier, a scholar of African traditional art, points out that the relationship between the *orisha* and the devotee is complicated, but never is understood as a matter of ultimacy. That is reserved only for allegiance to the supreme deity. But there are distinctions.

For example, Beier says that when the term *olorisha* is translated into English, it is often rendered as "*orisha* worshipper." However, the term actually has several meanings. It more nearly means "one who has *orisha*," "one who is *orisha*," or "one who makes *orisha*."[22] "To have *orisha*" means the person or group has inherited the *orisha*, neglect of which would be perilous and the source of eventual disorder in interpersonal relationships and in the wider community. Such disaster results not because of vengeance on the part of the *orisha*, but because things get out of joint when the relationship with the *orisha* is not nurtured according to the tradition.

"To be *orisha*," on the other hand, means offering one's body to the *orisha* as a vehicle, as in possession when the *orisha* "mounts" the person (called "mounting his head"); the person in turn no longer has his or her own personality but becomes in effect the visible herald for a particular *orisha*. "The limits of human existence have been extended and man has become divine for a brief moment. Man has been reassured of his participation in creation, man has reassured himself that he is part of god...."[23]

Finally, "to make *orisha*" indicates intimate interdependence between the devotee and the *orisha*, reinforced through daily dialogue: greetings, drumming, singing, special intercessions, dancing, small sacrifices, divination. This is the most difficult and taxing level of *olorisha*, for it involves knowing the language and music of all the elements of the universe, such as the rocks, rivers, leaves, bones, and trees, so that the person can grasp which forces are congenial to certain types of people and to particular *orisha*. Possession at this stage is described by Susanne Wenger as "like an invasion by human beings of the world that is normally reserved for the gods, and some divine forces are brought back home."[24]

22. Beier, *The Return of the Gods*, 44.
23. Ibid., 47.
24. Cited in ibid.

J. Omosade Awolalu, however, does not make a sharp distinction between spirits and divinities, but he does divide the divinities into three groups purely for analytical purposes: (1) primordial divinities, which, like the "begotten" divinities named by Idowu, exist before the creation of the earth and are the council of the supreme being; (2) historical divinities, which are former kings, heroes and heroines, brave warriors, founders of cities, who have been deified; and (3) nature divinities, found in natural phenomena like rivers, lagoons, trees, wind, the sea, mountains, and rocks.[25]

An important question is the theological character of the relationship between God as supreme deity and the spirits and divinities. This is not an easy question to answer because it is asked usually from a perspective shaped by a Graeco-Roman concept of deity or divinity, with God having the only true attributes of divine deity, which is shared with the Holy Spirit, but not lesser spirits. Afro traditional religions, as has been pointed out, are quite content to live with a supreme God who manifests a many-sided relationship with humankind, earth, and nature through divinities and spirits without ceasing to be the divine supreme and sovereign deity. Spirits and divinities have their jurisdiction and their mandates on assignment from God as intermediaries and subordinates, even though within their own jurisdictions and spheres they are supreme and sovereign. God as supreme deity is not always as visible in the ceremonies invoking the spirits and the divinities; however, as the ceremonies and rituals proceed, God as supreme deity is acknowledged, even if the acknowledgment is not shaped into words. It may occur in dance or gestures, in sayings, greetings, and the praise-names at such ceremonies. Or God's sovereignty may be expressed in people's names, at shrines, in reciting creation legends or idioms recalling God's attributes, or in salutations. That is, the dynamics of everyday culture as well as articulated concepts testify to the varied relationships between God and the spirits.

Kwesi Dickson of Ghana provides a useful description of the theological character of this relationship, using Akan-speaking ethnic groups in Ghana (which include the Ashanti, Fante, Ahantas, Akwamu, and the Akwapim) as paradigms. One expression describing the relationship between God as supreme deity and the lesser deities is *Nyankopawn ne mba*: that is, the deities are "sons of God."

---

25. J. Omosade Awolalu, *Yoruba Beliefs and Sacrificial Rites* (Harlow, England: Longman, 1979), 20.

"Son" in Africa may be used generically to refer to someone younger than the speaker in addition to someone in a familial relationship, much like many elderly people in the American South or in Appalachia address younger men as "son." This communicates that these deities as "sons" derive their deity from God and share God's spirit.[26]

Another expression, *abrafoaw*, "executioners," alludes to the role of the divinities as judges and patrons of the community's moral code and taboos. When they are violated, which is a breach of conduct, the wrath of God is incurred. The divinities, in this case, act as God's executioners in inflicting punishment on the offending community or person.

Still a third description of this relationship uses the Akan word *akyeame*, meaning "spokesman." In court the spokesman is an intimate associate of the chief and thus makes pronouncements and announcements of the favors of the chief with authority, albeit delegated authority from the chief. "Unlike the two other expressions this one is not experientially and ritually exemplified in Akan religion."[27]

But at times, even with subordination within the heavenly council, in some tribal traditions God is portrayed as having limited sovereignty. We saw how God the supreme deity made mistakes in creation or redid some previous creation. For the African, this does not compromise God's sovereignty, since God in divine freedom can be both an absolute monarch and a constitutional monarch at the same time. However, unlike the relationship between a prime minister and cabinet, there is no overruling God constitutionally. It is clear that God has the last word, that "the buck stops here," to use President Harry S. Truman's famous words. In African and Caribbean traditional religions, God as supreme deity also controls the categories for understanding God, even when expressed in anthropomorphic analogies. But they are only analogies — they are useful for communing and communicating with God, but they cannot exhaust God's being and action. To borrow a theological expression from Latin, which witnesses to this totally free God in African religion, God is understood as the *aseitas Dei*.

---

26. Kwesi A. Dickson, *Theology in Africa* (Maryknoll, N.Y.: Orbis Books, 1984), 56.
27. Ibid.

EVIL SPIRITS AND LORDSHIP IN AFRO CULTURES

Other cosmic powers and forces do mischief, cause mishaps, and do evil, particularly through witchcraft. Awolalu calls them "mysterious powers" rather than spirits because, whereas spirits are essentially good, these forces in Africa are seen as the personifications of evil; they are bent on inflicting harm, wickedness, and misfortune on human beings.

> In the mental and social attitudes of the Yoruba, and of the Africans in general, there is no belief more profoundly ingrained than that of the existence of witches. All strange diseases, accidents, untimely deaths, a lack of promotions on the job, failure in examinations and business enterprise, disappointment in love, barrenness in women, impotence in men, failure of crops and a thousand other evils are attributed to witchcraft.[28]

Afro cultures do not agonize as much as Graeco-Roman cultures about the origins of these powers and forces, just as the New Testament does not speculate about their origins. But both the New Testament and Afro cultures, even in black America, know and experience their existence. Identified by various names — witchcraft, mysterious powers, sorcery, evil powers — they cause the unpleasantries of life, such as anxiety, accidents, sickness, and death. Although good divinities and spirits may also bring about these ailments, they do so because a morality or taboo has been violated. Punishment from them is considered a penance and helps correct a relationship with the spirits for the good health of the offender.

Mbiti observes that while such mysterious powers may ultimately come from God, they are experienced practically through concrete physical and spiritual objects and beings. Some humans are capable of tapping into these powers for good or for evil purposes. Good purposes include curative, protective, productive, and preventive tasks. Evil purposes include destructive, death-bearing, and injurious tasks.[29]

> The reason why man believes in terrors and evils and mysterious powers is that terrors, evils, and mysterious powers are there and very real.... To the Yoruba nothing happens by chance — something is caused by someone directly or indirectly by the use of power; and

28. Awolalu, *Yoruba Beliefs*, 81.
29. John S. Mbiti, *African Religions and Philosophy* (Garden City, N.Y.: Doubleday/Anchor, 1970), 265.

they, also, believe that there are individuals who have access to these mystical powers.... This power is ultimately from a supernatural being, but in practice it is inherent in or comes from or through some physical object, except in the case of witchcraft which is psychic.[30]

The continued influence of these forces even in modern African society can be gleaned from an incident among the Yoruba several years ago; it occurred between the Aladura Church and the traditionalists and took place at the Iwo Festival in Ondo State. This festival, which honors the river spirits in the area, was opposed by the Aladura Church, protesting that such was witchcraft, and in turn the church organized a preaching mission and procession opposing the festival. Since it is believed that these river spirits travel by the wind, the uninitiated are strongly advised to remain inside in the evenings; otherwise an encounter with the spirits could cause paralysis and possibly death. Some Aladura members purposely ventured outside in the evening in defiance of the spirits, whereupon they were struck with paralysis and some even died during the festival almost at once. The people laid their affliction to the mysterious power of Oro, known to cause paralysis when invoked by traditionalist priests. No medical cause apparently could be found for this sudden paralysis.[31]

In Caribbean societies there are equivalents to these traditionalist priests: the Obeah doctor in Jamaica, the *bocor* (Fon: *bokono*, "priest") and the *caplata* in Haiti. Melville J. Herskovits differentiates between the *bocor*, who deals almost exclusively in black magic and "buys" his gods, and the *caplata*, who deals in anything on demand and for a price. The *houngan* makes Voodoo; the *bocor* makes what the Haitians call *wanga*.[32] In Haiti one goes to a *bocor* in order to capture a zombie by imprisoning a person's *ti bon ange* (the will and character):

> The zombie cadaver with its *gros bon ange* [energy peculiar to that person] and *n'âme* [the energy that allows each cell in the body to perform] can function; however, separated from the *ti bon ange*, the

30. Awolalu, *Yoruba Beliefs*, 91.

31. Ibid., 73. When I was a visiting professor in Nigeria in the autumn of 1983, some charms and other articles associated with witchcraft and magic were found in a vacant apartment reserved for members of Parliament on Victoria Island, Lagos. Those MPs already living in the building immediately moved out and demanded a ritual cleaning of the entire building before they would return.

32. Melville J. Herskovits, *Life in a Haitian Valley* (New York: Octagon Books, 1975), 222–23.

body is but an empty vessel, subject to the direction of the bocor or whoever maintains control of the zombie *ti bon ange*....It is the notion of alien, malevolent forces thus taking control of the individual that is so terrifying to the vodounist.[33]

In American southern black culture, as already mentioned, there is the tradition of the Hoodoo doctor (sometimes called a "root doctor" or a *wangateur*),[34] who is a conjurer of black magic and spells. The conjurer not only can conjure up evil spells and charms; he or she can also "fix" spells and remove the power of charms that have been put on a person. This role is similar to the ability of Myal priests (good magic) in Jamaica to counter evil spells and charms conjured by Obeah-men and Obeah-women (bad magic). During slavery, belief in conjuring was so powerful that local conjurers sometimes rivaled black preachers in authority. However, most slaves then, as many blacks in the Caribbean and South today, were quite clear that they fulfilled different needs. As Raboteau rightly observes: for the slaves, conjuring answered purposes that Christianity did not and Christianity answered purposes that conjuring did not.[35] Some scholars suggest that some black preachers on the plantations may have practiced conjuring.[36]

In some places people distinguish between *good* root doctors and *bad* root doctors. The former are comparable to herbalists in African and Caribbean societies, who do not inflict harm, whereas the latter conjure and deal in the "evil arts." In Louisiana one speaks of "mojo" and "canja" just as one hears the expression "juju" in

33. Wade Davis, *The Serpent & the Rainbow* (New York: Simon and Schuster, 1985), 186–87. See also Chapter 2, above, on the Jamaican belief in the "capturing" of a person's shadow.

34. The latter word may be derived from *wanga*, Haitian Creole for black magic, rather than *oanga*, as proposed by Albert J. Raboteau, *Slave Religion* (New York: Oxford University Press, 1978), 276; see also Herskovits, *Life in a Haitian Valley*, 222.

35. For a good summary of the role of evil powers in the slave community, see Raboteau, *Slave Religion*, 275–88.

36. Eugene D. Genovese, *Roll, Jordan, Roll: The World the Slaves Made* (New York: Vintage Books, 1976), 255–56; Gayraud S. Wilmore, *Black Religion and Black Radicalism: An Interpretation of the Religious History of Afro-American People*, rev. ed. (Maryknoll, N.Y.: Orbis, 1983), 10. Raboteau, on the other hand, is skeptical about such a link, saying there is thus far no evidence to support such a claim (*Slave Religion*, 287).

West and East Africa to designate those who practice conjuring and sorcery.[37]

The perception in Afro cultures that there are evil powers about in the larger cosmos is not peculiar to those cultures. Indeed, in non-Afro cultures in the West belief in witchcraft and mysterious forces of ill continued to be widespread some twelve centuries after Christianity as a cultural force helped shape Western culture under the guise of Christendom; such belief was present in non-Afro cultures in the United States in its early days and is present in some circles of the modern feminist movement, which have revived witchcraft as a feminist religious concept.[38]

What is the character of a theology that can speak to this deeply embedded cultural tradition? In a study of some 8000 sermon texts used in the Aladura Church, Harold Turner provides some clues. Trying to determine what are the "marks" of the church when considering Aladura liturgy, hymnody, and preaching, he applied the criterion that the World Council of Churches uses for defining church, although the Aladura Church is not a member of that body: "Any faith which rests upon and is permeated by [belief in Jesus Christ as the Son of God, as Lord and Savior] must be said to lie within the limits of Christendom."

He discovered preference for certain books and types of literature in the Bible: (1) Wisdom literature and practical moral and religious teachings, including the Book of James; (2) the Gospels and the Epistles, especially those stressing ethical teachings such as those presented in the Sermon on the Mount; (3) mythical narratives and sagas, as in Genesis and the historical books of the Old Testament; (4) apocalyptic books with their warnings, judgments, and promises of deliverance, especially vision/dream narratives in Daniel; (5) prophetic literature; (6) historical, legal, and personal accounts in both testaments.

Furthermore, the Aladura prefer New Testament texts to Old Testament texts and are drawn to recurring themes like the kingdom of God and justification by grace through faith. The person and work of Christ do not capture them as frequently as the ideas of new life

---

37. For a summary of the different cultural expressions about the evil powers and their connection with healing and conjuring, see Michel S. Laguerre, *Afro-Caribbean Folk Medicine* (South Hadley, Mass.: Bergin & Garvey, 1987), 52–56.

38. See Frank Smyth, *Modern Witchcraft* (New York: Harper and Row, 1973); Mary Daly, *Gyn/Ecology: The Metaethics of Radical Feminism* (Boston: Beacon Press, 1978), 190–97.

and the spirit in the Gospel and Epistles of John and texts about the resurrection of the body and the spirit. Additionally, Aladura sermons and liturgy underscored God's help through the Holy Spirit and the teachings of Christ for those who confess their sins, repent of them, and obey his teachings. As these findings are similar to those in other studies of sermons in other African indigenous churches, Turner concludes that the Bible plays the same role in the formation of Aladura beliefs, teachings, and rituals that it plays in most such churches.[39]

Generally, the overwhelming picture of Jesus Christ in indigenous churches is also evident among other African Christians: a Christ of triumph, victory, and conquest through his resurrection and his passion. The victory of Christ over the power of the devil, sickness, fear, and death impresses many African Christians, for it conveys hope in their overcoming dire circumstances. Many African Christians are especially interested in the temptations of Christ by the devil in the wilderness and his not yielding to the tempter by virtue of a strengthening through the Spirit.[40]

In the study of a liturgy of a Sierra Leone independent church, Turner noticed that the theme of *victory* had been added to collects probably taken from the Anglican Book of Common Prayer. The church prays "that those evils which the craft and subtlety of the devil or of man worketh against us, be brought to nought." Likewise, in the versicles of the litany, also an adaptation of the 1662 Book of Common Prayer, are prayers for victory over a range of personal evil powers and forces: wizards and witches, magicians and necromancers, wicked juju men, soothsayers, quack doctors and herbalists, talebearers and gossips.[41] In Ghana the indigenous churches attract large followings in part because they are popularly perceived as the "Witchcraft Eradication Movement."[42]

In a rather somber comment about the reality of evil powers in Africa, even for African Christians, Turner concludes:

39. Harold W. Turner, "Profile through Preaching: The Use of Scripture as the Criterion of a Church," in *Religious Innovation in Africa: Collected Essays on New Religious Movements* (Boston: G. K. Hall, 1979), 231–44.

40. John S. Mbiti, "Afrikanische Beiträge zur Christology," in P. Beyerhaus et al., eds., *Theologische Stimmen aus Asien, Afrika und Lateinamerika* (Munich: Chr. Kaiser, 1968), 77.

41. Harold W. Turner, "The Litany of an Independent West African Church," in *Religious Innovation in Africa*, 247.

42. John S. Pobee, *Toward an African Theology* (Nashville: Abingdon, 1979), 48.

It would be wrong to imagine that the preoccupation with evil powers in this litany is an archaic element, a reference to the insecurities
of life in the African past.... One of the chief signs of [the] increase
in insecurity is the widely remarked upsurge of witchcraft in those
parts of Africa where it was most expected to vanish before the impact of education, medical care, industrialization and urbanization. A
litany that is so extensively concerned with all the practitioners of evil
medicine and witchcraft and that repudiates them so strongly, is both
Christian and relevant to its own social environment.[43]

THE SPIRIT AND BLACK AMERICAN RELIGION

The Spirit experientially and conceptually exercises a very strong influence in black American religion and culture. There it is an untidy,
dynamic, and ecstatic power that in part is the legacy of the slaves,
who adapted the revelation of their traditional spirits to the biblical
Spirit after being freighted to the coasts of the Americas and the
Caribbean; this power is especially present in the traditional black
churches and among black Pentecostalists. Like the breath of God in
scripture, this power moves through slave songs and gospel hymns,
the rhetoric of the black preacher and the black trickster alike, the ex-
temporaneous and unrehearsed prayers of the unsophisticated, and
the written liturgical prayers of more sedate congregations. It is the
presence of the Spirit — revealed in the sounds and ritual of black
churches — that impresses black folk at a service, prayer meeting,
Bible class, or a revival. With the Spirit present they can say with
great sagacity and joy that they "really are in church" or are in
"spirit-filled worship."

The debate in the 1930s about whether African survivals
and remnants are retained in black American culture — a debate
principally between the sociologist E. Franklin Frazier, who denied their retention,[44] and the anthropologist Melville Herskovits,
who affirmed their retention[45] — is no longer an issue in intellectual circles. Most scholarship, particularly since the advent

43. Turner, "The Litany," 251.
44. "American slavery destroyed household gods [of Africa] and dissolved
the bonds of sympathy and affection between men of the same blood and household.
...Their children, who knew only the American environment, soon forgot the few
memories that had been passed on to them" (E. Franklin Frazier, *The Negro Family in
the United States* [1939; reprint, Chicago: University of Chicago Press, 1966], 21–22).
45. "That the African past must be included under the rubric 'traditions of
the past,' whether these traditions are held overtly or not, becomes apparent when
the religious habits of Negroes in the Caribbean and South America are anchored to

of African-American studies at universities, is in general agreement that indeed in spite of the discontinuity caused by slavery in the United States, many Africanisms have survived in black religion and black culture.[46] Likewise, both the large Caribbean immigration to the United States since the Second World War and studies of the Sea Islands off the coasts of South Carolina and Georgia, where a slave culture has remained almost intact, support the argument that black religion and culture include a goodly number of Africanisms, particularly the African worldview of spirits.

Interestingly enough, even blacks in churches with ordered liturgies, such as the Roman Catholic and Episcopal churches, and in the churches with more structured free-worship services, like the Presbyterian and Methodist churches, increasingly allow for explicit ejaculatory expressions of the Spirit in worship. In black religion, the model of the Spirit imbues a spirituality that is not the classic *imitati Christi*, but rather *participati Christi*, through performance, drama, emotion, and ritual. Of course, the most vivid expression of the Spirit in black worship has been the Pentecostal-Holiness movement, a largely twentieth-century movement with nineteenth-century pietistic antecedents; its origins lie also in congregations of the black Church of God in Christ, founded by Charles H. Mason (1866–1961), and in the Azusa Street Mission, founded under a black pastor named William J. Seymour (1870–1922) in Los Angeles in 1906.

In the worship of these churches, particularly the latter, a mark of the Spirit is speaking in tongues. But these churches also emphasize gospel music, which employs musical instruments (in addition to the traditional spontaneous foot-stomping and hand-clapping) to evoke and invite the Spirit; these instruments include tambourines, the piano, horns, and electronic instruments. Called "gospel" because many of the songs include texts and themes from the Gospels and the teachings of Jesus interpreted through black metaphors

---

both ends of the scale whose central portion they comprise — to Africa, the aboriginal home of all these varieties of religious experience, on the one hand, and to the United States, on the other, where the greatest degree of acculturation to European norms has taken place" (Melville J. Herskovits, *The Myth of the Negro Past* [Boston: Beacon Press, 1941], 224–25).

46. See also Raboteau, *Slave Religion*, 55–87; Wilmore, *Black Religion and Black Radicalism*, 15–28; Herbert G. Gutman, *The Black Family in Slavery and Freedom: 1750–1925* (New York: Vintage Books, 1976), 211–16; Vera Rubin, ed., *Caribbean Studies: A Symposium* (Seattle: University of Washington Press, 1957).

and experience, this music as an art form emerged from the urban black ghettos in the North. Two black hymn writers important
for moving this music from these churches into the mainstream traditional black denominations, albeit with much resistance within
those denominations, were the AME pastor Charles Tindley (1856–
1933), who wrote and first published many of these gospel songs
in 1905, and the Baptist layman Thomas A. Dorsey (1899–). Many
gospel singers later went over to popular soul music; these included
Aretha Franklin, Gladys Knight, Dinah Washington, Dionne War-
wick, Sam Cooke, Patti LaBelle, and Little Richard, to name a few.
Now this music has become familiar not only in black denominations but also in many black congregations in traditional white
mainline churches, such as the Episcopalian, Methodist, Presbyterian, and Catholic churches, some of which have published black
hymnbooks.

The Spirit in black piety, however, is less an intellectual concept of the academy and theologians, and much more an active,
engaging, life-giving, and possessing power to be experienced, witnessed, and testified to. W. E. B. Du Bois acclaimed Spirit as one of
the hallmarks of black religion, calling it "frenzy" and "shouting."
He wrote:

> It varies in expression from the silent rapt countenance or the low
> murmur and moan to the mad abandon of physical fervor — the
> stamping, shrieking and shouting, the rushing to and fro and wild
> waving of arms, the weeping and laughter, the vision and the trance.
> All this is nothing new in the world, but old as religion, as Del-
> phi and Endor. And so firm a hold did it have on the Negro,
> that many generations have firmly believed that without this visible
> manifestation of God, there could be no true communion with the
> Invisible.[47]

Du Bois did not particularly enjoy gospel music, deriding it
as a debased imitation of the classic Negro spiritual with the jingle
but not the music, the body but not the soul. But he grasped the
significance of the Spirit and the ecstatic behavior associated with it
in black religion.

The Spirit in black religion moves the worshiper to make noise,
for without noise, as an African theologian, John Pobee, once ex-

---

47. W. E. B. Du Bois, *The Souls of Black Folk* (Greenwich, Conn.: Fawcett Publications, 1961), 141–42.

claimed, there is no real community among blacks.[48] The most reliable evidence of the relationship between the Spirit and noise in black religion is the testimony of slaves. One slave described the relationship of noise to the Spirit in black worship as follows: "They used to have prayer meetings. In some places that they have prayer meetings they would turn pots down in the middle of the floor to keep the white folks from hearing them pray and testify. . . . I kinda think the Lord put them things in their minds to do for themselves, just like he helps us Christians in other ways."[49]

Such "noise" may occur in vigorous singing, articulated amens, repeated hallelujahs, ecstasy, and even doing a holy dance — all can be expressions of the Spirit in black worship. Even after converting to the Christian religion of their slave masters, the blacks infused their new-found religion with the Spirit. And although white clergy usually forbade exhibiting Spirit-induced frenzy and ecstasy, the slaves would do it anyway. As one slave protested about boring music in white churches: "Ef I sing an' it doan move me any, den dat a sin on de Holy Ghost; I be tell a lie on de Lord."[50] One northern white visiting a slave service with her driver was visibly moved by the exhibition of the Spirit and wrote in her diary afterwards:

> The Negroes sobbed and shouted and swayed backward and forward, some with aprons to their eyes, most of them clapping their hands and responding in shrill tones: "Yes, God!" "Jesus!" "Savior!" "Bless the Lord, amen," etc. It was a little exciting for me. I would very much like to shout, too. Jim Nelson [her driver] when he arose from his knees, trembled and shook as one in a palsy, and from his eyes you could see the ecstasy had not left him yet. He could not stand at all and sank back on his bench.[51]

Of course, not all black church leaders were pleased with the Spirit-filled frenzy in black worship. The AME Bishop Daniel Payne steadily labeled such worship heathenish, saying it put off refined

---

48. Address presented at the Afro-Anglican Conference, Codrington College, Barbados, June 17–21, 1985.

49. George P. Rawick, *From Sundown to Sunup: The Making of the Black Community*, Series One, The American Slave: A Composite Autobiography, Vol. 1 (Westport, Conn.: Greenwood Publishing Company, 1972), 39.

50. George P. Rawick, ed., *South Carolina Narratives: Parts 1 and 2*, South Carolina Federal Writers Project (Westport, Conn.: Greenwood Publishing Company, 1972), 2:87.

51. Mary Boykin Chestnut, *A Diary from Dixie*, ed. Ben Ames Williams (Boston: Houghton Mifflin Company, 1949), 149.

and intellectual Christians. He opposed the ring-shout ritual of the slaves, hand-clapping in worship, and the holy dances that he called "voodoo dances."[52]

The emphasis on the Spirit and its visible emotional expressions is not peculiar or even unique to American black piety. Camp meetings, largely among the Scotch-Irish, with their frenzy began at the famous Cane Ridge, Kentucky, site in 1800. Started by Peter Cartwright, a rather flamboyant itinerant Methodist preacher, camp meetings nonetheless often failed to impress most of the slaves watching on the sidelines, who seemed to feel that the whites did not have the Spirit. But even camp-meeting frenzy among poor whites was affected by black piety. One antebellum Methodist minister lamented that after public devotions, many whites gathered elsewhere and sang the whole night many of the emotional, ecstatic hymns that originated in the slave quarters:

> We have too, a growing evil in the practice of singing in our places of public and society worship, merry airs, adapted from old songs, to hymns of our composing: often miserable as poetry...most frequently composed and first sung by the illiterate *blacks* of the society. ...What in the name of religion, can countenance or tolerate such gross perversions of true religion! but the evil is only occasionally condemned, and the example has already visibly affected the religious manners of some whites.[53]

But unlike most white camp meetings or pietistic churches, the Spirit in black religion did not have simply an internal or personal function; it also functioned externally and socially. John Lovell, historian of Negro spirituals and slave songs, points out that the African understanding of Spirit and spirit possession is crucial in studying black religious music.[54] It allowed for defiance as well as insured confidence and triumph, as in the lament, "Sometimes I feel discouraged, And think my work's in vain / But then the Holy Spirit revives my soul again." It also empowered those daring to rebel against slavery, as in "Wade in the water / Wade in the water, children. Wade in the water / 'Cause God's gonna trouble the

52. Daniel Payne, *Recollections of Seventy Years* (1886; reprint, New York: Arno Press and New York Times, 1969), 225.

53. Cited in Eileen Southern, ed., *Readings in Black American Music* (New York: W. W. Norton, 1983), 62–63.

54. John Lovell, Jr., *Black Song: The Forge and the Flame* (New York: Macmillan, 1972), 28.

water. . . . / See that band all dressed in red / It looks like the band that Moses led / God's gonna trouble the water."

The ethical dimension of the Spirit in black religion was particularly empowering in blacks' struggle for liberation, in that it, first, refurbished the souls of the slaves for the constant struggle, and, second, established a solidarity during the struggle. A gospel hymn by Tindley captures the first theme very well: "Courage, my soul, and let us journey on. / Tho' the night is dark, it won't be very long. / Thanks be to God, the morning light appears / And the storm is passing over, Hallclujah." A spiritual also highlights this theme: "Jordan River is chilly and cold. / Chills the body but not the soul. / Ain't be one train on dis track / Runs to heav'n and runs right back." The expectations of set-backs and defeats were buttressed by the confidence that there is only one direction for the train, which appropriately refuels itself from a vision of heaven, a most important concept in black piety, and then re-enters the fray for liberation.

The theme of solidarity induced by the Spirit in struggle stood out also in the civil rights movement of the 1950s and 1960s. We see this in a very popular spiritual that made its rounds in the movement: "Walk together, children. Don't you get weary / There's a great camp meeting in the Promised Land." This same theme is also lifted up in a gospel hymn by Thomas Moore: "Come, ye disconsolate, where'er ye languish; Come to the mercy-seat, fervently kneel / Here bring your wounded hearts, here tell your anguish. / Earth hath no sorrow that Heaven cannot heal." The vibrancy of a Spirit-grounded solidarity in black piety was particularly attested to when many spirituals and gospel songs were adapted to fit the political realities during the civil rights movement. For instance, "Keep Your Hand on the Plow, Hold On," was altered to "Keep Your Eyes on the Prize, Hold On." The adaptation was done by an uneducated black woman during a voter-education training course on Johns Island, South Carolina, in 1956. The woman was attending the course in order to learn to read so that she could vote.

It may now be helpful to summarize some points about the Spirit in black religion. First of all, it is something active and acting, engaged and engaging, an act and an event, and it is evidenced in shouting, frenzy or possession, praise-songs and shouts, preaching rhetoric, and the joy and lament of spontaneous prayers in worship and outside worship.

Second, the Spirit refurbishes and fortifies for strife and struggle in the course of liberation. It reminds the worshipers that the storm is indeed a storm, and that it too will pass over.

Third, the Spirit establishes solidarity during struggles for liberation and survival: solidarity within the temporal community and within the larger community of the ancestors and deceased relatives. It dispels weariness and faintheartedness. It connects ancestors with the living, mothers with sons, daughters with fathers, the uneducated with the sophisticated, and the impoverished with the affluent.

Fourth, the Spirit links black religion and black culture in the fine arts, literature, oratory, music, blues, poetry, drama, etc. Black culture, intricately connected to black religion, cannot be fully understood without giving some attention to the role of the Spirit. The Spirit also establishes an affinity between the different locations of the black diaspora in the United States, from the Sea Islands along the coasts of South Carolina and Georgia, to New Orleans, to northern and western urban areas with their mixture of southern black culture, northern black religion, and Afro peoples from the Caribbean.

Some black churches, such as the Pentecostalist churches, also believe in a dark side to the spirits, and they believe that Jesus protects believers from those forces. A member with a bad temper or in a disgruntled mood is often spoken of as having an "evil spirit." An obstinate member perceived as obstreperous in the church is frequently said to possess the "devil's spirit." Likewise, as midnight is both a metaphor for and the actual time when a person is believed to be most vulnerable to evil spirits, it is also thought to be the best time to be in touch with God through prayer. Pentecostal prayers and testimonies are full of references to "God who came at the midnight hour." They insist that demons can still possess people and that a person can be a slave of Satan: "dirt diggers," "gossipers," "root workers," "Hoodooers," "rascals," and "half-handed folks." Even food is not immune to these evil spirits: one must be cautious that someone does not put something in his or her dumplings. The only way to react against these spirits is with "Holy Ghost power."[55]

---

55. However, "dumpling" is also a metaphor for goodness or cooperativeness; for instance, a female member was described as a "sweet dumpling," meaning that she was willing to support the majority or the pastor's program; yet such a person is still considered vulnerable to an evil spirit (Melvin D. Williams, *Community in a Black Pentecostal Church* [Pittsburgh: University of Pittsburgh Press, 1974], 138–41).

SPIRITS IN BLACK CULTURE

In black culture in the United States, particularly in the South, the African legacy of spirits in local Voodoo (or Hoodoo) continues to shape beliefs and practices.[56] The Sea Islanders, for example, continue the African belief that the spirits control and influence nature and human life; hence one of the most respected people on the island is the "root doctor," who is able to reveal these forces or direct persons in communing with these spirits. The root doctor acts as counselor, healer, and ritualist. "The Christian doctor believes his power is a gift of God to be used to help mankind, therefore he will never invoke evil power.... Usually he prays for seeing God's guidance before interpreting situations."[57] His opposite, the root doctor, "fixes" things, that is, consults evil spirits for conjuring spells and charms to do injury. Much of Sea Island worship in traditional black churches has a noticeable African character, particularly when the "Sperrit" possesses the worshipers. They frequently go into a holy dance, which may continue until, for some unexplained reason, they stop. Often someone else in the congregation or gathering will decide that the "Sperrit" should continue and resumes the dancing until he or she feels that it is time to stop. Often the Spirit is identified with Jesus, while at other times the spirits are said to live in springs and bodies of water.[58]

Zora Neale Hurston's field research documents belief in spirits (Hoodoo) both in Protestant states in the South (Alabama, Florida, and Georgia) and in the Catholic state of Louisiana, particularly New Orleans and along the Gulf coast. She also discovered black Spiritualist churches in New Orleans dealing with the spirits.[59] Brought by the slaves exported to Louisiana as early as 1716, Voodoo was

56. The concept and expression "Voodoo" as a generic term for evil spirits and negative magic are also used to malign Afro tradition, such as the charge by one scholar that the early black Muslims engaged in "Voodoo" human sacrifice. See Erdmann Doane Baynon, "The Voodoo Cult among Negro Migrants to Detroit," *American Journal of Sociology* 43 (May 1938): 894–904. None of the early pioneering research in the beliefs of the Nation of Islam identifies it with such practices. See C. Eric Lincoln, *The Black Muslims in America* (Boston: Beacon Press, 1961); E. U. Essien-Udom, *Black Nationalism: A Search for an Identity in America* (Chicago: University of Chicago Press), 1962.

57. Janie Gilliard Moore, "Africanisms among Blacks of the Sea Islands," *Journal of Black Studies* 10 (June 1980): 473.

58. Mary A. Twining and Keith E. Baird, "Introduction to Sea Island Folklore," *Journal of Black Studies* 10 (June 1980): 411.

59. Zora Neale Hurston, "Hoodoo in America," *The Journal of American Folk-Lore* 44 (October–December 1931): 317–417.

most firmly established by Haitian slaves accompanying their French refugee slave masters fleeing Haiti during the Haitian Revolution. By 1792 statutes were in place in Louisiana denying entry to Haitian slaves for fear that they would infuse other American slaves with a similar kindred spirit of rebellion. This restriction was lifted after the United States bought Louisiana in 1803. But in 1809 another influx of former Haitian planters came to Louisiana — this time from Cuba after France went to war against Spain — with slaves and their Voodoo from Haiti and other French Caribbean colonies.

Two legendary figures in New Orleans Voodoo are Marie Laveau and her daughter, also named Marie. The origins of Marie Laveau, called the "Queen of Voodoo" in Louisiana even to this day, are somewhat obscure. A free mulatto, she was born in 1794 in New Orleans. One of the few public records about her, a marriage certificate at St. Louis Cathedral in New Orleans, records that in 1819 she wedded Jacques Paris, a mulatto freedman from the famous Haitian town of Jeremie. She is listed as the illegitimate daughter of Charles Laveau, a wealthy white planter, and Marguerite Darcantel, whose ancestry included whites, blacks, and Indians.

At the time of their marriage neither she nor her husband was into Voodoo. In fact, she worshiped daily at the cathedral in New Orleans.[60] However, shortly after her husband died some five or six years later, she met Louis Christophe Duminy de Glapion, also a mulatto from Haiti, who had been honored as a member of the Company of Men of San Domingo in the Battle of New Orleans. He moved into her house on North Rampart Street, the house having been given to her by her father as a dowry when she married Paris. She and Glapion lived together until his death in 1855. He and Marie had 15 children. While living with Glapion, Marie Laveau got into Voodoo.

Zora Neale Hurston, initiated into Voodoo in New Orleans in spite of being the daughter of a Baptist minister from Florida, was an early pioneer in actually going to the field to do a research project. The subject of her study was Haiti and Voodoo, and she passed on the story about how Marie Laveau became a devotee of Voodoo. According to one of the famous "Hoodoo doctors" in New Orleans, called Turner, whom she interviewed, the snake *loa* in Haitian Voodoo and Dahomey traditional religion "came into her

---

60. Robert Tallant, *Voodoo in New Orleans* (Gretna, La.: Pelican Publishing Company, 1983), 52–53.

[Laveau's] bedroom and spoke to her," after which she studied with a Hoodoo expert.[61] (There may be some truth to this because many of the stories about Voodoo ceremonies in Laveau's time often focus on snakes in addition to other Haitian *loa* as well, like Legba, the spirit at the crossroads who is acknowledged at all Voodoo rituals in order that other spirits be admitted, and Agousssou, the spirit for good luck.)

Newbell N. Puckett, who describes himself as an "amateur Hoodoo-doctor," in his study of southern Negro folk beliefs observes that in general the black populace in New Orleans in the early twentieth century held the popular belief that Voodoo was a means for conjuring, spells, witchcraft, and what southern blacks call "Hoodoo." Based on his field research with Hoodoo-men, he disputes this popular impression, saying that many of the Hoodoo doctors he interviewed distinguished between their use of magic and conjuring and Voodoo with its spirit possession and ceremonies. In fact, though some in New Orleans insist that Voodoo disappeared with the death of Marie Laveau, Puckett found that it still survives, although underground.[62] He located some local Voodoo celebrations of Damballah, in which Liba (Papa Legba in Haitian Voodoo) functions as in Haitian Voodoo; the celebrations included spewing rum on the audience, spirit possession, and bits of Catholic ritual, possibly a carry-over from Laveau's time, as well as Haitian Voodoo.[63]

In fact it is thought that when Marie Laveau took over the Voodoo cult in New Orleans after having superseded the reigning queens at the time, such as Sanité Dédé and Marie Saloppé, she exacerbated the popular confusion between Voodoo rituals and conjuring rituals by adding new symbols to the ritual on her own (these included holy water, incense, and statues of saints), by selling her *gris-gris* and amulets, and by holding ceremonies in one of the public squares, Congo Square, now a part of Louis Armstrong Park.[64] Congo Square, near Laveau's house on North Rampart Street and

61. Zora Neale Hurston, *Mules and Men* (1935; reprint, Bloomington, Ind.: Indiana University Press, 1963), 201.

62. Newbell Niles Puckett, *The Magic and Folk Beliefs of the Southern Negro* (New York: Dover Publications, 1969), 91. Hurston claims that blacks in New Orleans and elsewhere prefer the name Hoodoo, while whites prefer Voodoo (see *Mules and Men*, 193).

63. Puckett, *The Magic and Folk Beliefs of the Southern Negro*, 192–96.

64. Her nephew disputes this and says this was a claim made by whites. According to him, these were dances for fun and recreation, not for Hoodoo. The

within walking distance of many plantations near the city, was the traditional place where the city allowed slaves to dance and entertain themselves on Sundays.[65] There amidst vendors selling lemonade, *biere douce* (ginger beer), and *esotomac mulatre* (ginger cakes), the slaves would entertain themselves by singing and dancing the bamboula and the calinda to the musical accompaniment of tam-tams, bamboulas, the semidried jawbones of asses, and, of course, drums, until sundown. Then they returned to their respective plantations.[66]

In June 1881 Laveau died, having not set foot for six years outside her second home; that home was on St. Ann Street and was reputedly given to her by a grateful father whose son was acquitted of a crime because of her intervention.[67] This house on St. Ann Street, since demolished like the house on North Rampart Street, was the scene of most of her Voodoo ceremonies until her death. The funeral of her mate Glapion was held in that house as well, suggesting strongly that both of them participated in Voodoo services during their time together.

She was accorded Catholic burial rites (no Voodoo rites were visible) and was reportedly buried in St. Louis Cemetery Number 1, where Glapion was also buried. (This grave has a marker engraved with her name given as "Paris," the name of her first husband; the marker also bears the name "Glapion." Further, there is a brass plaque from the Archdiocese of New Orleans celebrating her sobriquet, "Queen of Voodoo.") Flowers and markings with red brick continue to decorate this marked grave. However, in the same cemetery there is an unmarked wall grave (called an "oven") that some

---

beating of the drums at these dances may have misled the white spectators (see Hurston, *Men and Mules*, 201).

65. Originally called Place Publique, site of the Spanish Fort San Fernando, this square was officially named Circus Square because of visiting circuses performing there. However, it was popularly called Congo Square because of the slave gatherings, dancing, and music-making on Sunday afternoons, permitted after 1817 by the municipal council as a safety-valve from the harshness and brutalities of daily slave labor. This was intended to keep the slaves content and to be an alternative to dancing at Voodoo ceremonies (see J. Richard Shenkel, et al., "Archaeology and Design of Congo Square," in *Archaeology of the Jazz Complex and Beauregard [Congo] Square, Louis Armstrong Park, New Orleans, Louisiana*, Research Report No. 2, Archaeological and Cultural Research Program [New Orleans: University of New Orleans, March 1980], in the Historic New Orleans Collection).

66. Raymond J. Martinez, *Portraits of New Orleans Jazz: Its People and Places* (Jefferson, La.: Hope Publications, 1971), 16. A detailed description of the music and dances can be found in George W. Cable, *The Dance in Place Congo*, in the Historic New Orleans Collection.

67. Tallant, *Voodoo in New Orleans*, 58.

believe is her real grave; visitors leave two nickels and a penny on its ledges. Likewise, another grave in St. Louis Cemetery Number 2 also is said to be her resting place. All are adorned with crude crosses made with the dust of the soft New Orleans red brick as a petition for cleansing and warding off evil spirits.

One local paper, *The Daily Picayune*, on the occasion of her funeral editorialized:

> All in all Marie Laveau was a wonderful woman. Doing good for the sake of doing good alone, she obtained no reward, ofttimes meeting with prejudice and loathing. . . . Her last days were surrounded by sacred pictures and other evidences of religion, and she died with a firm trust in Heaven. While God's sunshine plays around the little tomb where her remains are buried, by the side of her second husband and her sons and daughters, Marie's name will not be forgotten in New Orleans.

On the other hand, the *New Orleans Democrat* would have none of this shrill rhapsodizing and wrote a counter-editorial:

> The fact is that the least said about Marie Lavoux's [*sic*] sainted life, etc., the better. She was, up to an advanced age, the prime mover and soul of the indecent orgies of the ignoble Voudous; and to her influence may be attributed the fall of many a virtuous woman. It is true that she had redeeming traits. It is a peculiar quality of the old race of Creole Negroes that they are invariably kindhearted and charitable. Marie Lavoux made no exception. But to talk about her morality and kiss her sainted brow — pouah!!![68]

After her death began the reign of her daughter Marie, born on February 2, 1827.

---

68. Cited in Raymond J. Martinez, *Mysterious Marie Laveau, Voodoo Queen, and Folk Tales along the Mississippi* (New Orleans: Hope Publications, 1956), 51.

8

Ancestors and Saints

"Let us make man in our own image," God says in Gen. 1:26, thought by most Old Testament scholars to be a reference to God as the supreme deity consulting a heavenly council of other divine beings. Gen. 3:22 and 1 Kings 22:19-23 portray God conversing with other heavenly spirits sitting around God's throne, and Isaiah 6 describes a liturgy among God and divinities. Therefore, the idea that other divinities exist alongside of but subordinate to a supreme God is known even in the Bible. The fact that this belief continues to reappear at different periods in Israel's history means that it is not simply a "flash in the pan" idea on the fringe of Israel's religious beliefs. And, as we shall see, the veneration of ancestral spirits even continued into the New Testament period when the Christian faith emerged.

Ancestors in African and Caribbean traditional religions are a part of the heavenly council under the governance of the supreme deity, along with the divinities and spirits. They make up an important link between the living and the dead, the eternal and the here and now. Indeed, a case can be made that they were adapted by slaves in the United States to Christianity via black religion, as can be seen in some spirituals and gospel songs. The continuing belief in the benefits of ancestral spirits is reflected in a host of customs. For example, in many parts of black Africa and the Caribbean when a new bottle of rum or other spirits is opened, a few drops are poured on the ground as a libation to the ancestors. Likewise, it is traditional often to place some food on the ground or in a special part of the house for the ancestors.

Ancestors in traditional religion are a community of divine intermediaries standing before God; their function is not dissimilar to that of saints in Christian traditions, who act as patrons, intercessors, benefactors, guardians, protectors, and, if need be, punishers in a particular constituency, usually family or a community. Since ancestorship plays such a pivotal role in Afro traditional religion, it is unlikely that any proposed theological model taking cognizance of African culture would be appealing to Afro Christians in Africa and much of the Caribbean without giving serious attention to the ancestors. "Until Christianity can penetrate [the world of] spirits," John Mbiti writes, "it will for a long time remain on the surface."[1]

Because the ancestors in African culture have such a pivotal role — just as in many Asian cultures, such as Japan, China, Korea, and India — the issue is whether links can be established between ancestorship in Afro cultures and the Christian faith, just as links were forged between Christian belief and the Graeco-Roman culture of ancient Europe. Some have proposed as a possible link the Christian concept of the "communion of saints" (*Communio sanctorum*). This phrase, first found in a sixth-century creed from Gaul and a part of the Western tradition since the Apostles' Creed (eighth century), was incorporated into the baptismal ceremony during medieval times. It has been interpreted variously. Among these interpretations are: (1) it depicts the spiritual union between Christians in heaven and on earth; (2) it expresses the solidarity among Christians as God's saints on earth; (3) it depicts the sharing of holy things on earth by Christians, such as the Eucharist or the Lord's Supper.[2]

Indeed, Edward Fashole-Luke (Sierra Leone) thinks "communion of the saints" is the appropriate concept for "Christianizing" African ancestorship, provided that union with God through Christ and not the ancestors is underscored. He cautions that the "communion of the saints" will not exhaust the concept of ancestors, but the concept does draw attention to the death of Christ having universal meaning for the entire world and cosmos, which encompasses all of the living and the dead.

> It is at [the Eucharist] that we can and do live with our dead.... It is also at this service, where we show forth Christ's death, that Africans can be linked with their non-Christian ancestors. This is so because we believe that the death of Christ is for the whole world

---

1. John S. Mbiti, *Eschatology in an African Background* (Geneva: Ecumenical Institute, WCC, 1977), 155.
2. F. L. Cross and E. A. Livingstone, eds., *The Oxford Dictionary of the Christian Church*, 2d ed. (Oxford: Oxford University Press, 1983), 323.

and no one either living or dead is outside the scope of the merits of Christ's death.[3]

Other African scholars have proposed that Jesus Christ himself as the God-man is the link and archetype for ancestorship and fellowship between the living and the dead, the eternal and the here and now. "Christ as Brother-Ancestor implies a relationship linked to eternal life and straight to God." As regards the ancestors, this link is based on belief in (1) the ancestors' consanguinity with the living; (2) the divine status and supernatural powers of the ancestors; (3) the ancestors as role models for exemplary morality and behavior; and (4) the threat of calamity if they are offended and disrespected.[4] Juxtaposed against African ancestorship are (1) Jesus Christ as the Second Adam, thereby establishing him as brother to all of humanity, living and dead; (2) the divinity of Christ as God and his humanity as a man, thereby establishing his supreme power and authority as intermediary to the supreme deity; and (3) Christ as the source of all Christian morality, making him the exemplar par excellence. The difference is that Christ's authority and kingship are rooted not only in his partnership with humanity, as with the ancestors, but also in the very godhead itself. His divine relationship to the Father establishes his superiority over the ancestors, who are related only to survivors through common earthly parentage.[5]

HAGIOLATRY AND THE ANCESTORS

Who are the ancestors in African traditional cultures? What does the concept *ancestorship* mean? Ancestors are a divine community of the noble and exemplary dead existing between those living on this earth and those no longer living on this earth. They have a unique relationship to human beings as "spiritual superintendents of family affairs"; this is a role that they alone exercise — it is not exercised by God, the divinities, or other spirits.[6] Not all who die become ancestors. In order to be a worthy candidate for ancestorship one needs to have led an exemplary life, to have not been infertile, and

3. Mark E. Glasswell and Edward W. Fashole-Luke, *New Testament Christianity for Africa and the World* (London: SPCK, 1974), 217.
4. Charles Nyamiti, *Christ as Our Ancestor: Christology from an African Perspective* (Gweru, Zimbabwe: Mambo Press, 1984), 16.
5. Ibid., 21.
6. E. Bolaji Idowu, *African Traditional Religion: A Definition* (London: SCM Press, 1973), 184.

to have not died of particular tabooed illnesses or conditions. If candidates fit these criteria, they join the number of those whose former natural relationships to family and community have been endowed with an a-natural status.

It is not clear how the deceased become ancestors or when, although it is thought that both God and the other ancestors make the judgment. Also many deceased apparently are deified as ancestors by absorbing the attributes of an original divinity; this happened to Shango, principal divinity in the cult of Shango in Yoruba, who is thought to have been a human king who took on attributes of Jakuta, the original divinity of thunder and the sun in that religion.[7] J. Omosade Awolalu observes that in Yoruba and other African traditions, the accolade "ancestor" is likely to be applied only to the deceased man or woman who lived an exemplary life, attained old age, and is survived by good children and a happy memory. "Children and youths who die a premature death, barren women, and all who die a 'bad' death — e.g., killed by Ayélála or Shango or Sooponnó — are excluded from this respectable group."[8] Idowu contends that even those who died when they were not old or who died in the prime of life can be venerated as ancestors, provided they had children before their demise and led good lives according to the community.[9]

The bond between the ancestors and the living is usually beneficial, but it can be troublesome when persons, descendants, or communities offend the ancestors by transgressing a taboo or showing disrespect to the deceased. One Roman Catholic missionary, dubbing African ancestorship as superstition, stressed the fear among Africans when a taboo is violated: "The ghosts of influential persons and near relatives and people one had wronged in some way are greatly feared. [The ancestors] were considered to be revengeful and a frequent cause of illness."[10] But the dynamic between ancestors and the living is also characterized by a dependence and an

7. Ibid., 186.

8. J. Omosade Awolalu, *Yoruba Beliefs and Sacrificial Rites* (Harlow, England: Longman, 1979), 54. On the basis of my conversations with Ashanti and other tribes in Ghana and Kenya, these criteria for the "good death" also apply in their cultures as well.

9. Idowu, *African Traditional Religion*, 187.

10. B. K. Taylor, *The Western Lacustrine Bantu* (London: International African Institute, 1969), 38 (cited in John O'Donohue, *Spirits and Magic: A Critical Look* [Eldoret, Kenya: Gaba Publications, 1981], 17); see also R. E. S. Tanner, *Transition in African Beliefs* (Maryknoll, N.Y.: Orbis Books, 1967).

interdependence: a dependence of the earthly community on the benefaction and protection of the ancestors and an interdependence in that a covenant between the ancestors and the living is established, obliging both parties to responsibilities: "[Ancestors] are believed to be powerful in the sense that they maintain the course of life here and now and do influence it for good or for ill. They give children to the living; they give good harvests; they provide the sanctions for the moral life of the nation and accordingly punish, exonerate, or reward the living as the case may be."[11]

Mbiti calls them the "living-dead." That is, they are still living within the active memory of a family or a community and interact with them even though dead. The libations and morsels of food placed on the ground for the ancestors are signs of this interaction and are "acts of hospitality and welcome, and yet inform the living dead to move away. The living-dead are wanted and not wanted."[12]

Many Western theologians are distressed about the veneration of ancestors in African and Caribbean Afro cultures, thinking it either a kind of worship or a kind of spiritual necromancy engaged in by the living. At the same time they say the influence of ancestors for ill in human affairs contravenes traditional Christian doctrines of love and good will, thus posing a severe dilemma for African Christians wanting to affirm traditional ancestors: "Christians cannot accept the view that ancestors have power over living family members, and they must emphatically deny that deaths are caused by ancestors. And divination, a primary occupation of the ancestral cult, is entirely unacceptable."[13] Idowu reacts vigorously to Westerners' confusing veneration of ancestors with worship and adoration. He protests rightly about dismissing African religion as "ancestor-worship," saying this is based on a misunderstanding of the respect due the ancestors in the daily life of most Africans. Still, he acknowledges that the line between popular piety and veneration of the ancestors is very thin:

> Among the Igbo in Nigeria, the morning ritual begins with the invocation: "Chukwu (Deity), come and eat kola nut; Ala (Earth Goddess), come and eat kola nut; Ndiche (Ancestors), come and eat kola

11. John S. Pobee, *Toward an African Theology* (Nashville: Abingdon, 1979), 46.

12. John S. Mbiti, *African Religions and Philosophy* (Garden City, N.Y.: Doubleday/Anchor Books, 1970), 109.

13. Jack Partain, "Christians and Their Ancestors: A Dilemma of African Theology," *Christian Century* 103 (November 26, 1986): 1067.

nut." . . . The Yoruba use the same word, *bo*, indiscriminately with reference to the worship of Deity or divinities, as well as with reference to the making of offerings to the ancestors.[14]

Likewise, Melville J. Herskovits points out that in the traditional religion of Dahomey and Haitian Voodoo, the latter largely a legacy of Dahomean traditional religion, ancestors constitute a third category of spirits. These ancestor-spirits play an especially important role in the daily life of the Dahomeans, but they also fulfill a religious function: "For though the ancestral cult, when looked at in terms of its setting in the total configuration of Dahomean life, must be treated as an aspect of social organization, yet, in the final analysis, it is as fundamental a part of religious life as it is of social life."[15]

To understand the interplay between the ancestors or the "living-dead" (Mbiti) and the temporal community in African cultures, non-Africans ought to keep several points in mind. First, ancestors are venerated because ancestorship and parenthood are highly prized social values in African cultures. Proper communal and filial relationships are shaped and monitored by ancestral sanctions.

Second, the chief filial obligation of males is to carry out correct funeral rites and customs for their parents, an important first step for beginning the transformation of the dead toward possible ancestorship, provided they meet the other criteria. Veneration of ancestors is really the "ritualization of filial piety."[16]

Third, as noted previously, it is important to emphasize the ancestors' role as overseers of a community's moral code, which at the same time is the basis of its stability. Observance of taboos and moral codes is not founded on fear or ignorance, although such often is the motivation for veneration and even worship by some Africans; rather observing them has to do with maintaining communal stability and proper social relationships among the living and between the living and the dead. Their observance means conformity to a basic morality that shapes the ethics and relationships in the family and the community. Disrespecting them deliberately can endanger

14. Idowu, *African Traditional Religion*, 183.
15. Melville J. Herskovits, *Dahomey: An Ancient West African Kingdom*, 2 vols. (New York: J. J. Augustin, 1938), 2:297.
16. Meyer Fortes, *Oedipus and Job in West African Religion* (Cambridge: Cambridge University Press, 1959), 29 (cited in Edward W. Fashole-Luke, "Ancestor Veneration and the Communion of Saints," in Glasswell and Fashole-Luke, *New Testament Christianity for Africa and the World*, 212).

the well-being of the public and can even risk death, so serious is this breach. Connecting death and disobedience parallels the biblical world. However, for Christians tension does occur between the traditional concept of ancestors and biblical faith if they rely on ancestors, rather than God, to determine death.[17]

Fourth, ancestors are the bands of cohesion and coherence in African society, acting as guardians of ethics, family traditions, and community customs. In the Ashanti culture, for example, this is illustrated in the tradition of the stools, beginning with the Golden Stool. The Golden Stool is an essential sign for the political well-being and governance of the entire Ashanti culture. Unified as a nation in the seventeenth century during the reign of Osei-Tutu, founder of Kumasi and first king (*asantehene*) of the modern Ashanti people, the Ashanti believe that they came together as a people *in* the Golden Stool, which contains the very soul and chords of unity of the Ashanti kingdom and its ancestors.

This stool was created initially as a wooden stool embellished with gold. Tutu's chief priest, Anokye, summoned all the paramount chiefs, kings, queen-mothers, and other chief nobility together to endow this stool with the *sunsum* ("soul")[18] of disunited, fragmented, and therefore vulnerable tribes in the Ashanti nation, thereby creating political unity. Today no one is permitted to sit on it; nor may it touch the ground. R. Sutherland Rattray, a noted British scholar of traditional religion in Ghana, says of the Golden Stool: It is "the shrine and symbol of the national soul; the great umbrella covering the Stool when brought out in a procession or during an open-air ceremonial is known as *katamanso* — 'the covering of the nation.'"[19]

The Ashanti also honor their ancestors in the "blackened stool," an honor allowed only deceased chiefs, queen-mothers, kings, and clan elders known for their exemplary behavior and morality. The candidates must also have died a "good death." For instance, those who died from disfiguring diseases, snakebite, drowning, lightning, or suicide are considered not to have died a "good

17. Fashole-Luke, "Ancestor Veneration," 212–14.

18. The Ashanti, like participants in most African traditional religions, believe a person has two souls: *okra*, the individual soul given by God at birth that returns to God at death; and *sunsum*, the soul that is unique to a particular person and gives him or her personality and character. See also Peter Sarpong, *The Sacred Stools of the Akan* (Tema, Ghana: Ghana Publishing Corp., 1971), 30.

19. R. Sutherland Rattray, *Religion and Art in Ashanti* (Oxford: Oxford University Press, 1927), 130.

death," and therefore cannot have their stools blackened after death. Blackened with soot from spider webs (as a sign of wisdom, which the spider represents), eggs (a sign of peace), and sheep's blood and fat, the blackened stools are visible monuments to ancestral spirits and are representative of them. Thus these stools, so sacred that they can be kept only in the house of the reigning chief, are both shrines and vessels of the ancestors.

But the blackened stools are also links in the political and ruling succession of the chiefs among the Ashanti. When a new chief is installed, an essential ritual is the lowering and raising of the chief-elect three times over the blackened stool of the ancestor who is the founder and guardian of the royal lineage. At the conclusion of this ceremony, the chief acquires a sacredness and new inviolability. These virtues are to be reinforced by his observing various taboos, such as not striking or being struck by anyone; he is obliged to wear sandals or shoes and not walk around barefooted as other members of the tribe; he should always walk gently and majestically.

> An Ashanti chief fills a sacred role as the "one who sits upon the stool of the ancestors."... He is the link, the intermediary, between the living and the dead; for according to the conception which the Ashanti share with other Akan tribes, the dead, the living, and those still to be born of the tribe are all members of one family, and it is the stool that binds the family together.[20]

Likewise, at the annual ceremony in Ghana called Odwera, which lasts from seven to fourteen days, or the Adae festivals, food and drink are offered to the ancestors, and the chief and people process to the royal burial house where among other prayers they petition for a strengthening of the link between the ancestors and the community:

> Here is food; all you ancestors receive this and eat; the year has come round again; today we celebrate it; bring us blessing; blessing to the chief who sits on your stool; health to the people; let women bear children; let the men prosper in their undertakings; life to all; we thank you for the good harvest; for standing behind us well [i.e., guarding and protecting us]; Blessing, blessing, blessing.[21]

---

20. K. A. Busia, "The Ashanti of the Gold Coast," in Daryll Forde, ed., *African Worlds: Studies in the Cosmological Ideas and Social Values of African Peoples* (London: Oxford University Press, 1954), 202.
    21. Cited in ibid., 204.

Fifth, ancestors are also spirits who communicate with their survivors through dreams, reincarnation, and visions. They may be reincarnated in grandchildren or great-grandchildren, while at the same time remaining in the community of spirits. Even if they are reincarnated, they continue to be recognized as the head of the family or community, and they continue to intercede on their behalf before the supreme deity and the divinities. Awolalu notes that in the worldview of most Africans a major benefaction of ancestors is protection from the effects of the evil powers of witches and sorcerers.[22]

Ancestors are recalled and celebrated very much in the sense of what liturgists call "anamnesis" or "remembrance." The word is linked to the Eucharist and its institution in the New Testament: "Do this is remembrance of me" (1 Cor. 11:23-25). This does not mean simply a memorial or a collective recalling of someone absent or some historical occasion; rather this remembrance is an actual re-presenting, a reliving of the person and his or her life; this person operates in the present and has influence on the here and now. The ancestors are living beacons that neither life nor community ends with death; both continue after death and in spite of death.

Ancestorship in the Caribbean

Ancestorship in the Caribbean comes in various forms — some directly reflect characteristics of African traditional religion and others do more to adapt those characteristics to conditions of New World Christianity. The burial services of the slaves, for example, were important occasions for honoring the ancestors, where libations and food offerings were made. In Jamaica the slaves had two burials for the deceased, the first after the third day of death and the second after 40 days, the progenitor of the current 40-day mourning period in parts of Jamaica. The first burial was considered temporary so that the soul could travel. The second was the occasion for "covering" the corpse in the grave completely with soil, signifying that the soul had finally found its resting place. Much celebrating, drinking, eating, and dancing accompanied the second burial. The Jamaican scholar Edward Brathwaite comments that when whites watched all the jubilation at slave funerals and the two burials, they often concluded that the slaves did not take death or care of their

22. Awolalu, *Yoruba Beliefs*, 61.

deceased very seriously.[23] But the slaves took death quite seriously, not only because of ancestorship, but also because they believed that after death, they would return reincarnated to Africa. The ancestors played an important role in this process of reincarnation because they were links with the Old World. As one Jamaican slave woman picturesquely put it: those who misbehaved and mistreated others while alive would return as mules, horses, and flies; those who led good and exemplary lives would return as freed blacks.[24]

As noted before, Jamaican Kumina holds to the African belief in ancestral spirits of the deceased, which they call "ancestral zombies." In the beyond, many zombies are thought to have become even more powerful, therefore increasing the munificence of their benefaction to the earthly survivors. In addition, Kumina holds to the Nine Night wake in Jamaica, also practiced by revivalists and Catholics as a way of giving respect to the souls of deceased members of families.[25] Many Afro Caribbean cultures have inherited the West African belief in two souls, even though people think this belief is dying out among the educated classes in Jamaica. According to this belief, each individual has a soul that returns to God at death, and a second soul or a "duppy" that stays behind after death.[26] A duppy can inflict good or harm upon survivors and others. If the duppy has been dismissed at the wake or in another ceremony, it cannot return on its own and do harm.

Nine Night is a series of wakes for the deceased that begins on the third day after the death, usually the day of the funeral, in accordance with the belief that Christ rose on the third day. A lighted candle representing "the rising light" is placed outside the residence of the deceased. The ceremony includes Christian hymns,

23. Edward K. Brathwaite, *The Folk Culture of the Slaves in Jamaica* (London: New Beacon Books, 1981), 10.

24. Ibid., 11.

25. I am depending mostly on the accounts of this ceremony in George Eaton Simpson, *Religious Cults of the Caribbean: Trinidad, Jamaica, and Haiti* (Rio Piedras, P.R.: Institute of Caribbean Studies, 1979).

26. The precise derivation of "duppy" in Jamaica is uncertain, although some think it came from an African word *bube* or *dupe*, meaning "ghost." First recorded in 1774 by British colonialists who heard slaves referring to their deceased friends as duppies, it is thought to have come from West African traditions that held that the soul goes to heaven after death, but its shadow remains near the body. Unless the corpse is properly laid to rest, its spirit becomes a duppy. Eventually duppy and shadow were identified as the same thing (see F. C. Cassidy, *Jamaica Talk* [London: Macmillan & Co., 1961], 245–46; F. C. Cassidy and R. B. LePage, eds., *Dictionary of Jamaican English* [Cambridge: Cambridge University Press, 1967], 164; and Edward Long, *The History of Jamaica*, 3 vols. [London: Lowndes, 1774], 2:416).

Bible readings, and spirit possession, as well as the favorite foods of the departed and a rum libation. In the morning after the ninth night service, the water used in the service to summon the spirits is thrown out to show that the corpse's spirit is now free. The house is then swept clean and any clothes of the deceased are given to relatives. Proper funeral rites make certain that the ancestral spirit can return in peace and not turmoil.

There are also burial dances that have different purposes, such as the memorial dances, which are intended to put the soul of the just departed to rest, and the entombment and crop-over dances, which mark the end of the Nine Night ceremony. These dances take place at the burial place of the ancestors and the recently deceased; otherwise the duppy will wander and steadily bother the family and the community.[27]

In Trinidadian Shango on the Feast of All Saints (November 1) and the Feast of All Souls (November 2), candles are lighted for the saints (the powers), a rum and sweet oil libation is offered, and incense is thrown on the ground of the place where the deceased is remembered. Participants march clockwise three times and counter-clockwise four times around a fire, each time throwing pepper and cloves into the fire, and songs are chanted, to Ogun (St. Michael) for protection against Eshu, a trickster and messenger of the divinities who can interrupt the ceremony, Osain (St. Francis), brother of and assistant to Michael as well as master of fire, and Shakpana (St. Jerome or Moses), a temperamental physician thought to control all evil spirits:

Ay la sen dah wah	Here is All Saints' night
Ay la sen dah wah	Here is All Saints' night
Ay la sen dah wah	Here is All Saints' night
Da Ogun la sen da wah	Ogun we want; All Saints' night
Osain la sen dah wah	Osain we want; All Saints' night
Shakpana la sen dah wah	Shakpana we want; All Saints night.[28]

At wakes for the dead in Trinidad, there is also a Nine Night service in some places. The people in these places believe that the deceased's "shadow" returns on the ninth evening after his or her death because it has not been dismissed. The dismissal may be a Christian committal service ("Ashes to ashes, dust to dust"), a curt

27. Cassidy and Lepage, eds., *Dictionary of Jamaican English*, 166.
28. Cited in Simpson, *Religious Cults of the Caribbean*, 52.

dismissal ("We don't need you anymore. Don't come back"), or a combination of both.[29]

However, the existence of ancestral spirits or duppies does not depend on remembrance or anamnesis by loved ones. Ancestral spirits have their own afterlife in a heavenly abode, independent of human remembrance. When ancestors are venerated at annual festivals in African towns and villages, they are often linked to the beginning of time, showing that their abode has an eternal character and is considered a "heaven" or "paradise." In Dahomean and Haitian traditional religion, when the soul leaves the earth, on the final trip to the afterlife, he or she must cross three rivers and climb a mountain to where the ancestors live in a valley; there the deceased is able to join them permanently, provided that the deceased has died a "good death" and been properly buried on earth.[30]

This is no doubt an adaptation of African traditions, since, as Herskovits points out, in African culture there are two reasons for giving a proper burial to the deceased. The first is positive: the prestige and status enjoyed by the family giving a resplendent funeral. The second is negative: fear of resentment by the deceased at an improperly provided funeral; that resentment can have an effect on the survivors and may result in the spirit of the deceased wandering without a final rest and thereby becoming vengeful.[31]

Ancestors and Black American Religion

Similar sentiments about the dead "going home" can be found in slave funerals and piety in black religion in the United States, that religion being an amalgam of Protestant Christianity, Africanisms, pietism, and slave religion. (It is noteworthy that funerals and burials continue to be important in contemporary black culture, particularly in the South and in some northern urban areas with large black populations from the South.) Many slaves decorated graves with favorite items of the deceased that could be enjoyed in the afterlife; this was done in order to induce good will toward the survivors.

In eighteenth- and early nineteenth-century Virginia this particular Africanism apparently influenced poor whites' burial rites. Many of their graves were adorned with seashells, overturned Mason

29. Ibid., 50–51.
30. Herskovits, *Dahomey*, 1:195.
31. Melville J. Herskovits, *The Myth of the Negro Past* (1941; reprint, Boston: Beacon Press, 1958), 198.

jars, wine bottles, children's toys, animals, dolls, and other memorabilia. Such an influence probably occurred because in Virginia blacks and whites often worshiped together in Baptist and Methodist churches. (In the more established Anglican churches the patricians and slave masters tended to restrict their slaves to galleries or separate services after the white service.)

> Placating their spirits [of the dead] was very important, and funerals remained the most significant transitional rites. Whites had come to share many African perceptions without being aware of this.... Spirits were perceived in a new way; life after death was seen as a "homecoming" and kin were expected to welcome the spirits. Funerals became far more important and graveyards were recognized as places where spirits should be honored.[32]

As we saw in the often curt and blunt "dismissal" of the duppy in Afro Caribbean cultures, many eulogies and sermons at black funerals both during slavery and in modern times are startling for their frankness and directness when speaking about the deceased; the speakers list the deceased's faults, weaknesses, the names of people with whom he or she disagreed, etc. Another characteristic of these rites is that during slavery the slaves insisted that at their funerals the preacher be black; this was believed to help insure a proper burial. Herskovits thinks these customs too are carry-overs from Africa and slavery when people spoke bluntly so that the spirit of the deceased would not hold resentments against some and so that its tranquil journey into the afterlife not be disturbed, thereby giving it no cause to return to bother the survivors.[33]

The role of spirits of the dead is more ambivalent in black American religion than in Caribbean traditional religion and even its Africanized churches, although it is quite clear that a great many of the historical American Negro spirituals and contemporary gospel songs express convictions about meeting up with the dead in heaven:[34]

32. Mechal Sobel, "'Wrasslin' Jacob': Black and White Understandings of Causality and Purpose" (Paper presented at the Northeastern Seminar in Black Religious History, Yale University, September 1985, 22–24).
33. Herskovits, *The Myth of the Negro Past*, 204.
34. The use of the category "Negro spirituals" to designate slave religious songs is a late nineteenth-century addition. Slave songs outraged whites, as did the slaves' gestures used to keep time and the "holy" dancing that the slaves engaged in during these songs.

I got a home up in that kingdom. Ain't that good news?
I got a home up in that kingdom. Ain't that good news?
I'm gonna' lay down this old world.
   Gonna' shoulder up my cross.
   Gonna' take it home to my Jesus.
Ain't that good news?

Likewise, gospel hymns in black churches announce a meeting with the dead in a "home" not made with hands:

O they tell me of a home far beyond the skies,
O they tell me of a home far away;
O they tell me of a home where no storm clouds rise,
O they tell me of an unclouded day.
O they tell me of a home where my friends have gone,
O they tell me of that land far away;
Where the tree of life in eternal bloom
Sheds its fragrance through the unclouded day.

Death therefore has a double meaning in slave and gospel songs: It is a liberation from the earthly bondage and oppression of slavery and it is a passage to the spirits of the deceased. Mostly, death was not feared in slave songs, according to some scholars, no doubt because the African ancestors were believed to have already paved the path with death and because death and life were partners. One of the spirituals expresses these sentiments:

Oh Deat' he is a little man,
And he goes from do' to do',
He kill some souls and he wounded some,
And he lef' some souls to pray.

Death he ain't nothin' but a robber, don't you see?
Death came to my house, he didn't stay long,
I looked in de bed an' my mother [father, sister, brother] was gone,
Death he ain't nothin' but a robber, don't you see?[35]

Thus it may be said that the afterlife in heaven in black religion, where loved ones will be reunited and seen again, resembles in some ways the afterlife in much of African traditional religion, where the

35. John Lovell, Jr., *Black Song: The Forge and the Flame* (New York: Macmillan Company, 1972), 307.

deceased expect to meet up with the ancestors. That is, in both belief systems, a bond of solidarity has been established between the living and the dead. For the slaves such a solidarity allowed for dignity and exaltation instead of indignity and humiliation bred by the system of slavery. John Lovell, Jr., studied 20 slave spirituals referring to family and relatives and found that mother, sister, brother, and father, in that order, were most frequently named, followed by grandmother, the Blessed Virgin, and friends.[36] So, for example, the slave sang of the "old ship of Zion" that was good for his or her dear mother or father:

> It has landed many a thousand.
> It has landed many a thousand.
> It has landed many a thousand.
> Git on board, Git on board.
>
> It will take you home to Glory.
> It will take you home to Glory.
> It will take you home to Glory.
> Git on board, Git on board.[37]

Given the similarities between ancestorship in Africa and the Caribbean and spirits in black American culture, why was ancestorship not more developed in black American culture, even given its more overtly Christian roots? Some insist that the evangelical Protestant nature of black piety chiefly caused the dearth or absence of this very important African legacy in black American Christianity. But both in Jamaica and Trinidad, countries ruled by the British, who certainly perceived themselves as Protestant, this Africanism survived among Caribbean Christian groups even with Protestant adaptations, such as Kumina, the revivalist churches, and Pocomania in Jamaica, and the Yoruba-descended Shango traditional religion in Trinidad. Others trace this dearth to demographics of the American slave system: (1) most plantations in the states with large slave populations, like Virginia and South Carolina, had fewer than 20 slaves per plantation; on those plantations, in spite of the master/slave stratification, the slaves and whites did have more frequent contact and therefore whites had more influence on the slaves' religion;

---

36. Ibid, 355.
37. J. Jefferson Cleveland and Veroigna Nix, eds., *Songs of Zion* (Nashville: Abingdon, 1981).

(2) whites outnumbered slaves in the South (only South Carolina [1850: 393,000 slaves] and Mississippi [1850: 310,808][38] of the 14 slave states had slave populations larger than the white population in the eighteenth and nineteenth centuries), while slaves outnumbered whites on Caribbean plantations (Jamaica: in 1703, 8,000 whites had 45,000 slaves; in 1768, 18,000 whites had 167,000 slaves; in the nineteenth century, the ratio was 1 white to 13 slaves;[39] Haiti: in 1791, 40,000 whites, 28,000 free blacks, 452,000 slaves);[40] (3) the large number of native-born slaves in the United States resulted in the death of the African gods because of the increased distance and diminished memory of African traditions;[41] (4) more widespread adaptation of Africanisms happened in the evangelical religious environment in America than in the Caribbean.[42]

However, I think the lack of this central feature of African cosmology in black American culture has to do with the absence of maroons, the slave freedom fighters in the Caribbean, among U.S. blacks. The maroons (Spanish: *cimarrón*, "domestic cattle which had run wild into the hills") were runaway slaves who hid in the mountains and hills of the various Caribbean islands, most especially Haiti, Jamaica, Cuba, and Trinidad. One of the most successful maroons was Boukman, a *houngan* who began the Haitian revolution in 1791 at a Voodoo service during which he appealed to the ancestral spirits for protection and fortification against the whites.[43]

---

38. *The Negro in Virginia*, comp. Workers of the Writers' Program of the Work Projects Administration in the State of Virginia (New York: Hastings House, 1940), 162.

39. Herbert S. Klein, *African Slavery in Latin America and the Caribbean* (New York: Oxford University Press, 1986), 54.

40. Alfred N. Hunt, *Haiti's Influence on Antebellum America: Slumbering Volcano in the Caribbean* (Baton Rouge: Louisiana State University Press, 1988), 9.

41. Klein disputes this claim. Without giving statistical data, he maintains that in the eighteenth century and during the first half of the nineteenth century, most of the slaves imported to the United States came directly from Africa, with their descendants accounting for four-fifths of the African-American community (Klein, *African Slavery*, 140). However, data show that after the abolition of the slave trade by the United States, the number of slave ships going from Africa to the United States diminished greatly, even though the United States was slow in enforcing the law and many ships from Africa carried "flags of convenience" in U.S. ports (see Philip D. Curtin, *The Atlantic Slave Trade: A Census* [Madison: University of Wisconsin Press, 1969], 72–74, 268).

42. Albert J. Raboteau, *Slave Religion* (New York: Oxford University Press, 1978), 89–90.

43. See the text of his prayer in C. L. R. James, *The Black Jacobins: Toussaint L'Ouverture and the San Domingo Revolution* (New York: Vintage Books, 1963), 87.

The maroons were what some call a "critical mass" in preserving and handing down African traditions in spite of unrelenting pursuit and restrictions of their movement by the whites. Maroonage began in the Spanish possessions, the first incident being traced to the insurrection of slaves on December 26, 1522, appropriately enough on the island of Hispaniola (present-day Haiti and the Dominican Republic). Escaping into the hilly terrain, the maroons were imaginative enough to use their harsh natural environment for their own defense and concealment, which in turn provided a barrier against colonial religion. One writer describes a community in Jamaica where descendants of maroons still survive: "Had it been entered by a line of men, it would not have been difficult for the maroons from the heights to have blocked them up in the front and in the rear, by rolling down large rocks at both ends, and afterwards to have crushed them to death by the same means."[44]

They became such a problem for the Spanish colonialists in the Caribbean that in 1540 a royal decree was issued that proclaimed:

> Maroons are to be punished according to the statutes of this book, and at no time shall such punishments be replaced by the amputation of those parts of the body which, in all decency, cannot be named.[45]

In 1685 King Louis XIV of France decreed in *Le Code Noire* the following punishment for maroons in the French Caribbean:

> A Negro who is absent for a month shall have his ears cut off and shall have a *fleur de lys* branded on his left shoulder. If he again runs away, his knees shall be lacerated and his other shoulder shall be branded. Finally, if he runs away for a third time, he shall be sentenced to death.[46]

There are various stories about the religious beliefs of the maroons, usually told by outsiders who had forced entry into their villages in the swamps, mountains, and secluded places in the Caribbean; these stories frequently relate the magical powers of the maroons — one tells of a nanny in Jamaica who was able to catch bullets in her buttocks and then defuse them; another tells of Haitians who

---

44. Richard Price, ed., *Maroon Societies: Rebel Slave Communities in the Americas* (Baltimore: Johns Hopkins University Press, 1979), 6.

45. Cited in José L. Franco, "Maroons and Slave Rebellions in the Spanish Territories," in Price, ed., *Maroon Societies*, 39.

46. Ibid.

could not be wounded because they were wearing amulets.[47] But there is little doubt that the divinities and spirits of their African forebears were retained and adapted for survival and wars of liberation against the system of slavery; those beliefs survived even though the maroons were of diverse African tribes. Maroon communities survived partly by maintaining their African traditions in the isolation of the mountains. They waged at least two great wars on the whites in Jamaica: one from 1725–1740 and the other from 1784–1832.[48] Descendants of the maroons continue to live in the mountainous areas of Trelawny in modern Jamaica. Martha Warren Beckwith describes the descendants of the maroons in Jamaica as "hardy, intelligent and, in the old English sense, aristocratic. They guard too jealously their old privileges and do not listen yet to the younger men who want to make an end of degrading superstitions."[49]

Roger Bastide, a noted student of Brazil's African religions, says there were two types of religious adaptation in the Caribbean and South America: that which preserved or conserved, like Candomblé in Brazil and Santeria in Cuba; and that which adapted, like Voodoo in Haiti. The first, he said, was a kind of "defense mechanism," seeking to preserve without acknowledging any change or adaptation; the second was like a "charge of the light brigade," flexible enough to adapt just enough to remain stable.[50]

Thus ancestorship in Africa and the Caribbean effectively joins what one scholar called three "communities": (1) a community of obligation, in that there are duties and respect expected of the earthly survivors; (2) a community of interdependence between the ancestor and the family and community; and (3) a community of "cosmic continuity," in that neither the spirit-human nor the life-death relationship ends with this earthly life but rather continues in the heavens of the divinities and ancestors.[51]

---

47. Ibid., 10.
48. Orlando Patterson, *The Sociology of Slavery: An Analysis of the Origins, Development and Structure of Negro Slave Society in Jamaica* (Rutherford, N.J.: Fairleigh Dickinson University Press, 1967), 268–73.
49. Martha Warren Beckwith, *Black Roadways: A Study of Jamaican Folk Life* (New York: Negro University Press, 1929), 144.
50. Cited in Price, ed., *Maroon Societies,* 29.
51. J. M. Berentsen, *Grave and Gospel* (Leiden, Netherlands: E. J. Brill, 1985), 243.

HAGIOGRAPHY:
CHRISTIAN SAINTS AND THE ANCESTORS

Christian scholars generally agree that the cult of saints in Christianity historically combines popular piety about "pagan" heroes (that piety often viewed those heroes as "successors to the gods") with efforts to Christianize such piety. It is known, for example, that when Constantine came upon the Temple of Poseidon in his new-found city of Constantinople in the fourth century, he dedicated it to St. Menas, a fourth-century Egyptian martyr. St. Augustine's shrewd observation about the compromises between an idealized Christian faith and popular piety in particular cultures touches on what is at play in this merger: "What we teach is one thing; what we tolerate is another; and what we are obliged to put up with is yet another."[52]

Opinions differ, however, as to how the veneration of Christian saints began. Some say the public veneration of particular Christian heroes and heroines first began with the martyrs, the earliest occasion being the commemoration of St. Polycarp's death; Polycarp, the bishop of Smyrna, was burned at the stake in his diocese for refusing to renounce his Christian faith. These martyrs were revered as "athletes and prizefighters in a supernatural combat" with the devil and the evil standing behind the political struggles and persecutions.[53] By the fourth century this custom of observing the anniversary of the death of the martyrs had extended to ordinary and unsung Christians whose exemplary Christian lives and faith amid seriously threatening political torment and persecutions had led them to be called "confessors." This group of unsung heroes and heroines included bishops, religious, theologians, and pastors.

The New Testament scholar Joachim Jeremias proposes that Christian veneration of saints stems originally from the first-century A.D. Jewish custom of decorating the graves of ancestors such as Elisha, Abraham, Isaac, and Jacob in Hebron. Evidence cited in the New Testament includes: Matt. 23:29-30 ("Woe to you, scribes and Pharisees, hypocrites! for you build the tombs of the prophets and

---

52. Augustine, *Contra Faustum* 20.21 (cited in Stephen Wilson, ed., *Saints and Their Cults: Studies in Religious Sociology, Folklore and History* [New York: Alfred A. Knopf, 1987], 436).

53. Robin Lane Fox, *Pagans and Christians* (New York: Alfred A. Knopf, 1987), 436.

adorn the monuments of the righteous . . . ") and Luke 11:47. Veneration served partly as atonement or penance for the sins of previous generations and partly to honor the dead who were thought to be of assistance as intercessors for the living before God. Although the rabbis opposed such a custom, they were unsuccessful in preventing it.[54]

But the Bible also describes some type of veneration or even worship of ancestors taking place in ancient Palestine at shrines connected to the patriarchs, such as the tree east of Shechem (Gen. 12:6; 35:2, 4), the holy shrine at Bethel (Gen. 12:8; 13:3; 28:11-22), and the sacred terebinth tree of Mamre in the vicinity of Hebron (Gen. 13:18; 18:1). This means that the patriarchs and remembrance of them and their deeds continued to have a place in the culture of their survivors, who worshiped them as recipients and agents of God's revelation. Such shrines and cults are also evidence that the patriarchs no doubt once existed historically, not too dissimilar from African belief about actual historical personages becoming ancestors.[55]

Remnants of early Hebrew views about spirits (or souls) can still be found in certain Jewish rituals about death and mourning.[56] Contemporary chassidic groups, for example, visit the grave sites of their deceased *rebbe*, who is considered one of the "holy ones" in accordance with Talmudic customs. The Bratslaver chassidim even journey to Uman in the Soviet Union to visit their founder's grave, while Moroccan Jews visit the grave of the Baba Sali in Israel. Both groups seek the intercession of the holy one in matters of better livelihood, increased fertility, and cures.

There is also the custom of praying for the "elevation of the departed's soul," as in the early Ashkenazic ritual of studying and fasting on the anniversary (*Yahrzeit*) of the departed's death as a petition for the soul's elevation. Likewise, the tradition of *Kaddish* (prayers for the deceased) is thought to have originated in a saying from Rabbi Akiba. Rabbi Akiba was approached by an orphan wanting to relieve his father's suffering "in the world to come." Akiba advised him to recite a prayer for "the elevation of his soul" that is

54. Cited in Berentsen, *Grave and Gospel*, 132.
55. See a fuller account of ancestor worship in ancient Israel in Martin Alt, *The History of Israel*, trans. P. R. Ackrouyd, rev. ed. (New York: Harper & Brothers Publishers, 1960), 122-27.
56. For this information I am indebted to a colleague, Michael Chernick, an orthodox rabbi, who is also professor of Talmudic studies at the Hebrew Union College — Jewish Institute of Religion in New York City.

thought to be an early version of the *Kaddish*. The prayer frees the deceased from eternal punishment for any sins unrepented for while living and allows them an even greater reward for acts of piety.

Still, others deny such non-Christian origins and maintain that the idea of sainthood for special people such as martyrs began with gatherings at the burial places of Christian martyrs; in the early church these burial places in turn became sacred spaces in which a commemoration Eucharist was held on the anniversary of the martyrs' deaths. Because of much vandalism and personal assaults on Christians during the time of the Goths and the Lombards, public ceremonies and festivals became practically impossible, so the bones of the martyrs were relocated at shrines inside churches, where the liturgy was celebrated.[57] In many ways these early Christian celebrations parallel the annual local festivals to ancestors celebrated in many African towns and villages today.

Peter Brown, looking at the place of saints in the Christian tradition, has related the idea of shrines to the custom of grave houses built by affluent families in the first century to honor idealized heroes. He researched graves in cemeteries, which were usually found outside the walls of the cities in the western part of the empire. These grave houses were often built architecturally to resemble the early Christian shrines where Christians remembered martyrs at their grave (or grace) houses; the pagan grave houses thereby assimilated the veneration of a shrine. But, cautions Brown, the similarity between the pagan heroes and the Christian martyrs stops here because Christians insisted that the martyrs' lives were particularly exemplary due to their "intimacy with God." "Their intimacy with God was the *sine qua non* of their ability to intercede for and, so, to protect their fellow mortals. . . . [The martyr] was an intercessor in a way which the hero could never have been."[58]

Eventually these shrines, due to their location outside the walls of the town or city, were also used by some bishops in the West to anchor their control and power base in the church and to expand their influence.

> Tomb and altar were joined. The bishop and his clergy performed public worship in a proximity to the human dead that would have

57. Dom Gregory Dix, *The Shape of the Liturgy* (London: Dacre Press, 1954), 371.

58. Peter Brown, *The Cult of the Saints* (Chicago: University of Chicago Press, 1981), 6.

been profoundly disturbing to pagan and Jewish feeling. . . . The tomb of the saint was declared public property as the tomb of no other Christian was: it was made accessible to all, and became the focus of forms of ritual common to the whole community.[59]

Brown also mentions that even Emperor Julian the Apostate noted the novelty of the Christian cult of martyrs in the Roman Empire, complaining that such festivals only added new names to the already established roster of heroes.[60]

The cultic character of venerating and even worshiping the martyrs and heroes underwent further change liturgically in the fifth century and doctrinally in the eighth. In the fifth century the churches in the East added antiphons to the saints in the liturgy, a step followed by the West some 300 years later. The Seventh Ecumenical Council at Nicaea, held in the eighth century, decreed that each consecrated church should have a relic of a saint permanently buried in its high altar. Now attention was focused on the saints at every celebration of the liturgy. This of course got out of hand when the church in the West formalized the worship of such saints in its Roman Martyrology of 1584; according to that martyrology, a saint or saints were assigned to each day of the year that was not a feast of Christ or the Blessed Virgin Mary. On many days during the year a number of saints' feasts were to be celebrated.

In addition to martyrs and confessors new classifications were added: monks and nuns, virgins, bishops, and even popes; because these had led the "good life," they were viewed as prototypes of Christians and were deemed worthy of saintly veneration. Such additions reflected a change in popular piety as well as in the church's understanding of holiness and sanctity. It is important to note that the process of "canonization" exercised both by the Roman Catholic Church and the Orthodox churches does not make a person a saint, just as the sacrament of marriage does not make a marriage. Rather it is an official recognition of many of the virtues in the person's biography, and it is a means by which the church commends those virtues to others as marks of the "Christian" or the "good life." The person's life may not have been blameless, but nonetheless was a commendable example of Christian faithfulness, generosity, and integrity. The person was a *hero* to others in his or her lifetime. "And this giving, this loving self-offering to Him who is Holiness itself,

59. Ibid., 9.
60. Ibid., 7.

is entirely independent of such circumstances as occupation in life, social or other status, education, temperament, natural abilities or lack of them."[61]

But the notion about the "good life" of the saint can also be correlated to the "good death" of the saint, which has parallels in the "good death" virtue of African ancestorship. We can see this in popular piety that held that the saint was still present in his or her shrine in a special way, so that favors and intercessions could be gained from some physical relationship to that shrine. This popular piety was later corrupted as indulgences in medieval Roman Catholicism. Thus at the shrine of St. Martin of Tours (315–397), miracles (a sure witness to a saint's sanctity) that occurred on his feast day were regarded as indisputable confirmation of his worthy death and continued living presence among and protection of the community.[62]

Christian saints traditionally have other functions that parallel those of African ancestors; among these are bringing help for the living, particularly in troubled times or when the supplicant thinks he or she has offended the saint. Women wanting to have children, men wanting to be potent, those looking for jobs and good fortune, the sick looking for healing, and those in need of help in times of crisis all bring their petitions to the saints. Like some African spirits, there are also saints with special functions, such as St. Margaret (whose veneration was suppressed by the pope in the 1960s), who protects women at childbirth, St. Nicholas (fourth century), patron of lawyers, and St. Catherine, helper of midwives.

Another parallel lies in the role saints play as patrons, intercessors, and protectors for particular classes or institutions, a function analogous to an advocate or a lawyer in the courtroom. A hierarchy of advocate-saints has developed with St. Mary the Virgin at the head as "arch-intercessor." After Christianity became the established faith of the empire, every locality took on a patron saint who replaced the previous local gods. This tradition continued throughout much of Europe even after the Reformation, although it did not continue in areas strongly affected by the Protestant Reformation with its suspicions and hostility toward the veneration of saints. So, for example, we are reminded that St. Genevieve (c. 420–500), patroness of Paris,

---

61. Donald Attwater, *A Dictionary of Saints* (New York: Penguin Books, 1979), 11.

62. Wilson, ed., *Saints and Their Cults*, 11.

was sought not only by the sick of the city, but also in times of economic or natural distress and crisis, such as in 1206 when her relics
were paraded through the city so that the flood waters of the Seine
might crest, a tradition still maintained in the city's annual festival
to the saint.[63]

A third saintly function similar to that of ancestors is the be-
stowal of political legitimacy. In African cultures the ancestors have
long been used to legitimize the political and moral authority of
chiefs and kings. The church, on its side, often used the cult of the
saints to defend political and social interests of monasteries, con-
vents, parish churches, and even the papacy. This was done at a
saint's shrine under the protection of a particular religious order or
monastery. Monasteries often petitioned for recognition as a shrine's
patron to insure canonization of their local patron saint, such as was
done by the abbey at Westminster for St. Edward the Confessor in
the twelfth century.[64]

Christian saints also have a scolding or punishing function,
which has been exercised ecclesiastically and politically in the past
and to some effect in modern times in parts of Catholic Europe and
South America. Popes have asked saints to exercise this function
in political quarrels with kings and political authorities, as in the
case of King Aldfrith of Northumbria (685–704), who declined to
follow the instructions of the pope. The pope in turn promised that
he would be "stricken down by the power of the Apostles for his
defiance of Rome."[65] Thus in popular piety the saints had a great
deal of power that was used mostly for good, but also, like the
ancestors, could be used for punishment in severe cases of offense
and violation of honor. St. Benedict of Portugal at his shrine in
Geres is still said to be particularly vindictive when a vow is not
maintained.[66]

One Brazilian sociologist has described the role of sainthood
within Christendom in a way that echoes the role of ancestorship:

> The saint's presence, whether in the form of relics or an "effigy,"
> symbolizes the community, encapsulating its history and acting as
> the focus of its energies. If it is a guardian presence and a permanent

63. Ibid., 24.
64. Ibid., 26–28.
65. Ibid., 32.
66. Pierre Sanchis, "The Portuguese 'Romarias,'" in Wilson, ed., *Saints and Their Cults*, 268–69.

guarantee of continuity, life and abundance at all times, it is because, *like a deified ancestor* it allows the group to be conscious of its own being, intensifies its self-awareness, creates a sense of being socially "rooted," and provides a sure identity. For the community to lose its saint would mean the abandonment of this identity and would present it with the prospect of being reduced to anonymity.[67]

There is another power of Christian saints which, though not a part of African ancestorship, has parallels in the Afro Caribbean, namely, *possession*. In the Christian tradition possession was and continues to be mostly associated with evil and demons, which called for exorcism. Exorcism was a time for public confession, much like the ritual in the witch trials in seventeenth-century New England. Therefore the saint's shrine was a place for people to be possessed or to seek possession by the particular saint in order to confess privately to the saint rather than "expose themselves to the hard justice of their fellows."[68]

In sixth-century Gaul the possessed were recognized as having a special status. They were given food, received daily blessings from the priests, and were granted the honor of being allowed to clean the floors of the basilica housing the shrine. "Late-antiquity and early medieval men...felt that in [exorcism] they witnessed more clearly and with greater precision the manner in which God, through his lords the saints, could stretch forth into their midst the right hand of his healing power."[69] Hence, possession linked with the rites of exorcism by the church provided for a cleansing when evil possession was suspected, but also reintegration into the community.[70] St. Augustine noted, for example, that at the shrine of Gervasius and Protasius — two martyrs whose remains Ambrose found in late fourth-century Milan, but whose biographies are unknown — thieves brought there were possessed by the saints, confessed their misdeeds, and then were allowed to make reparations for the robberies rather than face the justice or vengeance of the community.[71] Reintegration was a sign that harmony in God's creation had been restored (which also has a parallel in African traditional cultures' notion of the role of sacrifice to the divinities).

67. Ibid., 264. Emphasis added.
68. Brown, *The Cult of Saints*, 111.
69. Ibid., 107.
70. Ibid., 111.
71. Ibid., 112.

The Catholic Church has adapted some aspects of early ancestor veneration into its burial liturgy and customs, such as bowing toward the altar where a relic of a saint is kept upon entering the church or crossing in front of the altar, using ointment and oils to anoint the corpses of clerics and bishops, praying for the souls of the dead, receiving gifts and lighting candles on behalf of the dead, using incense at requiem Eucharists, and using flowers in the church at funerals. Indeed in the eighth century the veneration or possibly even worship of ancestors among Christians had become so widespread that it was discussed at the German Council in 742, which spoke in opposition to "offerings to the dead."[72]

The Catholic Church in the West continues to be concerned about providing some theological guidelines for veneration of the dead via the saints. Hence, it says that the worship of God and Jesus Christ is *latria*, the veneration or honoring of saints and angels is *dulia*, and the veneration or honoring of the Blessed Virgin is *hyperdulia*. As Vatican II wrote in the Constitution on the Church:

> Once received into their heavenly home and being present to the Lord, through him and with him and in him they do not cease to intercede with the Father for us, as they proffer the merits which they acquired on earth through the one mediator between God and men, Jesus Christ.... So by their brotherly concern is our weakness greatly helped.... This sacred council accepts loyally the venerable faith of our *ancestors* in the living communion which exists between us and our brothers who are in the glory of heaven or who are purified after their death.[73]

Thus sainthood — with its many roles paralleling African ancestry both in the past and present — conceivably could be the theological and religious keystone for constructing one Afro model of pneumatology. It has been demonstrated that the concept of sainthood can be transferred to African heroes, even if some African modifications are necessary. The 22 martyrs of Uganda — who appropriately enough include both Catholics and Anglicans in a continent where European and American historical divisions are not so keenly observed — demonstrate this. St. Mugagga, patron saint of

---

72. Berentsen, *Grave and Gospel,* 132.
73. "Dogmatic Constitution on the Church," in Austin Flannery, O.P., ed., *Vatican Council II: The Conciliar and Post Conciliar Documents* (Northport, N.Y.: Costello Publishing Company, 1975), 410, 412. Emphasis added.

tailors, St. Joseph Mukasa, patron of politicians, St. Mukasa Kiri-wawanvu, patron of hotels and bars, just to mention a few, show how Western-controlled concepts of sainthood can become a part of African Christian piety and veneration. The question is whether such a transferred concept can help build a model that will suffi-ciently address and incorporate the experience of African Christians and their ancestors. This issue is less of a dilemma for Africans than for some Western theologians, Catholic and Protestant, but it can become less a problem for those theologians if the concept of ancestorship is looked at afresh as a possible enrichment for a multi-cultural, pluralistic Christian hagiography. Certainly black churches in America and the Caribbean have witnessed this kind of accommo-dation through slave religion, and many of the indigenous African independent churches have also accommodated ancestorship with beneficial results. Their anticipation of a reunion with family and ancestors witnesses to the importance of life continuing after death in community and is a vital contribution of Afro cultures to Chris-tian piety and doctrine. It certainly suggests that for Africans and those in the African diaspora in the Americas and the Caribbean, in-dividual autonomy and self-esteem are not simply personal values, as the Enlightenment would maintain, but have particular signifi-cance culturally and theologically in tandem with the ancestors and those gone to the land depicted in the text of a spiritual: "where the wicked shall cease from troubling and the weary shall be at rest. / And every day will be Sunday, by and by."

However, ancestorship does raise some thorny issues for some Christians, particularly those in the classical Protestant tradition. The issue of ancestors acting as chief mediators for us to God may be seen by some as jeopardizing total loyalty to Jesus Christ, "the one mediator between God and men ... who gave himself as a ran-som for all ... " (1 Tim. 2:5). Likewise, the issues of other spirits and consanguinity between the living and spirits of the dead draw suspicions of false idols and adoration of false gods, although, con-ceptually, ancestors are not divinities with their own ceremonies and claims of ultimate loyalty. Nevertheless, the line between divinities and spirits in piety and practice is a very thin one, and crossing that line might be seen by some as eroding the sovereignty and deity of Jesus Christ. Yet, the traditional mediating role of saints resem-bles the mediating role of ancestors without compromising ultimate loyalty to Christ. On this issue, the matter of a plurality of beliefs within the Christian tradition is again at stake.

Epilogue

There is nothing new about examining the tensions and critical questions that arise from the fact that early Christian theologians tried to interpret the oriental biblical world through the medium of Greek and Roman philosophical thought. Tertullian first called attention to the matter with his poignant question: "What has Athens to do with Jerusalem?" And over the past 100 years or so these tensions have been studied in great detail. Adolf von Harnack has provided the most extensive study of these tensions in his monumental *History of Dogma* (1885; Eng. 1894); and the issue has also been taken up by Reinhold Seeberg, *Text-book of the History of Doctrines* (1905); Martin Werner, *The Formation of Christian Dogma* (1965); Bernhard Lohse, *A Short History of Christian Doctrine* (1966); and Jaroslav Pelikan, *The Christian Tradition: A History of the Development of Doctrine* (1971–78).

The present study of God-talk in Afro cultures has sought to raise critical questions about the very guardianship of the Christian doctrinal tradition, its vocabulary, concepts, and theology; further, it has sought to critique the power structures of the tradition and the ethnocentric influences shaping the intellectual framework of that guardianship. The ideas and conceptual character at play in that framework have been largely influenced by Graeco-Roman metaphysical and philosophical thought, which is intimately linked to cultural and social ideas of Greek and Roman antiquity. At the same time, this Graeco-Roman tradition and culture also are the foundation of what can be called Eurocentric cultures and intellectual history, meaning Western civilization and its American offsprings. The guardianship of Christian dogmas and doctrines thus reflects a convergence of, on the one hand, an ethnocentric philosophical and intellectual tradition and, on the other hand, a structure of control over the development of Christian doctrine and concepts that is guided by theologians, bishops, councils, and liturgists. These persons and bodies — themselves formed by the Graeco-Roman ethnocentric philosophical tradition — are entrusted with the task of identifying and verifying what is authentic, legitimate, and true in Christian thought. The poles of this relationship thus reflect one another, and the situation is a kind of ecclesiastical "Catch-22."

Hence, when churches, whether in the Catholic, Orthodox, or Protestant tradition, determine which doctrines and liturgies are more authentic than others, usually they appeal to what is "ancient" or "orthodox" or "reformed," and hence "true." The operative norms for identifying the consensus or mind of the church as revealed in its councils and synods acting under the Holy Spirit are shaped by the stranglehold of these same bishops, theologians, and liturgists who have important institutional self-interests in perpetuating the Eurocentric tradition through such an appeal. Consequently, definitions of what is authentic and true in Christian doctrine (which itself emerged from cultural, ethnocentric, and power struggles in the early churches) have been universalized for all of Christian belief regardless of culture and context.

This is aptly illustrated by how the Nicene Creed, "an exemplary and authentic summary of the apostolic faith,"[1] became the normative act of confession in Christian worship. Robert L. Wilken reminds us that this creed in the Eucharist was first inserted in the late fifth century, largely because of a power play by the maverick patriarch of Antioch, Peter the Fuller, who opposed the approved Chalcedon Definition. Not only did Peter make this innovation in an effort to legitimate his own episcopate and to mock Chalcedon bishops, but also "by accentuating the venerable authority of the creed of Nicaea, he hoped to subvert the 'additions' to the faith of Nicaea recently proposed at the Council of Chalcedon."[2] Once the Nicene Creed was universalized for all of Christendom, its definitions in turn became the frame of reference and filter system through which scripture, consciously and unconsciously, was and continues

---

1. *Confessing One Faith: Towards an Ecumenical Application of the Apostolic Faith as Expressed in the Nicene-Constantinopolitan Creed (381)*, Faith and Order Paper No. 140 (Geneva: World Council of Churches, 1987), 3.
2. Robert L. Wilken, "The Nicene Creed in Its Historical Setting" (Paper presented at the American Theological Society, Princeton, N.J., April 5, 1986).

to be read, heard, and interpreted. These definitions also shape the boundaries and guidelines for arguments about the tradition itself.

Thus, although the church revised tenets borrowed from Greek and Roman philosophical thought, its doctrines nonetheless continue to reflect ethnocentric philosophical ideas about the absolute, unchanging nature and transcendence of the divine, about how the divine can be related to flux and change in creation and humankind, and about the need to concoct a way of allying Greek thought with biblical thought about God and Jesus Christ. Such an alliance *ipso facto* today not only excludes the possible intellectual contribution and integrity of ancient African cultures south of the Sahara in conversations about Christ and the Spirit, but also establishes the agenda that determines how the worldview of these African cultures will be heard by the tradition's guardians. Is, therefore, the political concept of "neocolonialism" also not an appropriate charge to raise with regard to the Eurocentric guardianship and control of the Christian tradition? That is, even though demographics impress us that the Christian faith is growing rapidly in politically liberated African and Afro Caribbean Third World cultures, which have their own theologians and churches, still determination of the content of authentic Christian doctrine about Jesus Christ and the Spirit remains in the hands of their former Eurocentric and American overlords. Hence a kind of ecclesiastical neocolonialism.

Afro cultures, whose origins and worldview are not decidedly Graeco-Roman, thus ask the following key questions about the assumptions underlying this guardianship and legacy. First, what might doctrines about Christ and the Spirit look like if the concepts and intellectual frame of reference of Afro cultures — instead of Graeco-Roman thought — were used as vehicles for interpreting biblical narratives and views in the formation of Christian doctrine? Second, Christian doctrine about Christ has primarily focused on the issue of *cur deus homo?* — that is, on how Jesus Christ could be both human and God — and, once that puzzle is worked out, it has focused on the relationship of the God-man to our salvation and redemption as sinful humankind. God-talk in Afro cultures, however, asks: What is the significance of this redemption for creation and nature, where good and evil powers, forces, and principalities reign and shape the human situation? Third, since the founding of the World Council of Churches in Amsterdam in 1948, Eurocentric and American churches have moved and controlled the modern ecumenical movement, declaring as a universal Christian goal the "restoration of visible unity in one faith" among Christian churches. Yet God-talk in Afro cultures raises the serious question: What will be the nature of that unity, worthy as it might be in our fragmented ecclesiastical and political world? Given that the ecumenical churches, which are heirs of the doctrinal guardianship, have defined the content of this unity and have established it as an urgency, might this goal better be characterized as a theological and historical priority for churches sustained by their mutual Eurocentric heritage rather than an urgent priority and feature of Afro Christian doctrine? If the integrity of indigenous Christianity in Afro cultures is to be heard and is to make a contribution to the tradition, might not this priority of the Eurocentric ecumenical movement better be reexamined under St. Augustine's principle: "unity in necessary things, liberty in doubtful things, love in all things" (*in necessariis unitas, in dubiis libertas, in omnibus charitas*)?

These questions are not raised with a view toward dissolving the traditional Eurocentric underpinning in Christian thought. That is impossible. Rather the questions have been raised for two reasons: (1) to test the assumption that there must be a worldwide unity and consensus about Christian dogmas if the Christian faith is to survive and have integrity; and (2) to suggest that the nature of that unity has already been programmed by appealing to ancient Western philosophical concepts so as to exclude or patronize non-Western Christian theologies. The latter's intellectual claims for interpreting God's revelation, it might be noted, also are rooted in antiquity.

The importance of the above three questions demands that we expand our discussion of them. We might begin by rephrasing the first question as follows: Can there be alternative "right" doctrines about the nature of Christ and the Spirit within the Christian tradition?

The African independent (indigenous) churches, with all their variety and geographical differences, demonstrate that consensus and understanding of God's revelation in Christ and the Spirit can thrive on alternative models of unity that do not conform to a Roman monarchical, or an Orthodox autocephalous, or a Protestant Reformation and ecumenical model. From these indigenous churches and Afro cultures have emerged doctrines about Jesus Christ as the anointed one, as the Lord of the heavens and all powers (good and evil) on earth, as the healer, as the liberator and liberated, and these doctrines obviously raise different questions than those raised in the classical christological disputes about the divine and human natures of Jesus Christ. God-talk in Afro cultures, as we have seen, is just as anxious as God-talk in Greek and Latin cultures to deal with the ancient confession, "Jesus Christ is Lord." But whereas traditional Christianity embraces the filter system of Graeco-Roman philosophical thought to interpret this confession and define christological doctrine, Afro cultures use the cosmological and anthropological concepts of Africa and its diasporan cultures in the New World, particularly in the Caribbean.

Throughout the history of Christianity a host of persons and groups have raised speculative issues regarding the nature of Christ. In the second century, Ebionism proposed that Jesus was fully human, was born of human parents, and would one day return as God's Messiah to establish his kingdom on earth. Docetism proposed that Jesus' humanity and suffering were not real, but only seemed real, because as the Logos of God he shared God's divine impassibility and only linked himself with the impurities of human flesh and matter until the crucifixion. The Gnostics and the Apologists were obsessed with the meaning of the Logos, a term itself imported from Greek philosophical thought. Origen questioned the existence of Jesus' soul before the incarnation. Apollinarianism insisted that Jesus Christ was *a composite being* — his flesh was the passive party and his Logos-soul was the active party; this had to be the case, it was claimed, because no man born of woman could be truly God and redeem sinful humankind as a man ("[only] one nature of the divine Logos, which became flesh").[3] Chalcedon's Definition of the Faith attempted to resolve the matter by stating that Jesus was "truly God and truly man, the same with a rational soul and body, consubstantial with the Father in Godhead, and the same consubstantial with us in manhood, like us in all things except sin...."[4] All these propositions and definitions reflect theological issues set aflame by power politics; they are claims and counterclaims rooted in ethnocentric Greek thought. But these need not be crucial christological issues and arguments for Afro cultures, even though they have been universalized and made root and branch of Christian doctrine by the Graeco-Roman guardians.

Similar observations can be noted in the classical disputes about the Holy Spirit and the Spirit. As we have seen, concern

3. H. Lietzmann, *Apollinaris von Laodicea und seine Schule* (Tübingen: J. C. B. Mohr, 1904), 251.

4. J. N. D. Kelly, *Early Christian Doctrines*, rev. ed. (New York: Harper & Row, 1978), 339.

and doctrines about the Spirit have almost been devotional after-thoughts. Christology — not pneumatology — has always been the area of study that generated the unique claims about God. But as claims and counterclaims circulated about the nature of the Christian God, in order to maintain some order among warring parties as well as the biblical claim that God is one, more attention had to be paid to the relationship between the one God and the Spirit revealed in scripture. The theological frame of reference operative in most of the classical controversies about the Spirit also reflected continuing tensions arising from filtering the biblical oriental world through the apparatus of Graeco-Roman metaphysics and questions. Hence, in the fourth century the Macedonians (also called Pneumatomachians) raised the issue of whether the Spirit is divine and therefore uncreated or created and therefore subordinate to the Son. Arianism asked whether the Spirit is created by the Father *and* the Son. Nicaea and Constantinople wrestled with the concept of consubstantiality — the Spirit being of the same divinity or substance as God and the Son. And Augustine proposed the concept of the Spirit coming from the Father and the Son (double procession). From an Afro perspective, all these disputes and propositions merely served to encase pneumatology in an intellectual formula.

This pneumatology may indeed continue to make sense within the heritage of Greek civilization and its Western cultural offsprings. However, it is bewildering and too speculative in civilizations and cultures of ancient non-Greek origins, where there are many spirits in the cosmos: ancestral spirits, divinities, good and evil powers, as in the Third World cultures of Africa, Asia, and the Caribbean. Again, I must caution that I am not suggesting that we jettison the Christian legacy of seeking to affirm unity within God and at the same time to affirm the biblical witness of the divine or deity in Father, Son, and Spirit. The concern is how to demythologize this legacy's sacrosanct Graeco-Roman character so that there is genuine conversation between Christian thought in Afro cultures and Eurocentric cultures. Is it possible that classical doctrines about the Spirit can become more inclusive in light of a multicultural Christianity liberated from theological as well as political neocolonialism and thought-control?

The second critical question that Afro God-talk raises is: How can classical belief in Christ's redemption for the world focus almost entirely on humanity (anthropology) and neglect Christ's redemption in creation and nature (cosmology)? As we have seen, the christology in the Epistles (e.g., in Romans, Colossians, and Ephesians) depicts Christ's victory over evil powers and spirits, and the healing stories in the Gospels depict the manifestation of spirits in disease and illness. Such is evidence for Afro cultures that a cosmological redemption was revealed by God in Jesus Christ as well as the redemption of sinful humanity. With the exception of parts of Eastern Orthodoxy and Maximus the Confessor (c. 580–662), who was deprived of his right hand and tongue because he resisted the orthodox interpretation of the Chalcedon definition, Eurocentric christology (especially after Augustine, Luther, Calvin, and Zwingli in the West) has emphasized Christ's central work to be the redemption of humankind and has neglected his redemption of nature and the cosmos. Maximus — who insisted that God's "enfleshing" of the Logos in Jesus Christ as a human at the incarnation was the original purpose of the creation — stressed that creation is not an autonomous entity apart from the Logos. Not only are the *logoi* (fundamental principles or purposes) of nature and the cosmos under Christ's sovereignty, but also all spirits, powers, and principalities dwelling in the cosmos:

> We believe that the *logos* of the angels preceded their creation; [we believe] that the *logos* of each essence and each power which constitute the world above, the *logos* of all that to which God gave being — and it is impossible to enumerate all things — is unspeakable and incomprehensible in its infinite transcendence, being greater than any creature and any created distinction and difference.[5]

Jesus Christ as the Logos removed the waywardness of nature that existed in opposition to God because of sin:

> He purified nature from the law of sin in not having permitted pleasure to precede his incarnation on our behalf. Indeed his conception wondrously came about without seed, and his birth took place supernaturally without corruption.... He frees the whole of nature from the tyranny of the law which dominated it in those who desire it and who by mortification of the sensuality of the earthly members imitate his freely chosen death.[6]

5. Maximus, *Ambigua*, col. 1081b. Cited in John Meyendorff, *Christ in Eastern Christian Thought* (Crestwood, N.Y.: St. Vladimir's Seminary Press, 1987), 134.
6. *Commentary on the Our Father*, in *Maximus Confessor: Selected Writings*, trans. George C. Berthold (New York: Paulist Press, 1985), 104.

Afro God-talk underscores this revelation in Christ's redemption. Interestingly enough, Karl Barth was one of the few influential Protestant theologians who also understood this link between creation and reconciliation in Jesus Christ:

> But if Jesus Christ is the content and form of the first and eternal Word of God, then that means further that the beginning of all things, of the being of all men, and of the whole world, even the divine willing of creation, is preceded by God's covenant with man as its basis and purpose. At the beginning of all things in God there is the Gospel and the Law.... Jesus Christ the incarnate Word, the baby born in Bethlehem, the man put to death at Golgotha and raised again in the garden of Joseph of Arimathea, the man whose history this is — is the unity of the two.[7]

The third question raised by Afro cultures has to do with the relative importance and the universalization of the "visible unity" that is being sought among mostly mainstream Eurocentric Protestant and Orthodox bodies. Might the emphasis on this search reflect more of a geopolitical priority and Eurocentric theological concern than a priority and theological emphasis of all of Christendom, especially those Christians and indigenous churches in Afro cultures? Many ecumenists speak of a "restoration" of Christian unity, referring to the time of the first six ecumenical councils before mainstream Western and Eastern churches divided theologically. But there never was a time of uniform or unified consensus about doctrine in all parts of the Christian church, even in the New Testament Christian communities. Likewise, as we have seen, making ancient conciliar Christianity (with its dependence on and adaptation of Graeco-Roman thought) normative explicitly excludes Afro thought and cultures. This simply institutionalizes Graeco-Roman God-talk, its definitions of antiquity, and its understanding of community, thereby casting a cloak of invisibility over the theological integrity and thought of Afro cultures south of the Sahara and in the Caribbean. They have been rendered homeless within the history of Christian thought and have been threatened with remaining so unless they first adopt Graeco-Roman presuppositions. But as Christianity has "come of age" among the younger churches in Afro cultures, those churches — which have their own criteria for interpreting Christian doctrine — have raised critical questions about the

---

7. Karl Barth, *The Doctrine of Reconciliation*, vol. 4/1 of *Church Dogmatics*, trans. G. W. Bromiley (Edinburgh: T. & T. Clark, 1956), 53.

nature of a Christian unity under Eurocentric dominance. Perhaps a more profound issue with regard to the goal of "visible [Christian] unity in one faith and in one eucharistic fellowship expressed in worship"[8] is whether — given the negativity explicitly and implicitly associated with blackness and black cultures in the history of Christian thought and Western consciousness — such a unity can ever be attained when the search for it is being conducted under the formula of *primus inter pares*. Can there be an alliance between Christian thought with its traditional Eurocentric negative views about blackness and black cultures and thought in Afro cultures with their own autonomous worldview? Can there be authority and integrity in a "community of communions" infused with Graeco-Roman claims that God must remain Greek? That has to remain a question for examination at another time.

---

8. *Constitution and Rules of the World Council of Churches*, as amended by the fifth assembly, Nairobi, Kenya, November 23–December 10, 1975 (Geneva: World Council of Churches, 1976), 1.

Selected Bibliography

Adeyemo, Tokunboh. *Salvation in African Tradition*. Nairobi: Evangel Publishing House, 1979.

Ajayi, J. F. A. *Christian Missions in Nigeria, 1841–1891: The Making of a Modern Elite*. Evanston, Ill.: Northwestern University Press, 1965.

Andersson, Efraim. *Messianic Popular Movements in the Lower Congo*. Uppsala: Almqvist & Wiksells Boktryckeri, 1958.

Appiah-Kubi, Kofi, and Sergio Torres, eds. *African Theology en Route*. Maryknoll, N.Y.: Orbis Books, 1979.

Ariès, Philippe. *The Hour of Our Death*. Trans. Helen Weaver. New York: Alfred A. Knopf, 1981.

Asante, Molefi Kete. *The Afrocentric Idea*. Philadelphia: Temple University Press, 1989.

Awolalu, J. Omosade. *Yoruba Beliefs and Sacrificial Rites*. Harlow, England: Longman, 1979.

Awolalu, J. Omosade, and P. Adelumo Dopamu. *West African Traditional Religion*. Ibadan: Onibonoje Press and Book Industries, 1979.

Badham, Paul, and Linda Badham, eds. *Death and Immortality in the Religions of the World*. New York: Paragon House, 1987.

Barnett, Leonard E. *The Sun and the Drum: African Roots in Jamaican Folk Tradition*. London: Heinemann Educational Books, 1976.

Barrett, David B. *Schism and Renewal in Africa: An Analysis of 6000 Contemporary Religious Movements*. Nairobi: Oxford University Press, 1958.

Bastide, Roger. *African Civilizations in the New World*. Trans. Peter Green. New York: Harper & Row, 1971.

———. *The African Religions of Brazil: Toward a Sociology of the Interpenetration of Civilizations*. Trans. Helen Sebba. Baltimore: Johns Hopkins University Press, 1978.

Bauer, Walter. *Orthodoxy and Heresy in Earliest Christianity*. Trans. and ed. Robert A. Kraft et al. Philadelphia: Fortress Press, 1971.

Becken, Hans-Jürgen, ed. *Relevant Theology for Africa*. Durban, South Africa: Lutheran Publishing House, 1973.

Beckwith, Martha Warren. *Black Roadways: A Study of Jamaican Folk Life*. New York: Negro University Press, 1929.

257

Beier, Ulli. *The Return of the Gods: The Sacred Art of Susanne Wenger*. Cambridge: Cambridge University Press, 1975.

Berentsen, J. M. *Grave and Gospel*. Leiden, Netherlands: E. J. Brill, 1985.

Bernal, Martin. *Black Athena: The Afriasiatic Roots of Classical Civilization*. New Brunswick, N.J.: Rutgers University Press, 1987.

Beyerhaus, Peter, et al., eds. *Theologische Stimmen aus Asien, Afrika und Lateinamerika*. Munich: Chr. Kaiser, 1968.

Boesak, Allan. *Black and Reformed: Apartheid, Liberation, and the Calvinist Tradition*. Maryknoll, N.Y.: Orbis Books, 1984.

―――. *Comfort and Protest: Reflections on the Apocalypse of John of Patmos*. Edinburgh: Saint Andrews Press, 1987.

Boff, Leonardo. *Church, Charism and Power: Liberation Theology and the Institutional Church*. Trans. John W. Diercksmeier. New York: Crossroad, 1985.

Brathwaite, Edward K. *The Folk Culture of the Slaves in Jamaica*. London: New Beacon Books, 1981.

Brereton, Bridget. *A History of Modern Trinidad 1783–1962*. Kingston, Jamaica: Heinemann, 1981.

Brown, Peter. *The Cult of the Saints*. Chicago: University of Chicago Press, 1981.

Burkett, Randall K. *Garveyism as a Religious Movement: The Institutionalization of a Black Civil Religion*. ATLA Monograph Series, no. 13. Metuchen, N.J.: Scarecrow Press & American Theological Library Association, 1978.

Campbell, Horace. *Rasta and Resistance: From Marcus Garvey to Walter Rodney*. Trenton, N.J.: African World Press, 1987.

Cassidy, F. C. *Jamaica Talk*. London: Macmillan, 1961.

Cassidy, F. C., and R. B. LePage, eds. *Dictionary of Jamaican English*. Cambridge: Cambridge University Press, 1967.

Chesi, Gert. *Voodoo: Africa's Secret Power*. Trans. Ernst Klambauer. Wörgl, Austria: Perlinger Verlag, 1980.

Choron, Jacques. *Death and Western Thought*. New York: Collier Books, 1963.

Courlander, Harold. *The Drum and the Hoe: Life and Lore of the Haitian People*. Berkeley: University of California Press, 1960.

―――. *Tales of Yoruba Gods and Heroes*. New York: Crown Publishers, 1973.

Crahan, Margaret E., and Franklin W. Knight, eds. *Africa and the Caribbean: The Legacies of a Link*. Baltimore: Johns Hopkins University Press, 1979.

Cronon, Edmund David. *Black Moses: The Story of Marcus Garvey and the Universal Negro Improvement Association*. Madison: University of Wisconsin Press, 1964.

Curtin, Philip D. *The Atlantic Slave Trade: A Census*. Madison: University of Wisconsin Press, 1969.

———. *Two Jamaicas: The Role of Ideas in a Tropical Colony, 1830–1865*. Cambridge: Harvard University Press, 1955.

Dawson, George Gordon. *Healing: Pagan and Christian*. London: SPCK, 1935.

Deren, Maya. *Divine Horsemen: The Living Gods of Haiti*. New York: Documentext, McPherson & Co., 1953.

Desmangles, Leslie Gérald. "God in Haitian Vodun: A Case in Cultural Symbiosis." Ph.D. diss., Temple University, 1975.

Dickson, Kwesi. *Theology in Africa*. Maryknoll, N.Y.: Orbis Books, 1984.

Dickson, Kwesi, and Paul Ellingworth, eds. *Biblical Revelation and African Beliefs*. London: Lutterworth Press, 1969.

Diop, Cheikh Anta. *The African Origin of Civilization: Myth or Reality*. Trans. Mercer Cook. Westport, Conn.: Lawrence Hill, 1974.

Dzobo, N. K. *African Proverbs: Guide to Conduct Vol. II*. Accra, Ghana: Waterville Publishing House, 1975.

Ellis, A. B. *The Tshi-speaking Peoples of the Gold Coast*. London: Frank Cass, 1894.

———. *The Yoruba-speaking Peoples of the Slave Coast of West Africa*. 1894. Reprint. Oosterhout, Netherlands: Anthropological Publications, 1970.

Erskine, Noel Leo. *Decolonizing Theology: A Caribbean Perspective*. Maryknoll, N.Y.: Orbis Books, 1981.

Fashole-Luke, Edward, et al., eds. *Christianity in Independent Africa*. London: Rex Collins, 1978.

Forde, Darryl, ed. *African Worlds: Studies in the Cosmological Ideas and Social Values of African Peoples*. London: Oxford University Press, 1954.

Fredrickson, George M. *White Supremacy: A Comparative Study in American and South African History*. New York: Oxford University Press, 1981.

Garvey, Amy Jacques. *Garvey & Garveyism*. New York: Collier Books, 1970.

Geffré, Claude, and Bertrand Luneau, eds. *The Churches of Africa: Future Prospects*. New York: Seabury Press, 1977.

Glasswell, Mark E., and Edward W. Fashole-Luke. *New Testament Christianity for Africa and the World*. London: SPCK, 1974.

González-Wippler, Migene. *Rituals and Spells of Santeria*. New York: Original Publications, 1984.

———. *Santeria*. New York: The Julian Press, 1973.

Gray, John. *Ashe, Traditional Religion and Healing in Sub-Saharan Africa and the Diaspora: A Classified International Bibliography*. New York: Greenwood Press, 1989.

Hamid, Idris. *Troubling of the Waters*. San Fernando, Trinidad: Rahaman Printery, 1973.

Hamshere, Cyril. *The British in the Caribbean*. London: Weidenfeld and Nicolson, 1972.

Harnack, Adolf von. *History of Dogma*. 7 vols. Trans. Neil Buchanan. New York: Dover Publications, 1961.

Herskovits, Melville J. *Dahomey: An Ancient West African Kingdom*. 2 vols. New York: J. J. Augustin, 1958.

————. *Life in a Haitian Valley*. New York: Octagon Books, 1975.

————. *The Myth of the Negro Past*. 1941. Reprint. Boston: Beacon Press, 1958.

Herskovits, Melville J., and Francis S. Herskovits. *An Outline of Dahomean Religious Belief*. Memoirs of the American Anthropological Association. Menasha, Wis.: American Anthropological Association, 1933.

————. *Trinidad Village*. New York: Alfred A. Knopf, 1947.

Horowitz, Michael H., ed. *Peoples and Cultures of the Caribbean*. Garden City, N.Y.: Natural History Press, 1971.

Hunt, Alfred N. *Haiti's Influence on Antebellum America: Slumbering Volcano in the Caribbean*. Baton Rouge: Louisiana State University Press, 1988.

Hurston, Zora Neale. *Mules and Men*. 1935. Reprint. Bloomington, Ind.: Indiana University Press, 1963.

————. *Tell My Horse*. 1938. Reprint. Berkeley, Calif.: Turtle Island Foundation, 1981.

————. *Voodoo Gods: An Inquiry into Native Myths and Magic in Jamaica and Haiti*. London: J. M. Dent, 1939.

Hyatt, Harry Middleton. *Hoodoo-Conjuration-Witchcraft-Rootwork: Beliefs Accepted by Many Negroes and White Persons, These Being Orally Recorded among Blacks and Whites*. 5 vols. Hannibal, Mo.: Western Publishers, 1970–78.

Idowu, E. Bolaji. *African Traditional Religion: A Definition*. London: SCM Press, 1973.

————. *Olódùmarè: God in Yoruba Belief*. Ikeja, Nigeria: Longman, 1962.

Isichei, Elizabeth. *A History of the Igbo People*. New York: St. Martin's Press, 1976.

————. *Igbo Worlds: An Anthology of Oral Histories and Historical Descriptions*. Philadelphia: Institute for the Study of Human Issues, 1978.

James, C. L. R. *The Black Jacobins: Toussaint l'Ouverture and the San Domingo Revolution*. New York: Vintage Books, 1963.

The Kairos Document: A Theological Comment on the Political Crisis in South Africa. Braamfontein, South Africa: The Kairos Theologians, 1985.

Kelsey, Morton. *Healing and Christianity in Ancient Thought and Modern Times*. New York: Harper & Row, 1973.

Kittel, Gerhard, and Gerhard Friedrich, eds. *Theological Dictionary of the New Testament*. Trans. G. W. Bromiley. 10 vols. Grand Rapids, Mich.: Wm. B. Eerdmans, 1964–68.

Knight, Franklin W. *The Caribbean: The Genesis of a Fragmented Nationalism*. New York: Oxford University Press, 1978.

———. *Slave Society in Cuba during the Nineteenth Century*. Madison: University of Wisconsin Press, 1970.

Laguerre, Michel S. *Afro-Caribbean Folk Medicine*. South Hadley, Mass.: Bergin & Garvey, 1987.

———. *Voodoo Heritage*. Sage Library of Social Research. Beverly Hills, Calif.: Sage Publications, 1980.

Lewis, Maureen Warner. *The Nkuyu: Spirit Messengers of the Kumina*. Kingston, Jamaica: Savacou Publications, Mona, 1977.

Logan, Willis H., ed. *The Kairos Covenant: Standing with South African Christians*. New York: Friendship Press; and Bloomington, Ind.: Meyer-Stone Books, 1988.

Lohse, Eduard. *Colossians and Philemon*. Trans. William R. Poehlmann and Robert J. Karris. Hermeneia Commentary Series. Philadelphia: Fortress Press, 1971.

Long, Edward. *The History of Jamaica*. 3 vols. London: T. Lowndes, 1774.

Lovell, John, Jr. *Black Song: The Forge and the Flame*. New York: Macmillan, 1972.

Martinez, Raymond J. *Mysterious Marie Laveau, Voodoo Queen, and Folk Tales along the Mississippi*. New Orleans: Hope Publications, 1956.

Mbiti, John S. *African Religions and Philosophy*. Garden City, N.Y.: Doubleday/Anchor Books, 1970.

———. *Bible and Theology in African Christianity*. Nairobi: Oxford University Press, 1986.

———. *Concepts of God in Africa*. London: SPCK, 1970.

———. *Eschatology in an African Background*. Geneva: Ecumenical Institute, WCC, 1977.

Metuh, Emefie Ikenga. *God and Man in African Religion: A Case Study of the Igbo of Nigeria*. London: Geoffrey Chapman, 1981.

Moore, Basil, ed. *Black Theology: The South African Voice*. London: C. Hurst & Co., 1973.

Moore, Joseph G. "Religion of Jamaican Negroes: A Study of Afro-American Acculturation." Ph.D. diss., Northwestern University, 1953.

Morais, Herbert M. *The History of the Negro in Medicine*. New York: Publishers Co., 1967.

Moreau de Saint-Méry, M. L. E. *Description Topographique, Physique, Civile, Politique et Historique de la Partie Française de l'Isle de Saint-Domingue*. 3 vols. Philadelphia, 1797. Abr. Eng. ed.: *A Civilization That Perished*. Ed. and trans. Ivor Spencer. Lanham, Md.: University Press of America, 1985.

Morrish, Ivor. *Obeah, Christ and Rastaman: Jamaica and Its Religion*. Cambridge, England: James Clarke, 1982.

Morrison, Clinton. *The Powers That Be: Earthly Rulers and Demonic Powers in Romans 13:1-7.* London: SCM Press, 1960.

Murphy, Joseph M. *Santeria: An African Religion in America.* Boston: Beacon Press, 1988.

Nettleford, Rex M. *Identity, Race and Protest in Jamaica.* New York: William Morrow, 1972.

Nicholls, David. *From Dessalines to Duvalier: Race, Colour and National Independence in Haiti.* Cambridge: Cambridge University Press, 1979.

Nyamiti, Charles. *Christ as Our Ancestor: Christology from an African Perspective.* Gweru, Zimbabwe: Mambo Press, 1984.

Okorocha, Cyril C. *The Meaning of Religious Conversion in Africa: The Case of the Igbo of Nigeria.* Brookfield, Vt.: Gower Publishing Co., 1987.

Parrinder, Geoffrey. *African Mythology.* New York: Peter Bedrick Books, 1982.

———. *West African Religion.* London: Epworth Press, 1949.

Patterson, Orlando. *The Sociology of Slavery: An Analysis of the Origins, Development and Structure of Negro Slavery in Jamaica.* Rutherford, N.J.: Fairleigh Dickinson University Press, 1967.

p'Bitek, Okot. *African Religions in Western Scholarship.* Nairobi: East African Literature Bureau, 1970.

Phillippo, James M. *Jamaica: Its Past and Present State.* 1843. Reprint. London: Dawsons, 1969.

Pobee, John S. *Toward an African Theology.* Nashville: Abingdon, 1979.

Price, Richard, ed. *Maroon Societies: Rebel Slave Communities in the Americas.* Baltimore: Johns Hopkins University Press, 1979.

Price-Mars, Jean. *So Spoke the Uncle.* Trans. Magdaline W. Shannon. Washington, D.C.: Three Continents Press, 1983.

———. *Une Etape de l'Evolution Haïtienne.* Port-au-Prince: Imprimerie La Prense, 1929.

Puckett, Newbell Niles. *The Magic and Folk Beliefs of the Southern Negro.* New York: Dover Publications, 1969.

Rattray, R. Sutherland. *Ashanti Proverbs.* Oxford: Clarendon Press, 1979.

———. *Religion and Art in Ashanti.* 1927. Reprint. Oxford: Oxford University Press, 1969.

Rawick, George P. *From Sundown to Sunup: The Making of the Black Community.* Series One, The American Slave: A Composite Autobiography. Vol. 1. Westport, Conn.: Greenwood Publishing Co., 1972.

Ray, Benjamin C. *African Religions: Symbol, Ritual, and Community.* Englewood Cliffs, N.J.: Prentice-Hall, 1976.

Rigaud, Milo. *Secrets of Voodoo.* Trans. Robert B. Cross. San Francisco: City Lights Books, 1969.

———. *Ve-ve: Diagrammes Rituels du Voudou.* New York: French and European Publications, 1974.

Rouget, Gilbert. *Music and Trance: A Theory of the Relations between Music and Possession*. Trans. Brunhilde Biebuyck. Chicago: University of Chicago Press, 1985.

Rowell, Geoffrey. *The Liturgy of Christian Burial*. London: Alcuin Club/ SPCK, 1977.

Sanneh, Lamin. *West African Christianity: The Religious Impact*. Maryknoll, N.Y.: Orbis Books, 1983.

Sarpong, Peter. *The Sacred Stools of the Akan*. Tema, Ghana: Ghana Publishing Corporation, 1971.

Sawyerr, Harry. *God: Ancestor or Creator?* London: Longman, 1970.

Sellers, R. V. *The Council of Chalcedon: A Historical and Doctrinal Survey*. London: SPCK, 1961.

Simpson, George Eaton. *Black Religions in the New World*. New York: Columbia University Press, 1978.

———. *Religious Cults of the Caribbean: Trinidad, Jamaica, and Haiti*. Rio Piedras, P.R.: Institute of Caribbean Studies, 1970.

———. *The Shango Cult in Trinidad*. Rio Piedras, P.R.: Institute of Caribbean Studies, 1965.

Sproul, Barbara. *Primal Myths: Creating the World*. San Francisco: Harper & Row, 1979.

Stavrianos, L. S. *Global Rift: The Third World Comes of Age*. New York: William Morrow, 1981.

Sundkler, Bengt. *Zulu Zion and Some Swazi Zionists*. Oxford: Oxford University Press, 1976.

Szwed, John F., and Roger D. Abrahams et al. *Afro-American Folk Culture: An Annotated Bibliography of Material from North, Central and South America and the West Indies*. Philadelphia: Institute for the Study of Human Issues, 1978. Pts. 1 and 2.

Tallant, Robert. *Voodoo in New Orleans*. Gretna, La.: Pelican Publishing Co., 1983.

Taylor, John B., ed. *Primal World-views: Christian Involvement in Dialogue with Traditional Thought Forms*. Ibadan: Daystar Press, 1976.

Taylor, John V. *The Growth of the Church in Buganda*. London: SCM Press, 1958.

Turner, Harold W. *History of an African Independent Church: The Church of the Lord (Aladura)*. 2 vols. Oxford: Clarendon Press, 1967.

———. *Religious Innovation in Africa: Collected Essays on New Religious Movements*. Boston: G. K. Hall, 1979.

Webster, James Bertin. *The African Churches among the Yoruba, 1888–1922*. Oxford: Clarendon Press, 1964.

Welbourn, F. B., and B. A. Ogot. *A Place To Feel at Home: A Study of Two Independent Churches in Western Kenya*. London: Oxford University Press, 1966.

Werner, Alice. *Myths and Legends of the Bantu*. London: George G. Harrap & Co., 1933.

Westerlund, David. *African Religion in African Scholarship: A Preliminary Study of the Religious and Political Background*. Stockholm: Almqvist & Wiksell International, 1985.

Williams, Eric. *From Columbus to Castro: The History of the Caribbean, 1492–1969*. New York: Vintage Books, 1984.

Williams, Joseph J. *Voodoos and Obeahs: Phases of West India Witchcraft*. New York: Dial Press, 1932.

Wilson, Stephen, ed. *Saints and Their Cults: Studies in Religious Sociology, Folklore and History*. Cambridge: Cambridge University Press, 1983.

Wink, Walter. *Naming the Powers: The Language of Power in the New Testament*. Philadelphia: Fortress Press, 1984.

Zahan, Dominique. *The Religion, Spirituality, and Thought of Traditional Africa*. Trans. Kate Ezra and Lawrence M. Martin. Chicago: University of Chicago Press, 1979.

Index

Acknowledgments

Excerpt from *Messianic Popular Movements in the Lower Congo* by Effraim Anderson copyright © 1958 Almqvist & Wicksells International, Stockholm, Sweden. Reprinted by permission.

Excerpt from *Rasta and Resistance: From Marcus Garvey to Walter Rodney* by Horace Campbell copyright © 1987 African World Press, Trenton, NJ. Reprinted by permission.

Excerpt from *Slave Society in Cuba During the Nineteenth Century* by Franklin W. Knight copyright © 1970 University of Wisconsin Press, Madison. Reprinted by permission.

Excerpt from *Voodoo Heritage* by Michael S. Laguere copyright © 1980 Sage Publications, Beverly Hills, CA. Reprinted by permission.

Excerpt from *Kimbangu: An African Prophet and His Church* by Marie-Louise Martin copyright © 1975 Oxford University Press, Oxford. Reprinted by permission of Basil Blackwell, Ltd.

Table from *The World Since 1500* by L. S. Stavrianos copyright © 1966 Prentice-Hall Inc., Englewood Cliffs, NJ. Reprinted by permission.

Excerpt from *Zulu Zion and Some Swazi Zionists* by Bengt Sundkler copyright © 1976 Oxford University Press, Oxford. Reprinted by permission.

273